Animal Others

SUNY series in Contemporary Continental Philosophy
Dennis J. Schmidt, Editor

Animal Others

On Ethics, Ontology, and Animal Life

EDITED BY

H. Peter Steeves

Foreword by
Tom Regan

State University of New York Press

Published by
State University of New York Press, Albany

For information, address State University of New York
Press, State University Plaza, Albany, N.Y., 12246

Production by Diane Ganeles
Marketing by Nancy Farrell

Library of Congress Cataloging-in-Publication Data

Animal others : on ethics, ontology, and animal life / edited by H.
    Peter Steeves ; foreword by Tom Regan.
        p.   cm. — (SUNY series in contemporary continental
    philosophy)
    Includes bibliographical references and index.
    ISBN 0-7914-4309-4 (hardcover : alk. paper).
    — ISBN 0-7914-4310-8 (pbk. : alk. paper)
    1. Animals (Philosophy)   2. Philosophy, European.
    I. Steeves, H. Peter.   II. Series.
B105.A55A55   1999
179'.3—dc21   99-17303
                                                          CIP

10 9 8 7 6 5 4 3 2 1

For Mi Pingüina and the memory of Snowball

Contents

Acknowledgments

This work, as all others, is the result of a community. Of course I take all responsibility for the shortcomings of the text; however, its success should be shared by many. For their help in a variety of capacities, I would like to thank: Will McNeill, Tom Regan, Jane Bunker, Diane Ganeles, Steve Ingeman, Joan Fearnside, Jim Slinger, Robert Maldonado, Karen Villarama, and the students enrolled in my independent study on Continental Philosophy and the Animal during the Spring 1998 semester at California State University Fresno. And, to my wife, Marinés, a debt of gratitude I could never repay. For having faith in this project from its inception, for sharing in the most important work of seeing it through in its various incarnations, and for providing me strength when I needed it most, she has my love and gratitude, now and always. Finally, my thanks to the contributors to this volume. How pleased I am to have a project of which I am truly proud to be a part. I can say with sincerity that their hard work and philosophic spirit and insight have inspired me. I am honored to appear on the page beside them.

It should also be noted that David Wood's use of "The Lizard," copyright © 1961 by Theodore Roethke (from *The Collected Poems of Theodore Roethke* by Theodore Roethke) is by permission of Doubleday, a division of Bantam Doubleday Dell Publishing Group, Inc., and Faber and Faber Ltd., London.

Foreword

In 1971, three young Oxford philosophers—Roslind and Stanley Godlovitch, and John Harris—published *Animals, Men and Morals.* The volume marked the first time philosophers had collaborated to craft a book that dealt with the moral status of nonhuman animals. At the time of its publication, the editors could not have understood how important their effort would prove to be. Or why.

As for the why: another young Oxford philosopher, the editors' friend, Peter Singer, was so impressed with the book that he submitted an unsolicited review to the *New York Review of Books.* Against all the odds, it was accepted. Published in 1973, Singer's review was something of a social bombshell. So large was the response, so intense the interest, that the editors of *NYRB* asked Singer if he would consider writing a book himself. It was an offer the young philosopher could not refuse.

Two years later, Singer's *Animal Liberation* burst upon the scene. From that day forward, "the animal question" had a place at the table set by Oxbridge-style analytic moral philosophers, and a legitimate place at that. In the past twenty-five years, these philosophers have written more on "the animal question" than philosophers of whatever stripe had written in the previous two thousand. Such an outpouring of focused scholarship, unique to the discipline's history, would never have occurred but for the slim volume, now largely forgotten, put together by John Harris and the Godlovitchs. Of such ironies is history sometimes made.

To make reference to "the animal question" is, of course, to oversimplify. There is no single "animal question," even among those philosophers who work in the analytic tradition. Difficult questions in the philosophy of mind and the philosophy of language demand attention. Is it possible for someone to have beliefs and desires while lacking the ability to use a language such as English or German? If nonhuman animals have beliefs and desires that are independent of such linguistic proficiency, how can we specify their content? Again, if nonhuman animals have minds, is it possible for us to understand what they are like? If so, how? If not, how can we avoid an unbridled skepticism about what it is like to be one of them—a bat, for instance?

In the wake of *Animal Liberation*, "the animal question" also has attracted the attention of moral and political philosophers in the analytic mold. Are any animals other than the human morally considerable? Singer, who answers this question from the perspective of a utilitarian, gives an affirmative answer: all sentient beings, whether human or not, are morally considerable. Others, like John Rawls, who answers from a contractarian perspective, give a negative answer: only beings who possess a "sense of justice" are morally considerable.

Why Singer and Rawls answer the question as they do is important certainly. Arguably, however, what is more important is that both recognize the necessity of asking it. Expressed another way, perhaps what is most important is the *centrality* "the animal question" has come to have in contemporary analytic moral and political philosophy. How very far these philosophers have come in less than a hundred years! It was 1903 when analytic philosophy's patron saint, George Edward Moore, published his classic, *Principia Ethica*. You can read every word in it. You can read between every line of it. Look where you will, you will not find the slightest hint of attention to "the animal question." Natural and nonnatural properties, yes. Definitions and analyses, yes. The open-question argument and the method of isolation, yes. But so much as a word about nonhuman animals? No. Serious moral philosophy, of the analytic variety, back then did not traffic with such ideas.

It does so now. The recognition that serious moral and political philosophy must address "the animal question" represents a change in the discipline it may take another hundred years for sociologists and anthropologists to understand.

It has been my privilege to be one voice in the choir of analytic philosophers pressing for consideration of "the animal question."

Very much a product of the analytic tradition, I have used what tools I have acquired, as best I can, even as I realized that, like all tools, there are some things—and these important things—my sort of tools are not suited to do well, or at all. Which is why (it must be almost ten years ago now) I began encouraging philosophers with a different set of tools to apply them to "the animal question," as they conceive it.

How very gratifying it is, therefore, to have been asked to write a short foreword to this important collection of papers. Here, for the first time, we have a volume where the tools of philosophy fashioned on the continent are used to explore the contours of our knowledge of, and encounters with, other than human animals. Not that continental philosophy's most influential thinkers (I have in mind philosophers like Heidegger, Husserl, Merleau-Ponty, Lyotard, Derrida, and Levinas) have had nothing to say on this topic. On the contrary, if this collection does nothing else, it will succeed in drawing attention to the large volume of extant work that takes up "the animal question" in a distinctively continental way.

I have no doubt, however, that this book will do much more than this. In particular, the rich assortment of continental voices that speak from these pages will, I think, help foster a larger conversation among those philosophers who prefer tools of continental design. Like *Animals, Men and Morals*, I believe *Animal Others* will help ensure that "the animal question" becomes as central to continental as it is to analytic philosophy. Only there will be this important difference: unlike *Animals, Men and Morals*, *Animal Others* will likely play a more durable role than any review, however impassioned or insightful.

TOM REGAN

Introduction

Joey is barking on the telephone. He knows several animal sounds; his parents tell me that he learned them at the same time that he learned to say "Mama" and "Daddy." He pretends to be different animals. He has books filled with pictures of animals, books in which animals are the heroes, the villains, the populators of the earth. He is surrounded with stuffed and plastic animals of dozens of species—dinosaurs, ducks, and Dalmatians, alone, are within view of the sofa. When a Disney video is on, he is hypnotized. Animals talk and dance and sing; he knows it to be true. And in all of this, Joey is no different from so many other human two year olds.

The process of becoming an adult is the process of conforming, of learning our concepts, our categories, and our places within them. It is a kind of dying, to be sure. The body becomes acceptably human; it must suppress its animality and mold itself appropriately. Whatever is *wild* must go. It will not be long until Joey does not want to be a frog—he will not want to jump around and be on the ground. He will take his place with us—up with us, on a pedestal of our own making—becoming a creature of upright posture and upstanding reason. The creature will be created rather than emerge. As he comes to think of his body as human it will become human, individual, and alone. Animals will die in the process—in his heart, his imagination, his stomach, his dreams. It is not inevitable; it is merely likely. I wish him more.

In Gene Myers' study of nursery schoolers' relationships to animals, he found that the children in his class had not yet acquired the variety of distancing mechanisms humans use to separate themselves from other animals.[1] They had learned some, but not all. When

1

animals were brought into the classroom, for instance, the children demanded to know what kind of animal it was as well as its name. Neither bit of information alone would suffice. A ferret had not yet become a ferret; a cow had not yet become a cow—as they have for us. For the children in the classroom, that animal *there* could still be somebody. What is it? Who is it?

When a cow is just a cow, McDonald's becomes possible. When posture becomes upright, the monkey house in the zoo becomes possible. These implications of our creation and categorization of humanity are surely and concretely important, but there are other, more intellectual consequences as well. In our "growth," there is a point at which the animal is no longer philosophically interesting. We relegate the animal to children's stories and children's thoughts. And we take up an academic of exclusion. We study the philosophy of language (as if our utterances were made in a world of silence). We analyze the philosophy of history (as if the tale of who owns the means of production at the poultry house were the whole story). We argue over logic (as if the classic modus ponens that tells us "Socrates is mortal" is worth greater study than the premise that he is a man— and thus not an animal?). We forget, and we live falsely.

I do not wish for philosophy to be practiced in a social vacuum. I would not wish for the impossible, even if I desired it. Neither do I wish to speak for the myriad of voices gathered on these pages. I hope to engage in philosophy in order to understand and learn, but to do and be as well. The process of living well involves eating well, acting well, being-with-Others well, and thinking well.[2] And so we begin in philosophy. We begin by reminding philosophy what we have become. We begin with the animal.

Animal Others is an attempt to found such a beginning. The new essays collected here—each especially written for this volume—deal with the general theme of the status of nonhuman animals from the perspective of continental philosophy. Within this broad topic are included various questions concerning the moral status of animals, the question of animal minds and animal phenomenology, the body of the animal, what it is to be an animal, what it is to be-with an animal, as well as the roles that animals play in the thought of such authors as Husserl, Heidegger, Nietzsche, Levinas, Merleau-Ponty, and Derrida.

In taking up "the animal question" from the perspective of continental philosophy, it is hoped that this anthology will fill a long-standing void in scholarship. As the authors brought together here apply the tools of continental thought to questions concerning animals, they seek not only to offer a better understanding of our world and ourselves, but to enrich continental philosophy with animal issues while at the same time expanding contemporary discussions on the status of animals by bringing the force of continental thought to bear on the topic. It is thus that we embark on something new—the first compilation of essays concerning animal issues written from the vantage point of continental philosophy. Although a variety of good books and essays on philosophical animal issues already exists, those works that are academic in nature tend to be analytic in nature as well. With *Animal Others*, we are attempting to break down barriers and open up new traditions.

But this is not just a book for continental philosophers, or, for that matter, just for philosophers in general. While it is true that the essays which follow often assume some background knowledge of philosophy, they can be read and appreciated on many different levels. William McNeill's essay on Heidegger and animals, for instance, is a rigorous piece of Heideggerian scholarship sure to interest Heidegger scholars; but like every other essay in this book, it makes a new contribution to animal issues in general and can offer insights even to the beginner. In general, those already immersed in continental philosophy will hopefully find the subject matter of the animal to be a new interest and a promising new venture. Analytic philosophers already embroiled in animal issues will hopefully be rewarded by a different approach to old questions. Lay persons engaged in thinking about animals will hopefully discover new arguments to back up their positions, new challenges which will force long-held beliefs into question. The environmentalist, ethologist, biologist, and social critic as well will hopefully be rewarded by the direction of this work and by the ways in which it draws attention to what it means to be human, what it means to be animal, what it means to be together in all of this. As the editor of this volume, I thus extend my general welcome.

David Wood begins our anthology by discussing the relationship between deconstruction and animals, especially as it involves questions of vegetarianism. After criticizing Heidegger and Levinas, Wood focuses his attention on deconstruction by analyzing Derrida's position on animals. Inevitably, Wood argues (against Derrida) that vegetarianism is not just about "substituting beans for beef"; but rather, the refusal to eat animals can be a first step toward resistance of the powers that perpetuate carnophallogocentrism.

Alphonso Lingis offers poetic insights into the ways in which being human is being animal. He argues that it is animal emotions that make our own feelings intelligible, and that animal ways of being give meaning to our own human actions and existence. Calling on us to recognize that every animal (including humans) has its mode of being in the pack, Lingis finds us in a world where we are always life in the midst of life, where human singing neither begins in silence nor simply imitates the songs around us, but rather answers the refrains which call to us. What we consider to be the finest human traits, he maintains, rise from our animal nature. It is thus that we learn to be courageous, forgiving, and generous. It is thus that we learn to be human.

Lynda Birke and Luciana Parisi write on the relationship between women and animals, seeking to move the debate beyond its previous incarnations (either separating women from their traditional ties to what is "natural," or tying together the plight of women and animals as oppressed Others). Arguing that any politics based on identity will necessarily include a displaced Other, Birke and Parisi turn our attention to the work of Deleuze and Guattari, whose concept of *becoming* is appropriated to better understand the unfolding of evolution and the inappropriate Western tradition of hierarchically categorizing humans and animals.

Monika Langer next offers an exposition of the role of animals in Nietzsche's thought, especially in *Thus Spoke Zarathustra*. Starting with the claim that Nietzsche adopted animal imagery in order to dissociate his work from traditional philosophy, Langer contends that the ploy fails in that it simply reinforces long-standing stereotypes and preconceptions of the animals involved. Far from being a "radical questioning," according to Langer, Nietzsche's philosophical use of animals maintains old hierarchies and perpetuates the devaluation of animals.

Elizabeth Behnke's objective is to make a step toward describing an interspecies/intercorporeal practice of peace. Using Merleau-

Ponty as a springboard, Behnke's chapter outlines how this may be possible in both a theoretical and practical manner. Her phenomenology of living-with cats leads her to a rich reading of Merleau-Ponty; and her application of theory to the real-life case of a (potential) cat fight offers new directions for understanding what it is to experience a world together with animals, as well as the moral call to live appropriately in that world.

Ralph Acampora further investigates sharing a lifeworld with animals, arguing that we can overcome the agnosticism associated with animal phenomenology (e.g., "it is impossible to know what it is like to be a bat") by appealing to Watsuji Tetsuro's notion of climaticity and the concepts of dwelling and bodily-being. To be flesh is to dwell in the world, in the earth-home, with other flesh. Offering a phenomenology of the park (Kissena Park of New York City, to be exact), Acampora grounds his theory by describing the ways in which the park residents—geese, squirrels, humans, etc.— form a carnal community.

My chapter offers a description of a particular mode of being-with animals—namely, being-in-fear. Relating to animals in fear is investigated through three lenses, each informed by an Husserlian and Heideggerian standpoint. First, I consider the social practices of hunting and zoos, suggesting that both are inauthentic ways of being-with. Second, I investigate animal sexuality, confronting the history, ethics, and metaphysics of bestiality as well as the moral and philosophical issues raised by our constant attempts to control the sex lives of our pets. Finally, I take up the question of eating-well by eroding the barrier between cannibalism and meat-eating, noting the fear that accompanies the crumbling of such boundaries.

James Hart contributes a detailed analysis of how we represent other animals. Working with an Husserlian concept of community, representation, and reference, Hart suggests that we inauthentically represent animals when we say "we" and that "we" appresents Others who have not empowered us to represent them as not immediate. The animal point-of-view involves an empty intention, and thus we must carefully consider our use of "we" and actions that effect "us." Since animals co-constitute the world—since the world appears as for-us-all—Hart argues for an authentic form of representation when we must speak for animals.

William McNeill writes on the topic of the animal in Heidegger's 1929–30 course, "The Fundamental Concepts of Metaphysics." Beginning with a critical analysis of the distinction between human life and animal life in Heidegger, McNeill provides a context for reading Heidegger's work on animals as part of his overall project involving the "retrieval and transformation of the philosophical (Platonic and Aristotelian) foundations of our scientific and technological conception of the world." Finally, McNeill defends Heidegger from the claim that his 1929–30 course is yet another essentialist and anthropocentric theory of animality—on the contrary, argues McNeill, it raises fundamental questions concerning animal-being and our responsibilities to Others of all kinds.

Carleton Dallery's work merges "popular" authors such as Vicki Hearne, Diana Starr Cooper, and Monty Roberts with classical phenomenological theory. Offering a phenomenology of the circus and of dog- and horse-training, Dallery suggests that each mode of being-with animals presents a truth about our own way of being. Challenging those who suggest "animal training" is always an exploitative relationship with animals, Dallery maintains that sentimentalizing animals—constructing them as cute or pretty or in need of loving strokes—is an improper reduction of animal-being. Hearne, who is an opponent of the animal rights movement for just such reasons, offers a description of appropriate communication with animals which Dallery builds on using the tools of phenomenology. The conclusion is a bold statement of a morality based on a general reverence within the intercorporeal world which houses us all.

Steven Laycock concludes the collection by challenging us truly to take the animal *as* animal. This, he argues, is only possible if we have an open conceptuality that does not annihilate the alterity of the animal Other even as it attempts to explain that alterity. Concepts, Laycock maintains, speak before they listen; they determine in advance what is to be seen and known. To stand without a conceptual intermediary in the presence of the animal requires an openness, a sensitivity, indeed a philosophic bravery to admit the possibility of true otherness. Drawing on the thought of such authors as Husserl, Merleau-Ponty, Baudrillard, and Zen Master Dōgen, Laycock consequently calls us to celebrate the animal as animal, the mystery of the Other as mystery.

Although the work which follows can be sliced up into chapters, allow me to suggest that there are benefits to be had from reading the book as a whole—as a continuous text. The variety of interwoven themes is intriguing; I will comment on three: the limits of the body; animal ethics; and the relationship between the animal and philosophy—between, essentially, the animal and thought.

We tend to think of our bodies as containers. Cartesian dualists are keen on seeing the mind as separate from and greater than the body. Many Christians see the body as a temple—some, a temple of sin (Saint Augustine disliked the seeming alterity and autonomy of certain parts of his body so much that he longed to snip away the offending nasty bits). Even continental thinkers—who can claim a tradition that recognizes the body to be a site of legitimate philosophic speculation and inquiry—are susceptible; although they rebel against dualistic epistemologies when they speak of consciousness embodied in flesh or of knowledge being incarnate, they often still see the body as a limit: the self contained within the limits of the individual flesh.

But we are not alone—even the body is many. Thousands of parasites make their home on my body; yet even to say that they are "on" my body is problematic. They partially constitute this body; we share it and we are it. The animal is not other.

Birke and Parisi remind us that the environment, too, is not an entity separate from the organism; rather, the two participate and adapt together. Individuality, if there is such a thing, is an accident. Echoing Lingis' claim that every animal has its mode of being in a pack, Birke and Parisi announce that individual bacteria, for instance, do not exist. Can we truly speak of individual bodies on any scale?

The boundary of the flesh need not mark the boundary of the self. Yet if we follow Lingis and cease to identify the body with the notion of a subject—if we follow Acampora and cease to identify the skin boundary as the edge of the self—with what are we left? In this spirit—the legacy of Merleau-Ponty—Dallery calls the result an overlapping of bodies. He celebrates its manifestations in the circus and in the horse training circle where humans and animals participate in something larger. It is the same intercorporeal way of being that Behnke celebrates in the midst of feline bodies, the same communal body she recognizes is in need of a new peaceful way of existing. Inevitably, multiple boundaries are eroded. The no-Man's-land between bodies as well as the distance between the self and the Other, the human and the animal, cannot be maintained. We recognize the chasm as false, and we fall together.

Space plays cruel tricks. It seems to separate us. It seems to provide a nexus of Here and There—an X Y Z of distinct points that makes a playing field in which we all meet. You always seem so far away. I can only hope: perhaps we will get together (perhaps not) within some neutral grid—we will converge on the marketplace as consumer units, we will meet in the State as Liberal selves, we will interact in the world as moral agents, we will go shopping at the Gap.

There has never been a neutral space of meeting! No space is neutral. No space is empty either. My human neighbors appear before me; and if I am attuned to them, birds and bugs and various beasts appear before me. But the space between us is not a conceptual vacuum. It is easier (yet still exceedingly difficult) to accept the parasites upon me and the bacteria within me as constituting my body. I can't shake them. They're here for good. But you? You are always so far away. The ducks are out there on the pond; the birds overhead are farther still.

The realization of our shared body comes partially with the realization of our shared well-being. It is a good thing we can't shake our parasites; we would die without them. And the same is true, though it is harder to see, of the ducks on the pond.

Still, the point is deeper. The truth of the matter is that the world does not appear *before* me. To assume such an epistemology is to beg the question. My eyes do not look outward (as if the brain is conveniently placed behind them, like a withered voyeur with a pair of binoculars peeping out for a glimpse of the Other). My hand does not reach out to stroke a cat, to scratch a dog's chin, to brush the hair from your face. It is never farther away from me than it is right now, hanging at my side—my hand in my lap, my hand extended, retains the same distance from me (which is to say that it is never any distance away). Space tricks us; false philosophy tricks us. My hand reaching for yours seems to move away from me, though it never does: it is me. Your hand, your paw, seems to be There and, hence, other. It is not: it, too, is me. We have met the animal's body, and he is us. There are no animal Others.

A rich ethic, I believe, is tangled up in all of this. In the past, I would have said "is founded by all of this," but I am no longer willing to maintain such a primacy of ontology, for ethics always unfairly becomes a second-class citizen. This is especially true in continental philosophy, so much of which is phenomenology in one of its manifestations. *Isn't phenomenology descriptive?*—comes the refrain. *How can it speak of values?* The worry centers on the descriptive/normative distinction, an unwanted child grown bitter in the aftermath of the is/ought divorce.

The book which follows manages to speak in many voices; continental ethics take many forms, some of them in the name of reconciliation. Dallery is, perhaps, most upfront with his rejection of both utilitarianism and rights-based ethics. They are too abstracted from being and living. We need something greater, something that recognizes the ways in which we are with animals and thus something that can begin to uncover the *appropriate* ways of being with animals. For Dallery—and Laycock—sentimentalism and paternalism are forms of violence. They reduce the animal, speak (inappropriately) for the animal, and fail to do justice to our being together.

When McNeill concludes his chapter with a description of the protoethical moment of presencing which founds respect, he claims that the responsibility we have toward living Others is boundless. Following Derrida, this is a problem that Wood recognizes in utility- and rights-based ethics: such ethics mistakenly allow our duties to be finite, figured, and stated. Once we complete these duties, we think we are good people, we think that we have calculated our responsibility and then fulfilled it. But a respectful responsibility is infinitely open, always vigilant in awaiting the call of the Other—a call that demands unbounded response. For this reason, Derrida discredits vegetarianism as an attempt to "buy good conscience on the cheap." It is as if to say that when we spare a cow—thus respecting her rights, or not increasing her suffering—we think we are done, we think we have done good. If ethics cannot adequately be expressed in a finite duty, we have not begun to act ethically when we simply refuse meat. Wood, however, sees vegetarianism as possibly being conceptually above such reductions of duty. Indeed, he sees it as a potential recognition of the expansion of duty and as a site for resisting numerous other evils.

These authors recognize that if there is alterity to be had in the animal, then it is radical alterity indeed. It is the voice of difference that calls to us when we listen for the animal. Thus our duty is made greater: no calculus can figure it; no rights can capture it. How can we know in advance what this Other may demand? The animal becomes the model and measure of the depth of our ethical duty.

There is, however, another possibility. The animal may not be so different from us; and thus an ethic of alterity may fail to realize the sense in which we are all together—all in this together. Birke and Parisi remind us how Nature, animals, and women have suffered due to dualistic thinking, a thinking which founds all politics built on *identity*, a concept that will forever require the presence of an Other. Hart's analysis of the proper use of "we" speaks to this same question in a different way. So often, the animal is assumed to be the "them" in opposition to "us." When we speak of an "us," we utter the exclusion of the animal. But the shared world, the mutually appearing world, the world co-constituted by humans and nonhumans is the site of our actions. "We" apperceives silent Others for whom we may not be empowered to speak. We make decisions about this world in the name of Others who have not given us their proxy. Realizing the senses in which we are together, and the phenomenological ways in which we properly or improperly speak for Others, is consequently a deeply ethical undertaking.

Perhaps it is the case that our finest ethical traits are not human traits which we need to polish up when we meet animal Others, but rather animal traits that we need to call forth and display proudly when dealing with Others of all kinds. Lingis' celebration of animal virtue pays special tribute to this ethical relationship. Here, courage arises from our animal nature; courage is on its finest display in penguins, wrens, and bees—we are destined to be called great if we are capable of living up to half their standard.

Typically, though, we are afraid. And we fail in our task. My own contribution to this text focuses on fear as an inappropriate way of being-with (at least when it is taken as the main and exclusive way of being-with Others) in terms of fearing death, eating, sex, and the nearness of animals. Fear, though, so consistently worries the authors on these pages that there is no doubt a much greater lesson to be learned. Lingis marvels at the lion's lack of fear over his parasites, at the human's ability to place justice before fear in times of strife that test our moral resolve. Behnke learns to stop fearing the possibility of a cat fight; and, newly liberated, she is able to note her rejection of fear as the first move toward peace and the construction of a peaceful communal body. Dallery, in his analysis of the immorality of sentimentalism, notes how often such mistreatment of animals is based on fear. And Laycock argues that we cannot accept the silence of animals—we *fear* the silence—and so we speak for them.

Like Hart, Laycock is concerned that we *improperly* speak for animals. As members of "us" who will never raise their voice and thus fill the empty intention by which they are marked, animals are an enigma. And so we speak on their behalf (how often, it seems, we merely mumble nervously). It is our failure that we do not accept silence as an answer. It is, perhaps, our failure that we seek an answer at all, that we demand the end of the mystery.

Some will see the death of philosophy in the acceptance of mystery, in the admission that there are questions to which only silence can respond. *What of the philosophic spirit? What of the quest to know, of the celebrated mind that shines a light into the darkest corners we encounter?* Yes, the animal calls into question all of our intellectual pursuits. But let us momentarily defer Laycock's point in order to address the larger role of the animal in philosophy. We must break the silence and speak of such things, if only for a moment as we move toward conclusion.

The animal is at the heart of all philosophy. The animal question is the first philosophical question. If philosophy seeks to understand "the world," it must understand the public world *for us all*, human and animal alike. If philosophy seeks to explore without preconceptions—to be an "elucidation of the functioning of our concepts," as Wood remarks—how can it do so without first recognizing how we assume the explorer to be human, how we assume the notion of "ours" is not already problematic. Wood's point is related to Hart's but is focused in a different direction: we cannot even begin to elucidate our concepts and categories without first resolving the function of "our," which is to say without first confronting the animal and the ways in which we are together.

Is this an impossible task? Langer's analysis of Nietzsche suggests that the latter's use of animal imagery in his philosophy could not escape the stereotypes and preconceptions associated with animals. Putting animals in the employ of philosophy did nothing to liberate either. Acampora has more confidence that philosophy can ask and provide answers to its important first questions concerning the animal. If Thomas Nagel was agnostic when it came to imagining whether philosophy could help us see across species boundaries—help us decide what it is like to be a bat, for instance—Acampora proselytizes in the park, announcing that faith in philosophy is well-founded if we know where to begin questioning.

If there is hope, where *do* we begin? Is it comfort enough to accept, as Laycock does, no answer at all as the answer to the animal question? To admit the mystery of the Other and then find solace in the silence, enlightenment in our realization of ignorance? Though it may sound anti-philosophical, it is within our tradition: Socrates' proclamation of his ignorance is a celebration of thoughtful not-knowing, an admission that philosophy's first step must be to withdraw from the security of knowledge, from the hubris of the intellect, from the complacency of dogmatic slumbers, from—if you will—the natural attitude. Too often, though, such revolutionary cries have caused the troops to charge in the wrong direction. Once withdrawn from the world, we forget our reason for battle and we take pride in our newfound knowledge of the terrain. Once out of the cave, we announce how well we can finally see, we find a nice spot in the sun, circle around a bit, and curl up for a nap. Perhaps a return to the things is a return to the world, and thus a return *to the animal himself*—and the accompanying insecurity of not-knowing.

I think of paleontologists facing distant animals—enormous Others who live only in the echoes of bones. Physically, the scientists reduce the temporal distance of the Other by reducing its spatial distance. The dinosaur is constituted today—its body is made, its identity is formed. We know the look of the calcified scaffolding holding them together, of the conceptual scaffolding that casts them as doomed past rulers of the world. But how best *to know* such creatures? Have we reached the velociraptor when we decide if she was warm or cold blooded, a caring mother or an absentee parent? Haven't we merely assigned her a quality that we went looking for in the first place, and then, having found it, we pause to celebrate our genius? The brontosaurus will not speak once we know more about his throat and larynx. Yet these beasts are not fully silent. Across millions of years they call to us, call back to us, in words we understand—precisely because they are the words for which we listen, the words we use to try to reach them: our own voices bouncing off a canyon wall, returning, sounding foreign yet familiar, mistakenly taken to be an answer to their own question. Scientists, though, are an easy mark; the natural attitude is their habitat. Philosophers, too, dig up exactly that for which they go looking.

Behnke strives to live appropriately with cats by abandoning the desire to know. In its place she adopts an attitude of responsiveness to an open future. By admitting her lack of knowledge (here, a lack of knowledge concerning how the future will unfold when certain cats come together) she proceeds—not without preconceptions, but from an appropriate starting point. She desires peace; she is aware of her body and those around her; she knows phenomenology. This author is not a blank slate. But she has attempted to move beyond pre-judging the future and the Other. If we think we know such things in advance, we fool ourselves. Perhaps the mean cat will defeat the submissive cat in the most brutal of fights. Perhaps the less territorial cat will become submissive and avoid the cat-fight altogether. Either way—any way—the future is understood as a cat fight (a bloody one, a short one, one that didn't end up happening but almost did) and the Other is "understood" as well (as mean, submissive, territorial, "cat"). When this is the sort of understanding we gain, we have done nothing more than what Laycock refers to as a cheap magician's trick. We *learn* that the card is the Ace of Spades, when in fact that was the card we had palmed earlier. We now know how cats act and what cats are, when in fact the moment unfolds exactly as we set it up and the cats play the part in which we cast them from the start. Only if we allow the moment to unfold itself and allow the Other to become whatever he or she will, do we gain knowledge that is worthy of pursuit.

I am still trying to figure out if this is true. It seems on the surface too individualistic, as if it all comes down to choice, that most important of modern Liberal values. But I know there is more. It is not about letting a kitty decide for herself who she wants to be. Perhaps it is about realizing that we are all constructing each other. The responsibility seems overwhelming. Lately, I have taken to thinking about silence, but I continue to talk to animals.

I am convinced of this, though: we need to begin to reclaim the animal—not to steal them from children, but to share them in our stories, our imagination, our lives together. If the animal is "first philosophy," there is much that needs to be done. So we turn to our task, and, on the pages beyond, we mark an attempt to speak to the questions at hand. Some voices sing of our community; others, our distance. Together, I think they are a fine chorus.

These days, I am told, Joey has stopped barking. But he's trying tofu sausage and learning to roar like a T. rex.

The rest is silence.

H. PETER STEEVES

Notes

1. Gene Myers, *Children and Animals: Social Development and Our Connections to Other Species* (Boulder, CO: Westview Press, 1998).

2. Please note that "Other" will be capitalized throughout the chapters in this book when it refers to an other being. It should not be assumed that this implies a Levinasian flavor to all of the texts. It is, instead, a matter of aesthetics, coherence, and conformity. Of course, we are too sophisticated today to accept that a disclaimer can change the way that language works, but it is offered here with sincerity.

ONE

Comment ne pas manger—
Deconstruction and Humanism

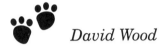 *David Wood*

1.

Coming to terms with the nonhuman animal, or indeed, knowing when to leave one's terms aside, is the reef on which, arguably, the originality of both Martin Heidegger's and Emmanuel Levinas' thinking founders. Jacques Derrida's repeated charge against Heidegger is that when it comes to his treatment of the animal, the revolution in thought comes to a halt and the deep currents of humanism reassert themselves. I shall be arguing that something similar happens to Derrida himself in his long discussion with Jean-Luc Nancy, "Eating Well."[1]

But first I would like to explain why this repeated failure matters. If we think of philosophy as an elucidating exploration of the ways in which we already think, then we might not be surprised to find a moral and metaphysical line being drawn between Man and the Animal. A Rortyean neopragmatism would support this: we are men, how could we want to do any more than write and think as men? Indeed, if we consider, as we must, the importance of history, culture, tradition, and language, perhaps we should declare all our interests and involvements. Our philosophical output could all then

15

be subtitled, for example: What it is like to be a WASP (white, Anglo-Saxon, Protestant). And Richard Rorty encourages just such modesty. If it were not for the fact that this project is dialectically unstable, we would be looking the end of philosophy in the face. The dialectical instability arises from the fact that pragmatist self-declarations are already modes of reflection that as such contaminate and exceed their proclaimed limitations. To be able to define our identity and the limited validity of our claims is already to move in a space in which those limitations are being breached. There are other instabilities too. There is no one map of the ways in which we plot the animal/human relationship. The consequences of sentimentality toward animals, of our fear or disgust, of our symbolic deployment, of our culinary habits, are such as to give us a laminated set of superimposed maps of that relationship. Further instabilities arise when we begin to think through the implications of both the words "Man" and "Animal." Each suggests an unproblematic universalization. So, Man includes Woman, and occludes racial, historical, and other differences. And Animal covers everything from cows to caterpillars, apes to anchovies, and more. The instability arises not just because of species diversity, but because its obvious supposed unimportance makes us realize that these terms are, to put it bluntly, metaphysical categories requiring all sorts of police work, and not simply useful conceptual tools, biological generalizations, etc. If they are metaphysical categories then they are subject to the deepest forms of scrutiny that philosophy can devise.

Philosophy cannot just be an elucidation of the functioning of our concepts or categories because the very word "our" is already problematic. It is problematic whether or not we are explicit about how we intend it. If we are explicit, we make philosophy into *Weltanschauungtheorie* (an account of a world view) in which its critical edge vanishes. If we are blind to the question of "we" or "our," we run the risk of projecting a parochialism.

I am claiming that philosophy has to maintain a critical function if it is to avoid a fate worse than death—that of having actually died but seeming to live on (in an emasculated form). So, the first reason why this failure to think the animal or animality matters is that it is symptomatic of a wider failure in the philosophical project, or at least any conception of that project for which a serious reexamination of the whole man/animal nexus would be close to a top priority. And, to be quite clear here, the suspicion is that it is within this dyad (among others, especially man/woman, man/God) that the difficulties of thinking, rethinking, and defining man are distributed.

The second reason why it matters has to do with practical reason. If the fate of nonhuman animals (and here I include both individuals and species) is dependent directly and indirectly on the actions and technologies of human beings, and if these actions and technologies continue at least in part because they seem justified, and if humanism of some sort is always the framework for such justifications, then practical consequences could flow from a persistent scrutiny of such humanism. Allow me, if I may, just a couple of brief reflections on this bit of scaffolding. First, of course, the argument is only as strong as its premises. And it might be argued that I have more faith than I should both in reason and in its practical relevance. How far do our animal practices survive because they seem justified? Would anything change if we could no longer justify them? The current coexistence of various forms of horrific interhuman violence around the world with a massive moral and political consensus that condemns it is not a hopeful precedent. And the manipulability of international law to justify counter-terror (for example, in Somalia and Iraq) gives us no clear promise that right will prosper. Worst of all, there is more than a faint worry that the very concern with justification might not survive the deconstruction of humanism. Our treatment of the animal kingdom, in other words, might eventually be recognized to be the acid test of our true humanity only at the point at which that value has lost all credibility.

Compare the following argument: Man is said to be different from animals. Q: But if he is so different, why does he act so beastly toward animals? A: He is not acting beastly: morality has always had a practical dimension, reflecting human and other more specific interests. Reason is and should only be a slave to morality. Comment: On that account, Man would be sacrificing reason in the cause of meat-eating. . . .

Let me return to Derrida. Derrida's most powerful readings of philosophers have been devoted to certain of those—I have in mind especially Husserl, Heidegger, and Levinas—who have attempted a revolution in philosophy, who have diagnosed a certain systematic difficulty, inadequacy, or failure in the tradition, and tried productively to overcome it. The shape of Derrida's readings of these thinkers is such as to bring out recursive difficulties in the radicalism of their new beginnings. The point of these readings, however, has often been misunderstood. People have talked about Derrida's deconstruction of Husserl, his critique of Heidegger, etc. What is clear, however, is that what is called deconstruction did not fall fully formed from the sky onto Derrida's desk, but has been developed through these various readings. Derrida is deeply committed to a version of the very philosophical radicalism that Husserl, Heidegger, and Levinas attempted, but one that builds on a certain recursive openness as antidote to the natural tendencies toward closure of any method. And here I would explicitly link Derridean deconstruction to phenomenology's inaugurating opposition to naturalism and psychologism, Heidegger's allergy to vitalism, life-philosophy, and philosophical anthropology, Levinas's rejection of ontology, and the principle of totality. Deconstruction is, *inter alia*, the most powerful attempt to preserve philosophy against plausible complacencies. What it preserves philosophy for, I believe, is a certain capacity to respond, and particularly to respond to what has not been adequately schematized, formulated, etc.—perhaps to the inadequacy of any schematization or formulation. In this way, philosophy's critical function makes way for something more receptive and responsive.

It is in this context that the question of humanism arises as a question. It has an interesting history within twentieth century European philosophy. In his *Existentialism and Humanism*,[2] Jean-Paul Sartre chose to interpret existentialism as a form of humanism when the alternative was nihilism, even if he was careful to distinguish it from such essentializing humanisms as Christianity and communism. He later repudiated this essay. Heidegger, on the other hand, in his "Letter on Humanism,"[3] sees the humanistic tradition as preserving a mistaken primacy of subjectivity against the more primordial analysis of Man's relation to Being that he himself is offering. But it is clear from his lectures in the early 1930s (as Derrida[4] and David Farrell Krell[5] have shown) that Heidegger continued to struggle with the question of how properly to characterize Man or *Dasein* in relation to animality without the traditional appeal to reason, subjectivity, or language. Derrida argues that Heidegger's thinking is in the end circumscribed within "a certain anthropocentric or even humanist teleology."[6] The lizard lies on the rock, but does not know it as a rock. The lizard has a world, but it is poor in world (*Weltarm*); it has a world in a privative or deprived sense. Heidegger has displaced the question of the animal and the question of whether or not the animal possesses some special feature, to the question of the animal's fundamental relation to the world. But as soon as the word "poor" (*arm*) appears, we have a comparison in which man's relation to the world sets the standard. And when Rainer Maria Rilke talks about the fundamental openness of the animal to the world—a kind of innocent, vulnerable being-out-there-amongst—Heidegger will insist that there is still a missing "as such." Of Levinas, I will only say that the tale of missed opportunity, of aborted radicalism, repeats itself. The thinker of otherness, of the most radical alterity, of the unassimilability of the Other, can accommodate the animal only by analogy with the human being, and indeed constructs the distinctiveness of the human being—the unreasonable animal—by contrast with the struggle for survival of the animal, the aim of whose being "is being itself." For a thinker for whom phenomenology is the jumping off point rather than a continuing method, it is revealing that he recognizes the value of "a specific phenomenological analysis" of our experience of the animal.[7] We might be tempted to say here, as elsewhere, and with apologies to Voltaire, that if animals had not existed it would have been necessary to invent them.

I have described deconstruction as the most powerful attempt to preserve philosophy against plausible complacencies. Derrida's diagnosis of Heidegger's thinking as anthropocentric, even humanist, is not, I think, offered in the spirit of the triumph of deconstruction. Rather it suggests that whatever we may have thought of Heidegger's radicalism with regard to the tradition, he has not succeeded in escaping from the very anthropocentrism that substituting *Dasein* for Man in *Being and Time* was to have signaled. There is no suggestion that this would be easy, or that Heidegger's failure is not instructive. But where does it leave us?

It is perhaps worth considering a wholly pessimistic verdict at this point—namely, that anthropocentrism in some sense is *logically* unavoidable. If Heidegger were the latest in a line of thinkers who had attempted to square the circle and failed, the proper response would not be to try harder, or find some more subtle, more radical approach, but to lay to rest the whole sad episode. But the sense in which it is logically unavoidable, is precisely, and for that very reason, an empty sense. The logically unavoidable sense is this: that any account we come up with of "our" relation to "animals" will be from "our" point of view. The challenge, however, remains to construct a point of view that is not just "ours," or one that allows us to practice a subtle and multilayered differentiation among animals as well as between various animals and various human beings, which is not subordinated to any hidden teleology.

There is, however, a more complex logical unavoidability thesis thrown up by the very attempt at such a practice. The kind of abstinence from anthropocentric projection described here is something to which no nonhuman animal could even begin to aspire. Surely the aspiration to it, let alone success in achieving such a rare and complex attitude, would, paradoxically, provide the best possible proof for the superiority of the human species. This is a fallacy. No one is disputing that there are many things that many humans can do that no other animal can do, and that there are many attitudes and capacities of humans that nonhuman animals do not share. What is being disputed is the move from these and other facts to the judgment of animals as only partial realizations of the human ideal, as subhuman, rather than as importantly different.

If I am right, then, about these pessimistic verdicts, we do not need to conclude that Heidegger's failure to avoid humanism is trivial. If I am right about deconstruction, it is just such doctrines as humanism that qualify for the status of a plausible complacency. Plausible, clearly. Complacency in the philosophical sense of being a structurally invisible commitment that as such resists critical interrogation.

What does Derrida himself have to say about the animal?

To answer this question I shall turn to the extended discussion between Derrida and Nancy ("Eating Well"). I argue that Derrida fails deconstruction at a critical moment and that the question of a humanist teleology hangs, if not over deconstruction, over Derrida's failure of nerve.

2.

"I am a vegetarian in my soul."

—Derrida (Cerisy Conference, 1993)

I would like to begin this section by quoting Derrida's opening to *The Other Heading.*

> A colloquium always tries to forget the risk it runs: the risk of being just another one of those events where, in good company, one strings together a few talks or speeches on some general subject.[8]

If this meeting had any chance of escaping repetition, it would be only insofar as some imminence, at once a chance and a danger, exerted pressure on us.[9]

Allow me, then, to invoke some of the silent or virtual or possible future conditions that exert "pressure" on us now:

(1) From the point of view of natural science, the man/animal boundary is already being breached through genetic engineering. Could not the practical consequences be as great as splitting the atom?

(2) Biological diversity is being threatened faster than the concept is becoming current; and this is due mainly to the destruction of habitats (especially the rain forest).

(3) Our concerns with each of these points are themselves bound up with a curious technoscientific displacement in which we human beings come to see our fate, indeed, our very being, increasingly bound up with our biological existence.

(4) We human beings live, still live, despite significant dietary shifts, in a carnivorous society fed largely by the biofactory flesh of nonhumans. This is not a secret, but it is usually treated as a background truth. Allow me, if I may, to disturb its recessive status by quoting from a paper I presented at *The Death of the Animal* conference at the University of Warwick (England) in 1993: "Since I started teaching at Warwick, and within two and a half miles of this room, 20 million unnamed cows have been killed for food. I calculate that would fill a four lane motorway from John O'Groats to Lands End, with cows standing nose to tail. But I have not met anyone on campus who has ever seen a single cow in the vicinity, dead or alive, coming or going."

Philosophy is not practical in the way that engineering and medicine are, but it does and can respond to what presses. Is it enough for us to say that the pressure, the imminence, is just truth, or philosophy itself? What would it mean for us to have escaped repetition? We perhaps never think except in response to such imminences, pressures, or as we might say, calls or appeals.

Much of Derrida's recent work—in *The Other Heading*,[10] in "Force of Law,"[11] in "Afterword: Toward an Ethics of Discussion," in *Limited Inc.*,[12] and in "Eating Well"[13]—has been devoted to thinking through what we might call the ethical dimension of deconstruction in terms of justice or more frequently, responsibility. (Responsibility is thought of in terms of a response or openness to what does not admit a straightforward decision.) If deconstruction is, will be, or may have been responsibility (or justice), the urgency of *this* moment can be found not only in particular topics, issues, etc., but also in the continuing response to the call of philosophy itself, reactivating perhaps a certain tradition of philosophy as responsibility. Not everyone will share my sense that the fate of philosophy and our own capacity for philosophizing is bound up with that of deconstruction. But the ethical and political dimension Derrida has more recently explicitly given to deconstruction answers at least those critics who have thought it alien to such concerns.

In order to assess Derrida's discussion of the problem of the animal in "Eating Well," I need to show how the concept of responsibility is developed into such a central term.

I have already remarked on the formative influence on Derrida of his reading of Husserl. And Husserl's linkage of philosophical method—its historical and cultural significance—with the idea of responsibility is well known. Responsibility for Husserl meant living and thinking within the possibilities of the reactivation of our original intuitive grasp of phenomena, even if his idea of a community of scholars living in "the unity of a common responsibility" and contributing to "a radically new humanity made capable of an absolute responsibility to itself on the basis of absolute theoretical insights" is now honored only in the breach.

Heidegger's meditations on the task of thinking at the end of philosophy, on the plight of the West, on the call, and on the appeal are moving in the same element. Heidegger's destruction of the tradition, of ontology, is in the service of what is first a program of renewal. Later, less of a program.

Derrida writes:

> Now we must ourselves be responsible for this disclosure of the modern tradition. We bear the responsibility for this heritage, right along with the capitalizing meaning that we have of it. We did not choose this responsibility, it imposes itself upon us, and in an even more imperative way, in that it is, as other, and from the other, the language of our language.[14]

The filiation is clear. Derrida is *taking responsibility for responsibility* as Husserl had originally laid it out, rethinking reactivation in terms of language rather than intuition, rethinking language in terms of the trace, chance, the proper name, signature, rather than in Heidegger's more poetized ontological way, and insisting on the original displacement wrought by the Other—but conceiving the Other, beyond Levinas, not as limited to the other man, but as the dimension of initial and permanent ruination of all presence. Being responsible for responsibility, reactivating—it is in such expressions that the importance for deconstruction of the phenomenological tradition in its broadest sense appears.

The relation between responsibility and language is an enduring theme for this tradition on many levels. It is a central issue, for example, in judging Heidegger's now infamous "Rectoral Address." Our first dismay is at what he is saying, our second at his saying it. But perhaps the lingering worry is about his willingness to use a language we had thought of as bound up with the project of reinterpreting the texts of the tradition for overtly political purposes. *The Other Heading* raises this question about Derrida. When he writes "it is necessary to make ourselves the guardians of an idea of Europe . . .," it is not difficult to feel a certain astonishment. But what Derrida has done is to enter the realm of public discourse by converting the old principle of writing under erasure into an insistence on bringing to the surface the aporetic structure of central philosophical concepts. Instead of new words, or old words with displaced meanings, Derrida works to develop the contradictory implications of concepts central to the tradition. Responsibility is one of these concepts, and like "justice" it is privileged in being able to guide our very reception of it. When Derrida writes "Now, we must ourselves be responsible for this discourse of the modern tradition," he is of course putting a weight on a word that is part of the modern tradition. When he writes "we bear the responsibility for this heritage," his words are inseparable from the tradition itself. Responsibility is obligation, burden, duty, etc. No words are forbidden, if ever they were. Indeed, if anything, Derrida is increasingly willing to draw the most traditional words within his embrace—because it is the disturbing embrace of ex-appropriation, of dislocation. For each word he chooses, deconstruction will be its undoing and its restoration as a word with which to think. The word "responsibility" is a case in point; there could be no more potent entrance into ethical and political discourse.

Although many people will associate responsibility with moralism or with some neo-Kantian account of the subject, for Derrida neither of these could be further from the truth. Accordingly, I will try to get clearer about what is at stake in "responsibility" by reconstructing (what it is hard not to call) Derrida's philosophical "program" as laid out in "Eating Well."

The full title of Nancy's interview is "Eating Well, or the Calculation of the Subject—an interview with Jacques Derrida."[15] We could talk here about the interview format and its limitations and opportunities, but I see nothing to caution against taking these formulations wholly seriously.

First the context. The 1970s and 1980s in particular hosted numerous pronouncements of "the death of the subject." The general idea was that the concept of the human subject, as agent, as seat of consciousness or experience, or as origin, had lost its capacity to underwrite philosophical inquiry. Ferdinand de Saussure, Claude Lévi-Strauss, Michel Foucault, and Jacques Lacan were obvious influences here. The book in which this interview appears followed a conference devoted to discussion of how to fill the supposed gap in the conceptual map. In beginning to answer the question "Who comes after the subject?" Derrida takes the opportunity—naturally—to raise the level of discussion from that of the absence or presence of the subject (the life or death of the "subject") both to the broader philosophical tradition dealing with consciousness and subjectivity (from René Descartes onward) and to the more recent trajectory of the phenomenological tradition which, within Husserl's work, already came to recognize an essential passivity of the subject in the studies of passive genesis. And interestingly, especially for those who despair of references to *the* Western metaphysical tradition, Derrida makes it clear that to speak of *the* subject, at least, is a fiction, a fable—it always has been a scene of real differentiation. Moreover— and in ways that recall the ambivalent imaginary conversation with

Christian theologians within which Derrida suspended Heidegger at the end of his book *Of Spirit*—he sets up, without resolving, a tension between those who would try to reconstruct a subject "as the finite experience of non-identity to self," and those who would "still have reservations about the term." What is striking, however, is the way Derrida sets up our relationship to the Heideggerian legacy and all its dangers. It is in the recognition of these dangers that Derrida answers those critics who would charge deconstruction with political and ethical irresponsibility. I am reminded, again, of Husserl, comparing those who are afraid of solipsism with children afraid of what is lurking in a dark corner. We should not turn away, he argues, but shine the light into the corner.

Derrida's view of the Heideggerian legacy on the subject has the following crucial double dimension. He writes:

> I believe in the force and the necessity (and therefore in a certain irreversibility) of the act by which Heidegger *substitutes* a certain concept of *Dasein* for a concept of subject still too marked by the traits of the being as *Vorhanden*, and *hence by an interpretation of time*, and insufficiently questioned in its ontological structure.[16]

Heidegger's thinking, in other words, is a necessary step in a process which it does not complete—which in brief we could call the deconstruction of the subject. Not only is the process incomplete, but its completion is internally threatened because "the point of departure for the existential analytic remains tributary of precisely what it puts in question."

Despite Heidegger's avoidance of the words "subject," "consciousness," and so on, what Derrida calls the "logic" of Heidegger's thought still betrays a commitment to "the axiom of the subject." I quote again:

> The chosen point of departure . . . is the entity that we are, we the *questioning* entities, we who, in that we are open to the question of Being and of the being of the entity we are, have this relation to self that is lacking in everything that is not *Dasein*.[17]

In other words, Derrida is insisting on the persistence and domination in Heidegger of the value of the proper, of self-relatedness, of identity, and of presence in the very way in which Heidegger sets out on his journey. This is not, of course, news. What makes it important is that Derrida restates despite everything the necessity of Heidegger's moves, and affirms the seriousness of their consequences for ethics and politics.

So Derrida's response to Heidegger's politics is that Heidegger did not go far enough and his challenge to us is to rework—dare one say reactivate—Heidegger's own origin. This is how Derrida puts the question, and I should add that it seems to me quite successfully to lay out Derrida's philosophical program.

First—where we stand with Heidegger:

> [T]he time and space of this displacement opened up a gap, marked a gap, they left fragile, or recalled the essential ontological fragility of the ethical, juridical, and political foundations of democracy and of every discourse that one can oppose to national socialism.[18]

Second:

> Can one take into account the necessity of the existential analytic and what it shatters in the subject and turn towards an ethics, a politics (are these words still appropriate?), in any case towards an other type of responsibility that safeguards against what a moment ago I very quickly called the "worst?"[19]

It is here that Derrida makes an extraordinary claim. The claim is that through his reading of Heidegger in *Of Spirit*, and some assistance from others (especially Françoise Dastur), he has located a point within Heidegger which breached the original starting point: Heidegger's reference to a *Zusage*, an original promise or pledge of language, a moment in Heidegger parallel to Husserl's discovery of passive genesis.

The importance of the claim is that this *Zusage* (Derrida will also speak of an original affirmation, or a "Yes") displaces the priority or privilege accorded by philosophy, and indeed by most of Heidegger's own work, to the question, and hence to questioning. If we can link the privilege of the question (interrogation) to that of the subject (who sets the questions, insists on answers) then anything that displaces that privilege will perhaps open up a new (post-deconstructive) determination of the responsibility of the "subject."

In beginning to answer this question: "Who comes after the subject?" Derrida, as usual, and in the context quite appropriately, problematizes the question itself. The very word "who" already suggests something human, does it not? In trying to pin him down, Nancy provokes one of the longest responses of the interview.

For our purposes, what I would like to draw attention to are his references to calculation and excess, for it is here that the concept of responsibility enters. Traditional dissatisfaction with Derrida's line of argument has often run along these lines: What is at stake in thinking of the subject is indeed its relation to ethical and political questions. In particular, it commonly has been suggested that as the central category of both the ethical and the political is action, and as action requires agency, and as all agency requires a subject that can get it together, Derrida's contribution here is negative, nihilistic. Deconstruction is the death of the subject, the death of politics, and the utter irresponsibility of thought.

Derrida's response is classical in its form. He claims that the subject is not just a given agency whose potency might be impugned by skeptical reflection, but a deeply complex concept inseparable from networks of concepts, from "a multiplicity of traditional discourses," from "the whole conceptual machinery." Now we could conclude that Derrida is saying that because we cannot decide what our responsibilities are until we have sorted out all these conceptual confusions, we must act cautiously with what Nancy later calls a "provisional morality." But this is not Derrida's position at all. Rather, he converts the condition in which we find ourselves from a negative to a positive one. It is not that we cannot yet sort out or calculate our responsibilities. Rather, to believe that we could do this would be to fail to grasp a responsibility that exceeds all calculation. Derrida identifies the spirit of calculation (classically represented by such Utilitarians as Jeremy Bentham, whose motto was said to have been "Let us calculate," but also includes anyone who could prescribe a hierarchy of duties and thus would also have a calculating machine) with that of the subject itself: "the subject is also a principle of calculability." We see later the shapes that the incalculable will take, but it is worth pausing at this particularly sharp formulation:

> I believe that there is no responsibility, no ethico-political decision that must not pass through the trials of the incalculable or the undecidable. Otherwise everything would be reducible to calculation, program, causality, and at best "hypothetical imperative."[20]

I said that Derrida's response to the charge of political impo-
tence was to argue for a two-stage responsibility—both of relentless
questioning—following out the structure of predicates traditionally
associated with the concept of subject, and their linkage to self-pres-
ence, but also a beyond of questioning, a vigil. We have of course
been here before. But the turn that it makes in his work is most
important. Let me fasten on just one sentence:

> Such a vigil leads us to recognize the processes of *difference*, trace,
> iterability, ex-appropriation . . . at work everywhere . . . well beyond
> humanity.[21]

Heidegger used the language of Being, of *Dasein*, to try to avoid traditional humanistic formulations. Perhaps unsuccessfully. Husserl's
epoché too was capable of an extreme radicalization, opening up a
sphere of transcendental consciousness that was in principle quite
as much nonhuman as human. And in the reference to this "well
beyond humanity," Derrida signals that he too will be trying to overcome the silent humanism to which Heidegger and Husserl in all
their radicalism succumbed. Derrida is saying this: that if we already
know or determine the call of the Other as human, then we have
failed to understand its radicalism. It is not another device in the
humanistic program. It is not, in that or any other sense, program-
mable, co-optable.

To abbreviate violently Derrida's story, we could say that in his
view, Heidegger rules out from the beginning the possibility that "the
call heard by *Dasein* [might] come originally to or from the animal";
or that "the voice of the friend be that of an animal." As Derrida
reminds us, Heidegger follows Aristotle in denying that we could
have a responsibility toward the living in general. Even Levinas, in
this respect, for all his apparent radicalism, seems to be following all
too carefully the contours of the human.

At this point, it is not unusual for people to say or to think and
then refuse to say (but this is not surprising): "we are human—is it
so odd that our thought reflects this?" It is worth spelling out the difficulties with this response: we are human. For all its obviousness, it
is an extraordinary remark. I will make two observations:

(1) The very issue of what it is to be human is precisely what is
at issue deep down in all of philosophy. To assert it in this way is to
refuse philosophy, and much more.

(2) It has a certain formality to it, which means it can be rewritten "we are male," "we are white," "we are European"—with whatever self-justifying consequences are meant to follow. But equally, "we are living beings," "we are animals." In other words, the performative force of the claim is radically undercut by the equally plausible substitutions it allows. Perhaps if it is repeated, we should add "all-too-human."

3.

Perhaps, however, we are missing something.

It is Derrida's thesis that a particular discourse, or a range of discourses, can be identified here. "[W]e are beings locked into a carnophallogocentric structure of subjectivity, governed by sacrificial discourse." And if this does not determine what it is to be human, it does describe the structure of Western humanistic subjectivity.

What Derrida is doing is at the very least drawing the question of the animal within what I have called the program of the "deconstruction of the subject," and in effect saying that we cannot pursue the responsibilities it enjoins without this incorporation. It is instructive, of course, and yet perhaps as necessary as it is a limitation, that Derrida uses the words "animal" or "the animal"—as if this were not already a form of deadening shorthand. Human/animal (or Man/animal), is of course one of a set of oppositions which anaesthetizes and hierarchies at the very same time as it allows us to continue to order our lives. And when man/God was still a good, working opposition, it too could be drawn into the game. What man is to God, animals are to men (and indeed woman to man)—that is, dependent beings. But I must break off. My point is just this: there are no animals "as such," rather only the extraordinary variety that in the animal alphabet would begin with ants, apes, arachnids, antelopes, aardvarks, anchovies, alligators, Americans, Australians. . . .

Our responsibility exceeds the limits of calculation. And, if Derrida is right, it is excessive or nothing. Such a list as this is a form of witness.

But I am deviating from the frame within which Derrida's discussion is set. Allow me, if I may, to return to it. Derrida defines the sacrificial structure of

the whole canonized or hegemonic discourse of Western metaphysics or religion, in which the most original form that this discourse might assume today [as discourses that leave] a place open,
in the very structure of these discourses (which are also "cultures")
for a non-criminal putting-to-death. Such are the executions of
ingestion, incorporation, or introjection of the corpse.[22]

But this sacrificial operation can take place symbolically or actually
(and in the case of our treatment of many animals, both). I will not
rehearse the way in which he shows how Heidegger and Levinas replicate this structure—his reference to the complicity of "Heidegger's
obstinate critique of vitalism" is particularly illuminating. Suffice it
to say that Derrida offers a massive project in which the deconstruction of the subject (that is, the human subject) would be linked to eating flesh, virility, the possession of nature, the privilege of the head
and the head of state—the general scheme of dominance condensed
in that ugly neologism "carnophallogocentrism."

> Th[is] subject does not want just to master and possess nature
> actively. In our cultures, he accepts sacrifice and eats flesh.[23]

Aware that I risk a half-digested regurgitation, I would add that
Derrida also alludes to a psychoanalytical graft of a whole discourse
on interiorization which would perhaps account not only for the formation of such subjects, but also symbolically for the religious and
philosophical dreams of interiorization (sublimation, appropriation,
etc.). To pursue all this here would be to bite off more than we could
chew.

There will be some, I am sure, who have concluded that my
response to Derrida is far from being an openness to an excessive
responsibility, and much closer to that of the worst kind of carnivorous ingestion. But of course Derrida is not arguing for vegetarianism at all. For the way he sets up the issue is so as to incorporate
and interiorize the actual eating of animals inside the symbolic eating of anything by anyone. The title of the paper, *"Bien manger,"* is
very difficult to translate: *"Il faut bien manger"* means straightfor-
wardly "we have to eat," and perhaps less obviously "we have to eat
well." The *"bien,"* in other words, operates first as an emphatic, and
only more obscurely as an adverb. So, many of the translations here
are as ambiguous as Derrida's attitudes to other animals are
ambivalent.

The argument of the interview seems to conclude in this way:

> [A] pure openness to the [O]ther is impossible—*and certainly* in this culture. We can no more step out of carnophallogocentrism to some peaceable kingdom than we can step out of metaphysics. Put another way, violence of a sort, "eating [O]thers," is not an option, but a general condition of life, and it would be a dangerous fanaticism (or quietism) to suppose otherwise. The issue is not *whether we eat, but how.*[24]

And if we try to fill out what eating well would consist in, what then? Derrida seems to be replacing Heidegger's *mitsein* (a deep Being-with) and Levinas' conception of the subject as hostage, with the idea that "one never eats entirely on one's own"—a "rule offering infinite hospitality."

Derrida shows how these considerations open onto a vast range of questions about bioethics, the state's attempts to regulate medical advances, etc. I will not pursue these here. But I would pause for a moment with the claim that "one never eats alone"—for it is unclear who the Others are here. Words like "hospitality" sound human; wars (of religion) sound human too. And one does wonder whether Derrida is not reverting to the very humanism he has tried to outflank.

In other respects, Derrida's argument is deeply disappointing and needs careful attention. First he assimilates—there is no other word for it—real and symbolic sacrifice so that real sacrifice (killing and eating flesh) becomes an instance of symbolic sacrifice. With this change of focus, the question of eating (well) can be generalized in such a way as to leave open the question of real or symbolic sacrifice. And to the extent that in this culture sacrifice in the broad (symbolic) sense seems unavoidable, there would seem to be little motivation for practical transformations of our engagement in sacrificial behavior. Derrida does have one overriding concern which sometimes seems equivalent to all he says about responsibility; and it is a concern that would align him with all the great diagnosers of human self-deception. It is the concern to avoid "good conscience" at almost all costs. To suppose that we could know our responsibility (and act on it) would be "good conscience," however heavy the burden taken on. Good conscience would allow that my responsibility be calculable, and hence limited, but everything Derrida says about responsibility points in the opposite direction. Responsibility is primarily a willingness and capacity to respond, hence an indeterminable openness. And it is here that Derrida parts company with vegetarianism. Noncannibalistic cultures are still symbolically cannibalistic. "Vegetarians, too, partake of animals, even of men. They practice a different mode of denegation."[25]

A carnivorous diet, it is true, is only the most visible and violent front of our undeclared war on the creatures with whom we share the planet. Although Derrida may seem to be bringing deconstruction down to earth when he says, for example, that "deconstruction is justice,"[26] this formula actually reinforces the separation between deconstruction and any particular concrete practice. Deconstruction is a practice of vigilance and cannot, as such, become some sort of alternative ethical seal of approval. Why then am I tempted to declare, in the face of Derrida's sidestep on this issue, that "vegetarianism is deconstruction"? Vegetarianism, like any progressive position, can become a finite symbolic substitute for an unlimited and undelimitable responsibility—the renegotiation of our Being-toward-other-animals. But it can also spearhead a powerful, practical, multidimensional transformation of our broader political engagement. Derrida's ambivalence toward vegetarianism seems to rest on the restricted, cautious assessment of its significance; one which would allow vegetarians to buy good conscience on the cheap. But Derrida does not thereby avoid entanglement in the paradoxes of "good conscience." For the avoidance of that widening path of resistance to violence that is vegetarianism could end up preserving—against the temptations of progressive practical engagement— the kind of good conscience that too closely resembles a "beautiful soul."

The question of the other animal is an exemplary case of responsibility in Derrida's sense, even if for that very reason it may seem too good. It is an exemplary case because once we have seen through our self-serving, anthropocentric thinking about other animals, we are and should be left wholly disarmed, ill-equipped to calculate our proper response. It is exemplary because the other animal is the Other *par excellence*, the being who or which exceeds my concepts, my grasp, etc.

Derrida is reported to have said at the Cerisy conference in the summer of 1993, "I am a vegetarian in my soul." The proper place for vegetarianism is not in the soul but in a complex reworking of the investments of the oral sphincter and all its personal and political ramifications. Carnophallogocentrism is not a dispensation of Being toward which resistance is futile; it is a mutually reinforcing network of powers, schemata of domination, and investments that has to reproduce itself to stay in existence. Vegetarianism is not just about substituting beans for beef; it is—at least potentially—a site of proliferating resistance to that reproduction. If we allow the imminences and pressures (and ghosts and cries and suffering) to which I have been yielding to have their say, we might well end up insisting that "deconstruction is vegetarianism."

There is a place for argument, proof, and demonstration in philosophy. I have insisted on its critical function, and claimed that deconstruction's relation to humanism has such a critical aspect to it. But I have also suggested that what this critical function opens onto are more or less motivated *possibilities of response*. As far as our relations to other animals are concerned, nothing is prescribed. Or if there is a prescription—thou shalt not kill—we are not obliged to listen. Or if we are obliged to listen to this prescription, this proscription, we do not have to respond. And if we do have to respond, nothing determines how we respond.

And yet there is something that moves in Derrida's account of schemas of dominance, something that it is hard not to be moved by. In "Eating Well," Derrida writes as though he is on the brink of a kind of historico-psycho-anthropology that would displace Heidegger's existential analytic, would reveal human subjectivity as something like surplus repression, and would give philosophy—deconstruction—the infinite task of reworking these archaic structures. But would not deconstruction be in danger of ending up as a kind of back door naturalism? For all its echoes of what Gianni Vattimo calls weak thought, the account I have given of deconstruction as a certain kind of critical vigilance opening possibilities of response is worth preserving. My sense, however, is that the poverty of Derrida's response to vegetarianism suggests that the resources of deconstruction are not being fully deployed here.

One last word. Before Heidegger, the history of philosophy zoo would have sheltered bees, asses, monkeys, bats, and fish. After Heidegger, snails become famous. But especially lizards. And it is especially for Heideggerians that I would like to quote part of a poem by the American poet Theodore Roethke.

The Lizard[27]

He too has eaten well—
I can see that by the distended pulsating middle;
And his world and mine are the same,
The Mediterranean sun shining on us, equally,
His head, stiff as a scarab, turned to one side,
His right eye staring straight at me
....
To whom, does this terrace belong?—
With its limestone crumbling into fine grayish dust,
Its bevy of bees, and its wind-beaten rickety sun-chairs.
Not to me, but this lizard,
Older than I, or the cockroach.

Notes

1. Jacques Derrida (with Jean-Luc Nancy), "'Eating Well,' or the Calculation of the Subject: An Interview with Jacques Derrida," *Who Comes After the Subject*, ed. Eduardo Cadava et al. (New York and London: Routledge, 1991).

2. Jean Paul Sartre, *Existentialism and Humanism*, transl. Philip Mairet (London: Methuen, 1957).

3. Martin Heidegger, "Letter on Humanism," *Martin Heidegger: Basic Writings*, ed. David Farrell Krell, transl. Frank A. Capuzzi and J. Glenn Gray (London: Routledge and Kegan Paul, 1978).

4. See, for example, Jacques Derrida, *Of Spirit: Heidegger and the Question*, transl. Geoffrey Bennington and Rachel Bowlby (Chicago: University of Chicago Press, 1989).

5. See David Farrell Krell, *Daimon Life: Heidegger and Life-Philosophy* (Bloomington: Indiana University Press, 1992).

6. Derrida, *Of Spirit*, p. 55.

7. See Emmanuel Levinas, "The Paradox of Morality," *The Provocation of Levinas: Rethinking the Other*, eds. Robert Bernasconi and David Wood (London: Routledge, 1988).

8. Jacques Derrida, *The Other Heading*, transl. Michael Naas (Bloomington: Indiana University Press, 1992), p. 4.

9. Ibid., p. 5.

10. Ibid.

11. Jacques Derrida, "Force of Law: The 'Mystical Foundation of Authority,'" *Deconstruction and the Possibility of Justice*, eds. Drucilla Cornell et al. (New York: Routledge, 1992).

12. Jacques Derrida, *Limited Inc.*, (Evanston: Northwestern University Press, 1988).

13. See n.1

14. Derrida, *The Other Heading*, p. 28.

15. See n. 1

16. Derrida, "Eating Well," p. 104. Emphasis in original.

17. Ibid., Emphasis in original.

18. Ibid.

19. Ibid.

20. Ibid., p. 108.

21. Ibid., p. 109.

22. Ibid., p. 112.

23. Ibid., p. 114.

24. Ibid., p. 115.

25. Ibid., pp. 114-15.

26. Derrida, "Force of Law," p. 15.

27. Theodore Roethke, "The Lizard," *Collected Poems* (London: Faber and Faber, 1985), p. 218.

Bestiality

 *Alphonso Lingis*

Sea anemones are animate chrysanthemums made of tentacles. Without sense organs, without a nervous system, they are all skin, with but one orifice that serves as mouth, anus, and vagina. Inside, their skin contains little marshes of algae, ocean plantlets of a species that has come to live only in them. The tentacles of the anemone bring inside the orifice bits of floating nourishment, but the anemone cannot absorb them until they are first broken down by its inner algae garden. When did those algae cease to live in the open ocean and come to live inside sea anemones?

Hermit crabs do not secrete their own shells, but instead lodge their bodies in the shells they find vacated by the death of other crustaceans. The shells of one species of hermit crab are covered with a species of sea anemone. The tentacles of the sea anemones grab the scraps the crab tears off when it eats. Since sea anemones have stings on their tentacles, the crab is protected from predator octopods, which are very sensitive to sea anemone stings. When the hermit crab outgrows its shell, it locates another empty one. The sea anemones then leave the old shell and go to attach themselves onto the new one as the crab waits. How do sea anemones, blind, without sense organs, know it is time to move?

Small nomadic bands of people have long lived in the rain forests of the world. But until recently only two commercial ways were found for humans to live off the rain forest without destroying it—tapping rubber trees and collecting Brazil nuts. Rubber has many essential uses in industry, and Brazil nuts have always commanded good prices on the export market. But there are so many species of trees intermixed in the rain forest that rubber tappers and nut collectors often had to walk for an hour from one tree of a species to the next. It early occurred to settlers to cut down the wild forest and plant plantations of rubber trees and Brazil nut trees. The Brazil nut plantations always failed. The trees grew vigorously, flowered, but never produced any nuts. Only fifteen years ago did biologists discover why. The Brazil nut flowers can be pollinated by only one species of bee. This bee also requires, for its larvae, the pollen of one species of orchid, an orchid that does not grow on Brazil nut trees. When did Brazil nut flowers come to shape themselves so as to admit only that one species of bee? What we know as Brazil nuts are kernels which, on the tree, are enclosed in a very large wooden husk containing hundreds of them. The Brazil nut tree is hardwood, and the husk about its seeds is of wood hard as iron. There is only one beast in Amazonia that has the teeth, and the will, to bore into that husk. It is a medium-sized rodent, and when it bores through the husk, it only eats some of the seeds. The remaining seeds are able to get moisture, and push their roots into the ground. Without that rodent, the nuts would be permanently entombed, and Brazil nut trees would have died out long ago.

There is perhaps no species of life that does not live in symbiosis with another species. When did celled life, with nuclei, come to evolve? Microbiologist Lynn Margulis established that chloroplasts and mitochondria, the oxygen-processing cellular energy-producers in plants and animals, were originally independent cyanobacteria that came to live inside the cells of plants and animals. Colonies of microbes evolved separately, and then formed the symbiotic systems which are the individual cells, whether of algae or of our bodies.

Human animals live in symbiosis with thousands of species of anaerobic bacteria, 600 species in our mouths which neutralize the toxins all plants produce to ward off their enemies, 400 species in our intestines, without which we could not digest and absorb the food we ingest. Some synthesize vitamins, others produce polysaccharides or sugars our bodies need. The number of microbes that colonize our bodies exceeds the number of cells in our bodies by up to a hundredfold. Macrophages in our bloodstream hunt and devour trillions of bacteria and viruses entering our porous bodies continually. They replicate with their own DNA and RNA and not ours; they are the agents that maintain our borders. They, and not some Aristotelian form, are true agencies of our individuation as organisms. When did those bacteria take up lodging in our digestive system, these macrophages take up lodging in our bloodstream?

We also live in symbiosis with rice, wheat, and corn fields, with berry thickets and vegetable patches, and also with the nitrogen-fixing bacteria in the soil that their rootlets enter into symbiosis with in order to grow and feed the stalk, leaves, and seeds or fruit. We also move and feel in symbiosis with other mammals, birds, reptiles, and fish.

Let us liberate ourselves from the notion that our body is constituted by the form that makes it an objective for the observation and manipulation of an outside observer! Let us dissolve the conceptual crust that takes hold of it as a subsistent substance. Let us turn away from the anatomical and physiological mirrors that project it before us as a set of organs and a set of biological or pragmatic functions. Let us see through the simple-mindedness that conceives of the activities of its parts as functionally integrated, and it as a distinct unit of life. Let us cease to identify it with the grammatical notion of a subject or the juridical notion of a subject of decisions and initiatives.

How myopic is the notion that a form is the principle of individuation, or a substance occupying a place to the exclusion of other substances, or that the inner organization, or the self-positing identity of a subject is an entity's principle of individuation! A season, a summer, a wind, a fog, a swarm, an intensity of white at high noon have perfect individuality, though they are neither substances nor subjects. The climate, the wind, a season have a nature and an individuality no different from the bodies that populate them, follow them, sleep and awaken in them.

The form and the substance of our bodies are not clay shaped by Jehovah and then driven by his breath; they are coral reefs full of polyps, sponges, gorgonians, and free-swimming macrophages continually stirred by monsoon climates of moist air, blood, and biles.

Every animal has its modes of being in a pack; it is not a substance with its own properties. What would a wolf all alone do? A whale, a flea, a rat, a fly? What would be a cry independently of the population that it calls or that bears witness to it? Schools of fish, flocks of birds, prides of lions are not lower forms of society, rudimentary beginnings of the political and economic order of the polis. They are movements and affects, differentials of speed that compose, intensities that materialize their force.

A pack of wolves, a cacophonous assemblage of starlings in a maple tree when evening falls, a whole marsh throbbing with frogs, a whole night scintillating with fireflies exert a primal fascination on us. What is fascinating in the pack, the gangs of the savannah and the night, the swarming, is the multiplicity in us—the human form and the nonhuman, vertebrate and invertebrate, animal and vegetable, conscious and unconscious, movements and intensities in us that are not yoked to some conscious goal or purpose that is or can be justified in some capitalist program for economic growth or some transcendental or theological fantasy of object-constitution or creativity seated in us. Aliens on other planets, galaxies churning out trillions of stars, drops of water showing, under the microscope, billions of squiggling protozoa are mesmerizing. What is mesmerized in us are the inhuman movements and intensities in us, the pulses of solar energy momentarily held and refracted in our crystalline cells, the micro-organic movements and intensities in the currents of our inner coral reefs.

Movements do not get launched by an agent against masses of inertia; we move in an environment of air currents, rustling trees, and animate bodies. Our movements are stirred by the coursing of blood, the pulse of the wind, the reedy rhythms of the cicadas in the autumn trees, the whir of passing cars, the bounding of squirrels, and the tense, poised pause of deer. The differentials of speed and slowness liberated from our bodies do not block or hold those movements only; our movements compose their differentials, directions, and speeds with those movements in the environment. Our legs plod with elephantine torpor; decked out fashionably, we catwalk; our hands swing with penguin vivacity; our fingers drum with nuthatch insistence; our eyes glide with the wind rustling the flowering prairie.

These movements have not only extension; they surge and ebb in intensity. They are vehement, raging, prying, incandescent, tender, cloying, ardent, lascivious. It is by its irritability, its fear, its rage, its languor, its exuberance that an octopus in the ocean, a rabbit caught in our headlights, a serpent in the grass, a cat on the couch, a dolphin in the ocean become visible to us. Our movements become irritable with the insistent whine of a mosquito, fearful before the fury of a hornet whose nest we have disturbed, languid with the purring of a cat, exuberant in the sparkling of the coral fish in the tropical surge.

A tune is nowise launched by an advance representation of the final note, and its evolution is nowise purposive. In singing a tune or sauntering or patterning one's finger movements through one's hair into a kinetic melody, one is also not controlled by another movement. Tunes do not imitate but answer refrains that start and stop in the streets, in the fields, and in the clouds.

Crickets in the meadows and cicadas in the trees, coyotes in the night hills, frogs in the ponds and whales in the oceans, birds in the skies make our planet continually resound with chant. Human beings do not begin to sing, and do not sing, in dead silence. Our voices begin to purr, hum, and crescendo in the concerto and cacophony of nature and machines.

Jean-Marie Le Clézio was long puzzled by the particular features of the singing of the Lacandon Indians in Chiapas—a music of cries and noises, without melody or harmony, repetitious, made in solitude and clandestinity in the night, a music made with a monophonic bamboo tube, a pipe with but two holes, a drum, a scraper, a shell, a bell, a music that does not seek to be beautiful, that is not addressed to anyone. Then, during long rainy season nights, Le Clézio heard how the songs of Indians leave behind the chains of words and meaning and pick up and join the *basso continuo* of the frogs, the dogs, the spider-monkeys, the agoutis, the wild boars, and the sloths in the tropical night.

Insects sing with their torsos, their legs, and their wings; human animals sing with their throats, their chests, their torsos, their legs, and their fingers. Human animals sing with the terrestrial, oceanic, and celestial animals, and with the reeds and the ant-hollowed branches of didgeridoos, the catgut strings and the drum-hides, the brass and the bronze. Around the campfires of hunter-gatherers from time immemorial humans have sung with their bodies; the dances of the Maasai compose visual melodies against the staves of elephant grass; in the black slums of Salvador in Brazil people are sauntering the samba into the geometrical diagrams of cars moving in the streets, with the pulsating movements of the cats and dogs of the alleys. In the imposed silence in university libraries the bodies of students are bent over books, but how much of their bodies sing— their ant-antennae feet rhythmically tapping the floor, their hummingbird fingers dancing elegant melodies in their hair.

We assign special importance, in everyday life, to purposive or goal-oriented movement. Yet most movements—things that fall, that roll, that collapse, that shift, that settle, that collide with other things, that set other things in motion—are not goal-oriented. How little of the movements of the bodies of octopuses frolicking over the reef, of guppies fluttering in the slow currents of the Amazon, of cockatoos fluttering their acrobatics in the vines of New Guinea, of terns of the species *Sterna paradisaea* scrolling up all the latitudes of the planet from Antarctica to the Arctics, of humans are teleological! How little of these movements are programmed by an advance representation of a goal, a result to be acquired or produced, a final state! They do not get their meaning from an outside referent envisioned from the start, and do not get their direction from an endpoint, a goal, or result. Without theme, climax, or denouement, they extend from the middle; they are durations.

How even less are these movements initiatives by which an agent posits and extends its identity! They are nowise the movements by which a conscious being seeks to maintain and consolidate and stabilize itself, even less integrate itself.

In the course of the day, our bodies shift, lean, settle; agitations stir them. Most of the movements of our arms and hands are aimless; our eyes glide in their sockets continually buoyed up and rocked by the waves of the sunlight. Even most of the movements to which we assign goals start by just being an urge to move, to get the day going, to get out of the house. We leave our house for a walk in the streets, a stroll along the beach, a saunter through the woods. In the Ryongi Zen Garden in Kyoto, for five hundred years each morning the monk rakes again the sands into waves. The *campesina* in Guatemala occupies her hands with the rhythms and periodicity of her knitting as she sits on the stoop gossiping with her friends. The now old Palestinian who will never leave this refugee camp fingers his prayer beads.

Every purposive movement, when it catches on, loses sight of its teleology and continues as a periodicity with a force that is not the force of the will launching it and launching it once again and then once again; instead it continues as a force of inner intensity. The carpenter climbs up the roof to nail shingles; almost at once his mind lets loose the alleged objective and the rhythm dum-dum-dum-DUM dum-dum-dum-DUM continues his movements as it does the dancer in the disco. And the force he feels in those movements is not the force of his deciding will, but the vibrant and vital intensity of his muscles on the grip of the fine, smoothly balanced hammer he likes so much. The rhythm of his hammering composes with the rhythm of the wind currents passing in and with the falling leaves. And when he pauses, he, alone in the neighborhood, registers the nearby tapping of a nuthatch on a tree trunk.

The movements and intensities of our bodies compose with the movements and intensities of toucans and wolves, jellyfish and whales. Psychoanalysis is there to sanction as infantile every intercourse with other animals which it so quixotically interprets as representatives of the father and mother figures of its Oedipal triangle. But one is not aiming at an identification with the other animal. Still less is one identifying the other animal with another human.

The hand of the child that strokes the dolphin is taking on the surges of exuberance that pulse in its smooth body while the dolphin is taking on the human impulses of intimacy forming in close contact with the child's face. The woman who rides a horse lurches with the surges of its impulses while the horse trots with her prudent programming. The movements of her body are extending differential degrees of speed and retardation, and feeling the thrill of speed and the soothing decompression of retardation. These movements are not productive; they extend neither toward a result nor a development. They are figures of the repetition compulsion: one strokes a calf each night on the farm, one rides a horse through the woods with the utterly noncumulative recurrence of orgasm.

Parents with their first baby feel all sorts of feelings about that baby—astonishment, curiosity, pride, tenderness, the pleasure of caring for a new life, the resentment of the mother over the father's unwillingness to share the tedium and distastefulness of nursing the baby and cleaning its diapers, and also the jealousy of the father as the woman he so recently chose to devote himself to exclusively— just as she chose him—now pours most of her affection on the baby. What does the baby feel, aside from hunger and discomfort? Whatever feelings simmer in that opaque and unfocused body are blurred and nebulous. Brought up in state orphanages, he or she would reach the age to be transferred to the car or tobacco factory assembly line with still opaque, blurred, and nebulous feelings. Brought up in an American high-rise apartment where the parents stay home weeknights watching action movies on television while fondling their gun collection, and go for rides weekends through a landscape of streets, boulevards, underpasses, and highways, seeing only other cars outside the window, the baby would reach sexual maturity with the feelings of Ballard and Vaughan in J.G. Ballard's *Crash*.

Is it not animal emotions that make our feelings intelligible? The specifically human emotions are interlaced with practical, rational, utilitarian calculations which tend to neutralize them—to the point that the human parent no longer knows if she feels something like parental love, finding her time with the baby dosed out between personal and career interests, not knowing how much concern for her child is concern with her own image or her representative. It is when we see the parent bird attacking the cat, the mother elephant carrying her dead calf in grief for three days, that we believe in the reality of maternal love. So much of the human courage we see celebrated is inseparable from peer pressure and the craving for celebrity and for the resultant profit, that it is the bull in the *corrida* that convinces us of the natural reality of fearlessness.

Is not the force of our emotions that of the other animals? Human infants are tedious at the table, picking at their food, playing with it, distracted from it; they pick up voracity from the puppy absorbed with total Zen attentiveness at his dish. They come to feel curiosity with a white mouse poking about the papers and ballpoints on father's desk. Their first heavy toddling shifts into tripping vivacity with the robins hopping across the lawn. They come to feel buoyancy in the midst of the park pigeons shifting so effortlessly from ground to layers of sun-drenched air. They come to feel sullenness from the arthritic old dog the retired cop was walking in the park and that they try to pet. They contract righteousness and indignation from the mother hen suddenly ruffled up, her beak stabbing when they try to remove a chick. They pick up feelings of smoldering wrath from the snarling chained dog in the neighbor's yard, and try out those feelings by snarling when they are put under restraints or confined. Temper in a human infant dies away of itself; it is from finding reverberating in himself the howling of dogs locked up for the night, the bellowing of tigers, the fury of bluebirds pursuing hawks in the sky, that his and her rage extends to nocturnal, terrestrial, and celestial dimensions.

The curled fingers of an infant ease into tenderness from holding the kitten but not tight, and rumble into contentment from stroking its fur with pressure and periodicity that are responded to with purring. In contact with the cockatoo—who, though he can clutch with a vice-grip around a perch while sleeping and chews up his oak perch in the course of a month, relaxes his claws on the arm of an infant and never bites the ear he affectionately nibbles at, and who extends his neck and spreads his wings to be caressed in all the softness of his down feathers—the infant discovers that her hands are not just retractile hooks for grabbing, but organs to give pleasure. In contact with the puppy mouthing and licking his legs and fingers and face, the infant discovers his lips are not just fleshy traps to hold in food and his tongue not just a lever to shift it into the throat, but organs that give, give pleasure, give the pleasures of being kissed. In feeling the lamb or the baby skunk extending its belly, its thighs, raising its tail for stroking, the infant discovers her hands, her thighs, and her belly are organs to give pleasure.

Far from the human libido naturally destining us to a member of our species and of the opposite sex, when anyone who has not had intercourse with the other animals, has not felt the contented cluckings of a hen stroked on the neck and under the wings rumbling through his or her own flesh, has not kissed a calf's mouth raised to his or her own, has not mounted the smooth warm flanks of a horse, has not been aroused by the powdery feathers of cockatoos and the ardent chants of insects in the summer night, gets in the sack with a member of his or her own species, they are only consummating tension release, getting their rocks off. When we, in our so pregnant expression, *make* love with someone of our own species, we also make love with the horse and the calf, the kitten and cockatoo, the powdery moths and the lustful crickets.

Orgasm proceeds by decomposition of the competent body, the body upon which have been diagrammed and contracted the efficient operations for functioning in the environment of kitchen utensils, tools, machines. It begins in denuding oneself. Clothing is not only a defensive carapace against the heat, the cold, the rain, the sleet, and the importunate impulses, curiosity, and advances of others; and protection for our flesh from the grime, dust, and harsh edges of the implements we manipulate and machines we operate. Whenever we go out in the street or open our door to someone who knocked, we see someone who has first washed off the traces of the night, the anonymity and abandon of the night, from his or her face, who has rearranged the turmoil of his or her hair, who has chosen clothing for his or her departure into the public spaces. All clothing is uniform. He and she dresses punk or preppie, worker or executive, inner city or suburban; she or he dresses chic or wears the worn leather jacket of an outdoorsperson; he dresses up in a business suit or dresses down in jeans; she puts on a pearl necklace or a neckchain of Hopi Indian beads. He or she also dresses today like he or she did yesterday and last year; she maintains the two-piece crisp look of an active woman with responsibilities, a business executive. He keeps his masculine, outdoors look even when visiting the city or coming to our dinner party; he does not put aside his plaid shirt and jeans for a tie-dyed hippie t-shirt or an Italian designer silk shirt. When we see her, wearing a t-shirt or sweat shirt with Penn State on it, we see someone who is not only dressing in the uniform of a college student, but who has dressed her movements, thoughts, and reactions with those of a Penn State freshman, a dormitory rat, or a sorority sister. We also see in the uniform the uniformity of a series of actions, undertakings, thoughts, opinions, feelings maintained for weeks, months, years, and predictable for the weeks, months, years ahead. We see the time of endurance and respond to it.

Now he or she undresses before our eyes and under our embrace. In denuding him or herself, he or she takes off the uniform, the categories, the endurance, the reasons, and the functions. Of course in the gym-built musculature we see another kind of clothing, body-armor, uniformization, a body reshaped to fit a model. But in the slight sag of the full or undeveloped breasts, in the smooth expanse of the belly, in the contour of the ass, in the bare expanse of the inside of the upper thighs, we see flesh, carnality, and our eyes already caress it to make contact with what makes it real and tremble with its own sensuality and life. This carnality, this naked flesh, is only real in the carnal contact with it, dissolute and wanton.

As our bodies become orgasmic, the posture, held oriented for tasks, collapses; the diagrams for manipulations and operations dissolve from our legs and hands, which roll about dismembered, exposed to the touch and tongue of another, moved by another. Our lips loosen, soften, glisten with saliva, lose the train of sentences; our throats issue babble, giggling, moans, sighs. Our sense of ourselves, our self-respect shaped in fulfilling a function in the machinal and social environment, our dignity maintained in multiple confrontations, collaborations, and demands, dissolve, the ego loses its focus as center of evaluations, decisions, and initiatives. Our impulses, our passions, are returned to animal irresponsibility. The sighs and moans of another that pulse through our nervous excitability, the spasms of pleasure and torment in contact with the non-prehensile surfaces of our bodies, our cheeks, our bellies, our thighs, irradiate across the substance of our sensitive and vulnerable nakedness. The lion and stallion mane, the hairy orifices of the body, the hairy bull chest, the hairy monkey armpits, the feline pelt of the *mons veneris*, the hairy satyr anus exert a vertiginous attraction. We feel feline and wolfish, foxy and bitchy; the purrings of kittens reverberate in our orgasmic strokings; our fingers racing up and down the trunk and limbs of another become squirrelly; our clam vagina opens; our penis, slippery and erect and the oscillating head of a cobra, snakes its way in. Our muscular and vertebrate bodies transubstantiate into ooze, slime, mammalian sweat, and reptilian secretions, into minute tadpoles and releases of hot moist breath nourishing the floating microorganisms of the night air.

Human sexuality is not just what priggish suburbanites call animal sex, the random and mindless copulation of their domestic dogs; it elaborates, we are told, all the refinements of eroticism. Lust enlists all the Platonic eros which craves beauty and immortality, the beauty that looks immortal and the immortality of beauty; it elaborates the skills and the arts of seduction, the teasing and provocative usage of language, metaphor and metonymy, synecdoche and irony, the no that is a yes and the yes that is a no, the specific pleasure in appearance, simulacra, and masquerade, the challenge and purely imaginary stakes of games. The consummately feminine look, Charles Baudelaire said, is "that blasé look, that bored look, that vaporous look, that impudent look, that cold look, that look of looking inward, that dominating look, that voluptuous look, that wicked look, that sick look, that catlike look, infantilism, nonchalance and malice compounded."[1]

Not a female body perfectly adapted to the function of childrearing or nurturing or winning the World Tennis cup. Not the woman who proves her flawless intelligence in pursuing a successful career, the woman who demonstrates her integrated emotional composition, unblemished by erratic outbursts, in attaining to high political responsibility. A woman not striding in sensible walking shoes, but pirouetting in stork heels or gliding in water-buffalo sandals; not wearing laundromat-washed t-shirt and jeans, but clad in the silk made by moths with chains of Polynesian shells dangling in the way of her movements. Not muscled arms and bloated, milk-full breasts, but satiny breasts and a belly not destined for pregnancy and stretch marks. An abdomen not emitting the gurglings of digestion and a derrière not smelling of defecations. A woman who survives on celery stalks and champagne, or brown rice and water. We do not see the female, we see the feminine, obeying nothing but aesthetic laws of her own making. An astral woman who appears in the crowd like a mirage, and who drifts effortlessly through doors to wander in rose gardens and crystal pools the moonbeams create wherever she turns.

Males in the Middle Ages became erotic objects in the ostentatious garb of knights, in tournaments taking place in an enchanted world of sorcerers, stallions, dragons, and rescues, and in the siren songs of outlaw gypsies, predators on the organized feudal world. The male erotic objects on the silver screen are eighteenth century cavalry or naval officers who gamble away fortunes, duel and dance, and *bandidos*, or twentieth century outlaws and high-society con men. The starched white uniforms of naval officers, with their gold epaulets; the hats, capes, and mirror-polished boots of cavalry officers with never the least trace of the muck of the barracks and the gore of the battlefield make them appear as astral men, mirages from the outer spaces beyond society. Nineteenth century *bandidos* and twentieth century outlaws and high-society con men stud their black uniforms with silver and their bloody hands with precious jewels. They prowl in the outer region of sorcery and necromancy, consecrated in that other religion of amulets, talismans, luck, fate, omens, curses, spells, werewolves, and vampires.

But in this, the courtesan, specialized in the rites of eroticism, is in symbiosis with the resplendent quetzal whose extravagantly arrayed glittering plumage serves no utilitarian function; the cavalry officer is in symbiosis with the coral fish whose Escher designs do not outline the functional parts and organs of their bodies and whose *fauviste* colors are no more camouflage than are his white jodhpurs and scarlet cape. The ceremonies and etiquette with which courtship was elaborated among the courtesans in the court of the Sun King were not more ritualized than the rituals of Emperor penguins in Antarctica; the codes of chivalry in medieval Provence not more idealized than the spring rituals of impalas in the East African savannah; the rites of seduction of Geishas in old Kyoto not more refined than those of black-neck cranes in moonlit marshes.

Humans have from earliest times made themselves erotically alluring, as pietist and frigid old Immanuel Kant noted, by grafting upon themselves the erotic splendors of animals, the glittering plumes of quetzal-birds and the filmy plumes of ostriches, the secret inner splendors of mother-of-pearl oysters, the springtime gleam of fox fur. Until Versailles, perfumes were made not with the nectar of flowers but with the musks of rodents.

And today, in our Internet world where everything is reduced to digitally coded messages, images, and simulacra instantaneously transmitted from one human to another, it is in our passions for animals that we learn all the rite and sorceries, the torrid and teasing presence and the ceremonious delays of eroticism. The dance floors are cleared of vegetation and decorated with shells and flowers that birds-of-paradise make for their intoxicated dances; a cock fight exhibits the extravagant and extreme elaborations far beyond reproductive copulation into the eroticism that humans have composed with the other animals.

The Neanderthal cave paintings of Cosquer, Chauvet, and Lascaux demonstrate that the most ancient gods of humanity were other animals, perceived by hunter-gatherers as not bound by taboos, more sacred and more demonic than humans. Noble animals—tigers, lions, jaguars, eagles, condors, cobras, animals of courage. The caves of Lascaux contain but one depiction of a human—a stick figure with the head of a bird. Who cannot but be struck with these images and carvings of lion-headed humans, half-human-half-bull, half-human-half-stag, human with the head of a fox, ibis, or cat, in the ancient art of Egypt, Mesopotamia, South-East Asia, and America?

Human animals are sometimes gregarious as chimpanzees, sometimes solitary as orangutans, sometimes timorous and obedient as sheep, sometimes proud and beautiful as panthers.

Human beings, naked, with such slow-developing maturity, so easily intimidated by one another, can sustain a deep layer of lifelong fear and instinctual prudence. They acquire useful skills, acquiescent dispositions, and deferential postures and attitudes. These they pick up from others, pass on to others. They are jealous of rights, take on responsibilities that make others dependent on them. They learn to be useful, serviceable, servile. Feeling themselves under accusation, they elaborate justifications for everything they feel and do.

When such humans armed themselves in the service of their expansionist polis, nation, or religion, they rode thousands of horses to uncomprehending death under their feet. It was the vultures that came to bury their bodies in the sky. The Dutch, English, French, Russians, and Peruvians sailed as far as To Pito O Te Henua for slaves; and when these slaves sickened and died, they threw them into the ocean, where the sharks came to make them live again in their bodies. Today, the homing pigeons and the dolphins as conscripts of human warfare have been consigned to obsolescence; human armies fly at great heights in the stratosphere and at great distances at sea to launch the missiles of destruction, and it is viral and bacteriological life that is conscripted to spread their species hatred on the battlegrounds.

The global capitalist free-trade economy now in place guarantees that industrial powers will not again wage world war against one another. They are dismantling their thermonuclear and biochemical arsenals. Instead, the Third World War their industrial might is waging is a war on the world—on the great components of Nature, the fertile continents, the oceans, the stocks of freshwater 70% of which are piled up in the now melting ice of Antarctica, the atmospheres, the ozone shield, the ultraviolet-reduced light that generates life. The destruction of these components of Nature since the Second World War has already been equal to the destruction that a third, thermonuclear World War would have wrought. Each year sees the genocide of 17,500 species of plant and animal life.

The noble impulses—of physical splendor, of the great health that knows itself in the great quantities of corruption it absorbs and transfigures into vigor, of the thirst for truth that opens upon woe, hell, hatred, and disgrace crippling the world (this world, oh you know it!), of the thirst for justice which transcends itself into mercy— these noble impulses are nowise contrived to serve human needs and wants, human whinings. They are nowise contracted to serve our self-consolidation and self-aggrandizement. They are forces that expend themselves without return, impulses to give in the super-abundance of exultation without calculation of profit and loss.

Socrates, who claimed none of the intellectual or moral virtues, at his trial reminded his judges of his courage which they all knew, proved three times in battle. Aristotle made courage the first virtue, for without courage neither truthfulness nor magnanimity nor friendship nor even wit in conversation are possible. But Socrates erred in then setting out to formulate the ideas and beliefs—his arguments for immortality—that would make courage itself possible. For courage, *courage*, as the word indicates, is the force of the heart; and sociological studies are there to show that the same number of people who think that their death is the gateway to eternal bliss die bravely and die cowardly as those who think their death is just annihilation. Courage rises up in us, we are inclined to say, from our animal nature. But the courage of the *torero* rises in his confrontation with the black bull; the courage of the divemaster rises in respect for the damselfish, but a few grams of matter jellied in seawater, who nonetheless attacks him; the courage of the pilot of the Cessna rises fraternally to the condors soaring at 18,000 feet over the desolation and glaciers of the peaks of the high Andes.

Our ethics, from Socrates, whose physical ugliness Friedrich Nietzsche noted and made much of, to John Rawls has not known what to make of physical splendor. Our ethics, which has built up so extensive a vocabulary, has not given a name of virtue to the compulsion of a man to acquire the strong and proportioned musculature of bulls and elk, the compulsion of a woman to move with the grace of a panther. This compulsion does not derive from ethical culture, but arises on invitation from nature, in whom the primal drive for beauty decorates with designs and colors as splendid as that of a pheasant the shells of blind mollusks, and which arrays such a *carnaval* parade of coral fish, butterflies, and birds. The creative drive of beauty is so fundamental in nature that all our interest in nature is a marvel at her beauty. The servile among us want only to be efficient and dress in uniforms; those who commerce with sunfish and dragonflies, leopards and eagles, recognize the nobility of physical splendor in humans, too.

The male emperor penguins huddle on the ice shelf under raging blizzards for nine months of the Antarctic winter, all their metabolic processes devoted to keeping warm in $-70°$ F temperature the egg the female emperor penguins have given over to their care. When the egg hatches, they nourish it with the secretions of their throats until the winter breaks and the females can return with krill from the open seas. House wrens in Pennsylvania gardens hurl themselves shrieking into the eyes of predator cats that are climbing to their nests. The stings of bees are barbed, and the bee can detach itself from the enemy it stings only by tearing fatally its own body. Every bee that stings an importunate suburbanite gives its life for the life of the hive. The other animals give not of their surplus to the less fortunate; they give of the nourishing fluids of their own bodies; they give their very life. They do not think to imagine a prestige that repays them on another level for gifts given freely. They do not think to imagine an infinite repayment beyond the death they give that others may live.

Our theoretical ethics from Aristotle to Marcel Mauss and Jacques Derrida has not ceased to find intelligibility in gift-giving only by reinterpreting in an economy of equivalent exchange, even if that means it has to calculate prestige as recompense with interest. The impulse to give without calculation and without recompense, when it rises up compulsively in us, as it does every day, we have contracted in our commerce with animal nobility. How rarely do humans find the courage to say those fearful words *I love you—* fearful, because we are never so vulnerable, never open to being so easily and so deeply hurt, as when we give ourselves over in love of someone. But from early infancy we have come to understand this instinct—in our kitten that so unreservedly gave itself over to its affection for us, in our cockatoo that in all her excitement upon seeing us wants nothing but to give us all her tenderness and affection.

How awesome the thirst for truth when we contemplate it sovereign in the great scientist, the great explorer! Here is someone contemptuous of honors and wealth, craving to open her mind to the most tragic realities, to the cosmic indifference of the universe to the wishes of her own species and to herself, craving to know with the wounds, rendings, and diseases of her own body the expanses and alien populations of oceans and tundra, rain forest and ice sheets. Human culture sets itself up as the compensation for those who limit their curiosity and their research only to funded projects that will benefit the human species. It is not from human culture that those consumed with the thirst for truth learn to program their lives. It is from the albatross that leaves its nest to sail all the latitudes of the planet and all its storms and icy nights for seven years before it touches earth again, only to give its mature strength to raising offspring like it. Nietzsche wrote, you, researchers and consolidators of knowledge, have, like spiders, only turned the ways of the universe into a spider web to trap your prey. It is because your soul does not fly, like eagles over abysses.

How awesome the thirst for justice when we contemplate it in a man like Mahatma Gandhi, Che Guevara, Nelson Mandela. They knew before they began that at the end of the path they were blazing lay assassination, ambush, and extermination, a life tortured from youth to old age in dungeons. Of the *Sandinista* guerrillas who made a blood pact to fight for the liberation of Nicaragua in 1959, only one, Tomás Borge, was not gunned down in the jungle, and he was captured and held in Anastasio Somoza's prisons for years. After the *Sandinista* victory in 1979, Borge was selected by his comrades to be Minister of Interior. A few months later, his subordinates informed him that among the captured agents of Somoza's *Guardia Nacional* were identified the three men who had tortured him during the decades of his incarceration. He went at once to the prison where they were held and ordered them to be brought before him. He looked intently at them and verified that they were indeed his torturers. Then he ordered them to be liberated.

No reasoning, reckoning, calculation of how to most profitably manage life in human society, has ever provided the motivation for the thirst for justice to which a human sacrifices his life—so often in vain!—and even less for the justice that liberates its enemies. "Justice, which began," Nietzsche wrote, "with 'everything is paid for, everything must be paid for,' ends by winking and letting those incapable of paying their debt go free: it ends, as does every good thing on earth, by overcoming itself. This self-overcoming of justice: one knows the beautiful name it has given itself—mercy." This justice that overcomes itself the noblest and most courageous humans contract, Nietzsche went on to say, from their commerce with lions, who are always covered with ticks and flies that seek shelter and nourishment there. The lion does not rage against them: "What are my parasites to me? . . . May they live and prosper: I am strong enough for that!"

Notes

1. Charles Baudelaire, *Oeuvres complètes*, ed. Claude Pichois (Paris: Gallimard, 1961), p. 1256.

THREE

Animals, Becoming

Lynda Birke and Luciana Parisi

"Mother nature" is a familiar phrase; the earth as mother, too, is an image used to advertise environmental campaigns. Such associations between nature and femininity/women are deeply embedded in Western thought, and find expression, too, in some strands of feminist writing. Yet they are also troublesome. Not surprisingly, many women have objected to being likened to animals or to unruly "nature."

In this chapter, we want to explore some of that heritage, focusing on the relationship between feminism and ideas about animals. The relationship is a complex one, sometimes denying any closeness, at other times exploring and celebrating it. But underlying it is the problem of dualism—the predominant Western tendency to think in terms of either/or, self/Other, culture/nature, man/woman, human/animal. Such dualisms pervade our thought, and all are hierarchical. So, both feminism and the causes of animals must share a concern with the ways that the Other becomes subordinate.

We will refer here to two sets of ideas that can be helpful in challenging such dualisms. The first comes from people seeking alternatives to the dominant stories within biology—how, for instance, do we understand evolution and our historical relationships with other species? The second comes from the work of philosophers, in particular from that of Gilles Deleuze and Felix Guattari and their concept of becoming animal, and the related ideas of feminist biologist Donna Haraway.

1. Irrational "Others"

Troublesome dualisms have a long history in Western culture from Greek times onward. In Plato's myth of the cave, truth (a rational, masculine form) required the banishment of matter (feminine, chaos); in the origin of Western thought, the Platonic myth represents a foundational theory for the relationship between self and Other. The obscure and deceptive cave where "man" lived represented the untrue world of images. In order to reach the true, the light of reason, "man" had to go out from the cave and never return back.

Aristotle, too, described a "chain of being" listing animal and plant kinds, with those nearer the top having more reason and being closer to an immaterial God. We thus have a long history of prioritizing rationality. Our view of nature is also shaped by the development, during the sixteenth and seventeenth centuries, of the scientific revolution which brought in its wake dramatic changes in worldview and established a mechanical model of nature that also influenced later philosophical thought. This new conception of science reacted against earlier concepts of form and ideas, ensuring a passage from an animistic conception of things in nature to a mechanical biology. Nature therefore loses soul and becomes mathematized and quantified; natural beings become machines.

Such notions were developed further by René Descartes' separation of the rational human mind from the body (and his ensuing argument that animals are mere machines), and by Immanuel Kant in his *Critique of Pure Reason*. Kant affirmed the importance of rationality in establishing universal and necessary truths. To understand matter, for Kant, required the "I," which would shape inert matter according to given truths. Both Kant and Descartes thus emphasized the power of rationality and insisted on dualisms that represented the relation of power between the "I" and the "not I." The "I" shapes our knowledge of nature according to preestablished categories stemming from pure mathematical models based on geometry and quantification.

These views deeply inform how we think about our world and our relationships to nature. Nature, animals, and women—each likely to be seen as embodied and lacking mind or soul—stand as irrational Others to culture, human beings, and men. Exploring these issues, ecofeminist author and activist Val Plumwood emphasizes that

> it is . . . exclusion from the master category of reason which in liber-
> ation struggles provides and explains the conceptual links between
> different categories of domination, and links the domination of
> humans to the domination of nature. The category of nature is a
> field of multiple exclusion and control, not only of non-humans, but
> of various groups of humans and aspects of human life which are
> cast as nature.[1]

Whatever is excluded from reason—be that women, non-Europeans, disabled people, animals—is other to Western masculine selves.

How we come to understand and name nature is very much a product of our history. Western observers have read rationality onto nature, ensuring that rational man remains central to our systems of thought. How we classify the natural world thus reflects these, and other, preoccupations. Carl Linnaeus' classification of plants, for example, was deeply dependent upon prevailing ideas of gender and sexuality,[2] while animal taxonomists in the nineteenth century often used animal names as a vehicle for celebrating European imperialism and racism.[3]

Yet, however scientists have classified nonhuman organisms, human beings remain privileged. Evolutionary ideas undoubtedly challenged the centrality of "man" by insisting that we too had evolved from some other kind. Yet for all that, the cultural assumption of our difference from other animals remains strong. The tension between our similarity and our difference from other animals, moreover, informs much of the political and philosophical tension around debates on animal rights. In short, we are animals; but we are not like animals. We might admit, after Charles Darwin, that we "are" animals in some physiological sense. But we hasten to deny any "beastly" behavior on our part. We possess reason, the argument goes, so we are not "like" other animals.

2. Feminism, Nature, Biology . . .

There are, inevitably, many kinds of politics within feminism. With respect to the culture/nature binary, modern feminism includes those who argue for women's inclusion in culture, those who prefer to see women as closer to nature, as well as those who seek to transcend the binary altogether. The conceptual links between women and nature were eloquently expounded by Susan Griffin in her prose-poem *Woman and Nature* (1978) and have since become a theme emerging from much ecofeminist writing.[4] The association is one of shared oppressions: nature, animals, and women suffer through the combined actions of various systems of domination.

Yet, this association is troubling to other feminists because it continues to rely on the same self/Other dualism. If women identify with Others such as nature, then that presumes that we can identify with that which is alien. None of these categories are unitary (let alone simple); there are complex differences among women, among nonwhite people, among animals. Which women, for example, are we speaking of when we talk of shared oppression between women and animals? And which animals?

Modern feminism generally has tended to emphasize separation from animals. At the beginning, in the 1970s, the main concerns of Anglo-American feminism were with gender, paying particular attention to the ways in which gender is socially constructed. Politically, this was important in order to contest various claims about women's capabilities originating in biology. When told women were "naturally" or "biologically" predestined to be nurturing, feminists answered back by showing how femininity is socially shaped. While important, this stance led feminist theory to something of an impasse: denying any significance to biology meant also denial of anything biological. The body was thus left out of much theorizing, while nature and animals were largely ignored.

This began to change in the 1980s as environmental consciousness grew. The emerging ecofeminist literature now includes discussion of animals in its many considerations.[5] Nonetheless, there are two problems at a theoretical level that we need to address. First, the woman/animal association has long been problematic precisely because it is used in ways that devalue women. Moreover, it all too easily leads us to overlook differences among women—difference having to do with race or ethnicity, for example. Second, and relatedly, the use of the generic animal is problematic. As we argue below, the generic "animal" is no friend of feminism.

Being likened to animals is often derogatory; similarity to brutes has all too often buttressed sexism and racism. But we cannot sustain that objection by expecting to be admitted to "full humanity" while ignoring the ways in which that humanity is defined. Plumwood stresses this point: "women cannot base their own freedom on endorsing the continued lowly status of the sphere of nature with which they have been identified and from which they have lately risen."[6] Yet this is indeed what happens in many feminist arguments.

Separating ourselves from nature and animals has been tactically necessary for feminists. We have needed to challenge biological arguments about gender, sexuality, and race. Now, those who produce such arguments typically refer to animal societies to buttress their claims. If some sort of animal behaves thus, they argue, then that behavior must be built into us. But there are two problems with this simplistic line of reasoning (which was particularly evident in the 1960s in the form of "pop" ethology). The first is that animal examples are notoriously tricky. For every instance of animal societies in which alpha males strut their stuff, there are others which seem to be centered on cooperating females. Second, the animal examples themselves are built upon certain assumptions—one of which is that animals are inferior to humans. The chasm between human and animal, so beloved of Western culture, is written into the history of scientific observation of animal societies.[7] As a result, animal behavior is all too often seen as automatic, instinctual, the product of built-in imperatives. Everything about animals constitutes their biology. Lurking behind this assumption is the related presupposition that rational human beings somehow escape such imperatives; our behavior and capabilities thus seem to lie outside of biology, that is, in that other dualism, body versus mind.

Underlying all this is the human/animal distinction itself which posits one species (Homo sapiens) against a generic animal—presumably, the whole of the animal kingdom. Now, perhaps the assumption that animals lack, say, reasoning powers, *might* be true if we were talking about some quite simple animals such as jellyfish or nematode worms (though how would we know? Who says what reasoning is in creatures so incommensurate with ourselves?). But it is a more difficult case to argue when it comes to many mammals, particularly primates.

This tendency to distance ourselves from a generic animal is one instance of what Plumwood (following Albert Memmi) refers to as the "homogenization of the colonized," in which the colonized Other is always seen in ways that reduce individuality. They are faceless Others. To contrast human with animal is thus to invoke a contrast with a mythical beast. Homogenization is common in racist and sexist rhetoric; but it applies also to how we conceptualize animals. To which ones are we claiming to be superior? And in which behavior or capability?

3. . . . and Animals

Feminists can, however, also challenge biological arguments by questioning premises about animals. Those biological arguments that we so dislike are based on an assumption that everything about "the" animal is biological, pure instinct, natural. Yet we need to challenge the notion of animal societies as machinery writ large; we need to explore the possibility (for which there is mounting evidence) that many species are more complex and capable than mere bundles of instincts. These animal societies, in other words, could themselves be thought about in terms of social construction, thus challenging the human/animal binary at the heart of biological determinism. One example is how gender develops: in nonhumans, we might tend to assume that gender difference comes down to biology—different amounts of hormones, perhaps. But even this assumption is unwarranted, as such biological influences cannot readily be dissociated from influences coming from the animal's native society.[8]

Animal capabilities cannot so readily be dismissed by assuming them to be instinctive as many theorists of human society tend to do.[9] It is not surprising if we find that such creatures seem stupid if we ask them the wrong questions. It is also not surprising that some seem stupid when scientists pose questions of animals that have been kept in captivity, living in highly impoverished dwellings; human beings might not do so well if kept in similar deprivation.[10] And how stupid would we seem if nonhuman animals asked us questions? How well would we fare if required by our dog friends to find our way around New York City by smell alone?[11]

In making this move, we do not intend to deny particular human abilities: writing this essay on a computer and corresponding via the Internet are cultural practices that mark human beings out. Moreover, we must also recognize that the animal kinds with which we are most familiar are precisely those which we human beings have culturally and symbolically constructed as "Other." For example, however much we might say to you that pigs are highly social animals who should be better respected, the various practices associated with human relationships with pigs argue otherwise: we keep them in tiny cages and fatten the piglets; we subject them to breeding programs designed to ensure heavy build (or even genetic engineering, leading to the creation of pigs unable to bear their own weight); we kill them to eat; and now we have created the transgenic pig designed to provide organs for transplant surgery. What these actions signify is that pigs are considered inferior; they are *created* as Other and are powerless to change their fate. Their cultural meaning *is* as bodies, as flesh, as commodities to be consumed. They are not selves in the way that we see ourselves.

Companion animals are, by contrast, socialized to become part of human society. People, moreover, have expectations of how such animals will behave, which in turn influences our relationships with them and hence how they do behave. In this case, companion animals are only partly Others, and we are inclined to grant them some level of intelligence or consciousness. They are clearly not Others when they are part of the family; yet they are other to the body politic, in that they themselves do not have rights (which are accorded instead to the "owner").

So, different kinds of animals may become Others in different ways or contexts. Yet, they are all other to humanity in any claims we might make about ourselves (intelligence, rationality, and so forth). It is when we wish to dissociate ourselves from animality, from nature, that we typically invoke this generic animal. The generic animal is mindless, irrational, instinctual (quite unlike many of the animal kinds with which we might share our daily lives). It is no wonder that feminists have wanted to distance themselves from this creature.

4. Describing Animals

As we have noted, how science names and describes animals has a history of incorporating various social beliefs. Among these is the belief that animals—all kinds of animals—are perpetually stupid and inferior. The growth of cognitive ethology (the study of animal minds and consciousness) has begun to challenge the view of animals as mere bundles of instinct. Alongside this are alternative views of how organisms develop—accounts which provide a challenge to the simple binary of human versus animal by challenging beliefs that organisms might simply be genes writ large.

Associated with the rigid separation between human and animal in Western history is a set of beliefs about biology. In particular, there are specific—and highly popularized—accounts of how evolution works and of the role of genes.

Darwin's theory of evolution through natural selection explains change through time as a result of organic mutations (variations); these mutations affect survival so that only organisms with favorable mutations leave descendants. Darwin also affirms that there is no fundamental difference between mammals and "man"; the only difference between them is a difference of degree, as organisms evolve from simpler to more complex forms of life. Darwin's theory has been extensively analyzed and discussed over the last century; yet, there remains a persistent belief in a linear evolution toward perfection, and in "survival of the fittest." Ideas of (human) perfection have a long history in Christian theology, while notions of competition and survival have become central to the operation of capitalism.

Relatedly, there has been a recent, rapid development of what might be called the discourse of the gene.[12] In this discourse, it is "the" gene which reigns supreme. "It" determines who we are, and—in the popular books by Richard Dawkins—dominates the lumbering robots called bodies by which genes perpetuate themselves. This rhetoric gains further momentum in the context of the Human Genome Initiative (the massive international effort to "map the human genome") and recent work with recombinant DNA (creating transgenic organisms, for example, by incorporating a human gene into the genome of a sheep).

At the heart of these related ideas is the belief that genes are blueprints of what we are. So, becoming an adult means following a path specified in those genes (and by random natural selection). This image pervades many discussions of ethics. When frozen human embryos were required by law in Britain to be discarded there were outcries about the resultant murder of "children." Yet, embryos at this stage are only two or four cells. It is not a case of destroying "individual human lives" (as was claimed), since embryos and their genes can develop into babies only in specific contexts (including a maternal womb).

The gene as prime mover is a story that enables us to emphasize our individuality: we are our genes. What emerges from this linear set of processes is an essence, a finished being. Yet development and evolution are far from being the unfolding of genes. Development, for example, requires much more than genes; embryos themselves take an active part in the process, making, engaging, and changing their environments even as their environments do the same to them. Moreover, this active process of change occurs with one set of genes even though bodily forms may change drastically in a lifetime. Perhaps the most extreme cases are those species, like butterflies, that metamorphose; but even we ourselves undergo limited bodily change throughout our lifetime as environments change.

Seeing natural selection as an entirely passive process relying on random chance is also a story that conveys a sense of fixity. Successful species are said to be "adapted" to a specific niche in the environment. Yet randomness and passiveness are not the way evolution necessarily works, as some evolutionary biologists such as Judith Masters have argued.[13] Rather, we can better understand the process if we think of organisms and their environments adapting and changing together. Niches, Masters insists, are not passive addresses, but change themselves: evolution requires the coadaptation of the organism and those other organisms that comprise its environment. So, insisting on the linkage and exchange between genes and their environments in which one can change the other is, we would argue, not only a better description of how biology works, but also moves away from essential being and identities. Who we are is not a fixed identity, but a continual process of becoming. Becoming through the organism's own agency, moreover, is not necessarily left to pure chance. Becoming, in turn, is central to any rethinking of the meaning of animals.

A critical part of the challenge to the human/animal binary is to reject the profound determinism that lies in accounts of genes and evolution-as-progress. If animal Others are bundles of instincts then we are to assume that the cause lies in the genes. But if we emphasize animal abilities then a rather different story emerges—one in which individuals (or social groups) actively engage with environments. They are not essences, acting out an inevitable role; rather, they are constantly becoming, and changing their environments. And so are we. The idea of becoming is helpful if we are to break down rigid boundaries of what counts as individuals or species, for it is these boundaries that reinforce Western beliefs about animals as separate from ourselves.

5. Animals, Becoming

In order to challenge the prevailing hierarchical model of self and Other, and the association in some feminist writing with nature/ animal as Other, we want to emphasize difference and becoming. We will draw on the concept of becoming as intended in the philosophical work of Deleuze and Guattari (which in turn draws on Henri Bergson's idea of "creative evolution"), and use it in relation to the ideas about evolution and differentiation of organisms noted above. From there, we will move to consider the wider political consequences for animals and for feminism.

Deleuze and Guattari's work is complex. It is not intended to be read in the usual linear fashion, but weaves in and out of many disparate images and metaphors. Important concepts here include the two on which we draw: becoming and the metaphor of the rhizome. Becoming, as Deleuze and Guattari describe it, is a process. We can speak of "becoming animal" in the sense of alliances and symbioses. You or I can be in a process of becoming animal (for example, to ride a horse well, in the sense of creating a harmonious partnership, we must "become horse"; to work with a sheepdog involves "becoming dog," while the dog is "becoming sheep" and "becoming human"). Deleuze and Guattari use this notion of becoming as an asymptotic process: we can never "arrive." It is not an emphasis on relationships between species that is crucial here, for that would imply individuals. Rather, becoming is something that might be shared between orchid and pollinating bee.[14]

This line of thought emphasizes becoming rather than being, process rather than essence, alliances and multiplicities rather than unitary individuals, heterogeneous populations (such as ecosystems) rather than species. Becoming is also molecular, stressing the movements of molecules rather than the rigid boundaries of (molar) selves. To illustrate further, Deleuze and Guattari draw on the metaphor of a rhizome spreading through the earth. This metaphor plays with the horizontal connection as opposed to the vertical connection that predominates in narratives of evolutionary descent and inheritance. These metaphors are not easy to think with, so strong and powerful is our heritage of essential kinds whose boundaries cannot be sullied.

We can illustrate these difficult ideas by turning to some concepts in scientific thought that are opposed to the dominant ideas of neo-Darwinism. In doing so, we hope to make the discussion a little less abstract before returning to the political issues of feminism and animals. Neo-Darwinism draws on genetic determinism, presupposing a becoming of the same (that is, the insistence on the eternal survival of the most adapted genes) and an evolutionary system rooted in given truths and stable categories.

Becoming, by contrast, is not about the genetic blueprint, the eternal survival of genes, or the continuous "perfection" of organisms; nor is it about the linear and progressive narrative of human evolution. Rather, becoming, for organisms, is about development, epigenesis, processes of interchange with environments and of "making them over." It is about the creation of change.

Deleuze and Guattari's idea of becoming is thus multiple in the sense that it shifts the emphasis from the individual organism to organisms-in-relation—not only to each other, other kinds, and environments, but also to themselves. Haraway uses related concepts in her discussions of feminism, focusing on the semi-permeability of relationships between self and Other (rather than the hermetically sealed sense of self which Western culture tends to idealize).[15]

Here, we can think of the example of ecosystems—although not as assemblages of individuals or populations of different species as they are sometimes described. Instead, we might emphasize the transformations of energy central to ecosystems (analogous to Deleuze and Guattari's molecular becomings). Through these transformations, entities are continuously in states of becoming: even apparent equilibrium is dynamic.[16]

Another way of challenging prevailing views of organisms comes from alternatives to Darwinian evolution (or at least the popularized accounts of it). Although few would now accept the Aristotelian idea of species as fixed and as having essences, such sentiment is curiously persistent, even in the face of notions of evolution and change.

As biologist Steven Jay Gould has pointed out, the idea of species as fixed holds on—even among biologists.

We draw upon some of Gould's arguments here to emphasize difference as a matter of degree as well as of kind. Differences of degree make it harder to believe in rigid separations. So, if we are only somewhat different from other animals (instead of absolutely different), then we are also somewhat similar. Indeed, it is precisely such emphasis on differences of degree that has been mobilized by those arguing for special consideration for the great apes; it is just their similarities (or differences of degree) that are emphasized here in order to have them included in a particular moral circle.[17]

For Deleuze and Guattari, evolution refers to a process of interchange between populations rather than to a production of species. The genealogical tree is made more complex by rhizomatic, horizontal connections—more like a network or spider's web, actually, than a tree. Here they draw on Bergson's theory, which stresses the possibility of interactive lines of evolution rather than isolated lines or even branches. This allows more complex interrelations and differentiation; it also emphasizes a continuous transformation of organisms which does not aim to perfection, but which is constituted by shifts, ruptures, and breaks. Similarly, Deleuze and Guattari emphasize processes of interconnection and change—an "imperceptible becoming" that is quite unlike the linear perfection metaphor of evolution.[18]

Human (Western) beliefs in individuality and boundaries are also threatened by symbiosis—that is, mutually beneficial and cooperative living arrangements between two organisms. This is a kind of becoming in which an organism is opened to others and to change through symbiosis which "brings into play beings of totally different scales and kingdoms, with no possible filiation."[19] Symbiosis in biology is central to the hypothesis of evolution proposed by Lynn Margulis, who points out that bacteria and viruses are part of the heritage of all more complex living organisms: bacteria became incorporated into the cell structure of viruses very early in the history of life.

Who or what, then, is an authentic species or organism? What is an individual? And are humans so special and different? Our ways of thinking are deeply dependent upon concepts of individuals as separate entities. These assumptions permeate biological hypotheses as they do the rest of culture. But, as Margulis has pointed out, these are based on mammalian (indeed, human) individualities.[20] It is not meaningful, she insists, to talk about individual bacteria; individuality arose almost as an accident as cells began to cooperate: "An organism becomes an individual as it is comprised of different component organisms living together symbiotically in a mode requiring adjustment and integration. Individuality requires incessant reiteration."[21] Emergent individuality—or "singularity" as Deleuze and Guattari prefer—thus requires processes of becoming.

Deleuze and Guattari's notion of becoming, along with some important ideas drawn from modern biology, allow us to begin to think differently about ourselves and about animals. These ideas move beyond simple dualisms by insisting on connections and flows rather than on individual entities, and by insisting on transformation and change rather than essence. Becoming animal, in Deleuze and Guattari's work, is to experience interchange; it is to question the ideals of humanism and purity. Nevertheless, any challenge to the Western idealism of human purity can easily be appropriated. Within science, we have only to think of those new techniques that deliberately alter organismic boundaries—experiments in transgenesis, xenotransplantation, and interbreeding, for example. Yet such boundary transgressions *become* threatening to many precisely because we tend to think in terms of purity.

6. Women, Animals, Becoming

These ideas are certainly complex. In drawing on the philosophical work of Deleuze and Guattari and on the development of particular themes in theoretical biology, we have tried to connect points of overlap and similarity, noting that (1) their starting point is in disagreement with predominant ways of thinking about organisms, and (2) they stress the connections between organisms. So, rather than thinking in terms of the characteristics which separate species, interconnections (that is, rhizomatic connections) are critical to this line of thought.

The relationship between women and animals is not, then, about essences or identification. Rather, it is about an infinity of connections which we need to explore. Deleuze and Guattari's concept of becoming woman has not escaped feminist critique[22] because it still retains a sense of woman as Other. Yet, as Elizabeth Grosz has pointed out, their work does suggest ways of breaking down binaries by insisting on alternative ways of thinking about ourselves-in-relation. Simple binaries make no sense in a rhizomatic world.

In an explicitly feminist context, Haraway's work is relevant here. Haraway speaks of affinities rather than identities,[23] of fractured rather than stable identities, and of situated knowledges rather than mythical pure objectivity.[24] The concept of fractured identities, for example, allows recognition of difference even within the self: there is no stable "I" but only a process of becoming. These ideas allow us to begin to think across boundaries, to challenge the rigid separations—of self/Other, human/animal—to which we are heirs.

In her work on the language of immunology, Haraway reminds us that, in evolutionary terms, "the individual is a constrained accident, not the highest fruit of earth history's labors."[25] We are assemblages of lineages of cells with different histories; we are also vulnerable to engagement with whatever is inside or outside us. The immune system connects us. "Immunity can be conceived in terms of shared specificities," Haraway argues, "of the semi-permeable self able to engage with [O]thers (human and non-human, inner and outer)."[26]

These, then, are important ideas for those of us concerned to challenge the rigid dualism of human versus animal. Rather than emphasize common identities between women and animals, we would prefer to break down identities and describe points of affinity and becoming. Conceiving of the world in this way respects unique singularities while simultaneously moves away from thinking in terms of atomized entities (individual selves) and toward thinking of fluidity.

7. Affinities and Politics

Yet what does it mean to think about notions like fluidity? How does such a shift affect the political questions that have concerned feminists and those involved with animal rights? Perhaps the most fundamental issue to emphasize is precisely that a politics focused on a specific identity merely shores up the dominant language and politics; it does so by perpetuating those self/Other distinctions that ran us into trouble in the first place. There will always be some Other to a politics built on identity. That, indeed, was exactly why a feminism emerging primarily out of the experiences of white, middle-class North Americans and Europeans was so criticized by those outside of such experiences: they remained other to that experience of feminism.

In similar ways, arguing for animal rights can sometimes perpetuate the problems. The concept of rights is certainly tricky; but so too is the notion of extending such rights to the hypothetical and generic animal. Again, this seems to be based upon the idea of extending the boundaries, but never questioning that boundaries remain central. The problem here is made clear when the argument slides, as it usually does, into sterile debate about where we might "draw the line." Around the great apes? Around mammals? Around vertebrates? The implication is that there is a boundary that can be drawn, somewhere. And buried within that is the implication that species can be ordered linearly and hierarchically—for how else can we define a boundary?

To argue for a politics of affiliation is to see politics as networks and connections that are not rooted in essential kinds or boundaries. What (much of) feminism shares with the politics of animal causes is precisely the need to challenge rigid boundaries of self and Other. With regard to nonhuman animals (as well as those human beings who have been cast as Other), we must learn to experience connection and to think in terms of becoming. We can become horse or become dog in our relationships with them—just as in doing good science we can become one with the organism being studied.[27]

This is not just about being better able to imagine their suffering. It is also about an imagining that can become their knowing. Knowledges are situated—socially located. A better politics and a better science will emerge when we recognize this and include all special locations rather than accept the single vision we now expect. Indeed, Sandra Harding points out that what would emerge would be a stronger objectivity in science—stronger and more fully representative of different knowledges.

So, a better politics (of feminism and of animals) and a better science must include the situated knowledges of all of us, of whatever kind. It must also start from a premise of becoming rather than one based on individuals and their rights. Becoming animal is to experience interchange and interconnection, to think in terms of flows and transformation rather than fixity. Just as the pollinating bee and the orchid are deeply interconnected, so too is the feminist author who shares part of her life with three dogs. That deep interconnection goes beyond companionship or (worse) ownership: it is a series of becomings.

However, it is just the possibility of breaching boundaries which permits scientists literally to create new kinds of organisms—in the form of transgenic animals, for example, or the use of donor organs from nonhumans for transplant surgery. Some people who have received donor organs from other people have felt that they have acquired characteristics of the donor—truly a becoming-Other (scientists, of course, would roundly refute such claims, arguing that it is simply not possible; we are merely noting the claims here). But if that were the case, then what happens when it is a pig's heart that is transplanted?

To speak of affiliation and fluidity can, perhaps, seem overly liquid, as though "anything goes." Yet even liquids are constrained; their molecules do not go just anywhere. New ways of thinking about our relationships to nature are imperative given the way Western culture has behaved. But these do not have predictable limits. What does connect feminism and the causes of animals are the political connections *and* the constraints. We are all living in a culture that valorizes domination and colonization—this is why the use of animals as organ donors seems to some to be justified. Experiencing our interconnections and their location in a politics of domination is our shared goal. For feminist theorizing, this must include understanding how we, too, have played into ideas of animals as Others in our critiques of biological determinism.[28] We must broaden our approach so that we not only reject such crude ideas about women but also question them about other kinds of animals.

Any alliance between women and animals must take into account differences among women and differences among animals, focusing on singularity and transformation, localizing conditions and temporary actions. This is where we want to intervene in the debate on animals as Other, insisting on the importance of withdrawing from ideas of opposition between the self and the Other. Looking at alternative theories in science, as well as critical feminist analyses of science, we want to go beyond these dualisms and move the debate toward the materiality of becoming. We must insist on seeing nature as multiple and differentiated, and deny the linear models of evolution and genetics that currently have so much power. This is, we believe, the heart of a nondeterminist science and of political alliances between Others. Nonhumans may not have a political voice in Western culture; but they have political interests and can form alliances. We must pay more heed to the deep interconnections between many kinds of politics.

"If you wish to know why there are disasters
of armies and people in the world,
listen to the piteous cries
from the slaughterhouse at midnight."

(Ancient Chinese verse)

Notes

1. Val Plumwood, *Feminism and the Mastery of Nature* (London: Routledge, 1993), p. 4.

2. Londa Schiebinger, *Nature's Body: Sexual Politics and the Making of Modern Science* (London: Pandora, 1994).

3. Harriet Ritvo, *The Animal Estate* (London: Harvard University Press, 1987).

4. See, for example, *Reweaving the World: The Emergence of Ecofeminism*, eds. Irene Diamond and Gloria Orenstein (San Francisco: Sierra Club Books, 1990) and Greta Gaard, *Ecofeminism: Women, Animals and Nature* (Philadelphia: Temple University Press, 1993).

5. See, for example, *Animals and Women*, eds. Carol Adams and Josephine Donovan (London: Duke University Press, 1995).

6. Ibid., p. 23.

7. Lynda Birke, *Feminism, Animals and Science: The Naming of the Shrew* (Buckingham: Open University Press, 1994); Daisie Radner and Michael Radner, *Animal Consciousness* (New York: Prometheus Books, 1989).

8. Lynda Birke, "How do gender differences in behavior develop?," *Perspectives in Ethology*, Vol. 8, eds. Peter Klopfer and P. P. G. Bateson (New York: Plenum Press, 1992).

9. For examples, see Birke, *Feminism, Animals and Science: The Naming of the Shrew.*

10. Lesley Rogers, "They are only animals," *Reinventing Biology,* eds. Lynda Birke and Ruth Hubbard (Bloomington: Indiana University Press, 1995).

11. See, for example, Elizabeth Marshall Thomas, *The Hidden Life of Dogs* (Boston: Houghton Mifflin, 1993).

12. Dorothy Nelkin and M. Susan Lindee, *The DNA Mystique: the Gene as a Cultural Icon* (New York: Freeman, 1995).

13. See, for example, Judith Masters, "rEvolutionary Theory: Reinventing our Origin Myths," *Reinventing Biology,* eds. Lynda Birke and Ruth Hubbard.

14. Gilles Deleuze and Felix Guattari, *A Thousand Plateaus* (London: Athlone Press, 1987), p. 238.

15. Donna Haraway, "The Biopolitics of Postmodern Bodies," *Simians, Cyborgs and Women,* ed. Donna Haraway (London: Free Association Books, 1991).

16. For an analysis of the ecosystem concept, see Frank Benjamin Golley, *A History of the Ecosystem Concept in Ecology: More than the Sum of the Parts* (New Haven: Yale University Press, 1993).

17. *The Great Ape Project: Equality Beyond Humanity,* eds. Paola Cavallieri and Peter Singer (New York: St. Martin's Press, 1993).

18. Steven Jay Gould, *Wonderful Life: The Burgess Shale and the Nature of History* (Harmondsworth: Penguin, 1991).

19. G. Deleuze and F. Guattari, *A Thousand Plateaus,* p. 238.

20. Lynn Margulis et al., "We are all symbionts," *Gaia in Action: Science of the Living Earth* (Edinburgh: Floris Books, 1996).

21. Ibid.

22. Rosi Braidotti, *Patterns of Dissonance,* transl. Elizabeth Grosz (New York: Routledge, 1991).

23. Haraway, "The Biopolitics of Postmodern Bodies," and "The Cyborg Manifesto," *Simians, Cyborgs and Women.*

24. Haraway, "The Cyborg Manifesto," and "Situated Knowledges," *Simians, Cyborgs and Women*; see, also, Sandra Harding, *Whose Science? Whose Knowledge?* (Buckingham: Open University Press, 1992).

25. Haraway, "The Biopolitics of Postmodern Bodies," *Simians, Cyborgs and Women,* p. 220.

26. Ibid., p. 225.

27. Evelyn Fox Keller, *A Feeling for the Organism* (New York: Freeman, 1983).

28. Birke, *Feminism, Animals and Science: the Naming of the Shrew.*

FOUR

The Role and Status of
Animals in Nietzsche's Philosophy

Monika Langer

Thus Spoke Zarathustra is the most popular of Friedrich Nietzsche's works and contains all the major themes of his philosophy. It abounds in animal imagery; and animals play a greater role here than in any of Nietzsche's other books. In order to assess the role and status of animals in Nietzsche's philosophy, it is therefore best to consider how animals figure in *Thus Spoke Zarathustra*.

Nietzsche claimed that traditional philosophers were concept worshippers and "sick web-spinners" who murdered and mummified everything that entered their grasp.[1] These "sterile" scholars coldly "unplumed" "every bird" and sat "like spiders" in "dusty rooms," "preparing poison" for their victims. Their so-called wisdom stank of "swamps"; and "frogs" croaked out of their solemn truths. Instead of being eagles, such traditional philosophers were "clever like asses," writing treatises that pulverized insights "to white dust."[2]

Nietzsche opposed this traditional philosophy, and employed several strategies to dissociate his philosophy from it. Among these strategies was the rejection of the scholarly treatise, which had typically been solemn, abstruse, dispassionate, and pallid. Instead, Nietzsche chose an aphoristic, narrative style in *Thus Spoke Zarathustra*, and made his writing witty, accessible, passionate, and colorful—his animal imagery helping to produce these features. *Thus Spoke Zarathustra* teems with metaphors and similes involving: birds (eagles, falcons, vultures, owls, songbirds, doves, crows, roosters, hens, peacocks, flamingos, a heron, a goose, and an ostrich), snakes, lizards, crocodiles, frogs, toads, worms, leeches, glow-worms, flea-beetles, lice, spiders, ants, flies, bluebottles, mosquitoes, bees, butterflies, moths, fish, crabs, oysters, bats, mice, moles, hedgehogs, rabbits, sheep, a goat, swine, cattle, buffalo, camels, horses, asses, mules, monkeys, apes, whales, bears, lions (and lionesses), tigers, panthers, wolves, dogs, cats, and an elephant. We also find references to: "maggots," "winged worms," "bugs," "vermin," "parasites," "evil birds," "evil beasts," "savage beasts," "wild animals," "beasts of prey," "beasts of burden," "monsters," and "dragons."

A few examples will show the wit of much of this animal imagery. Nietzsche (via Zarathustra) describes the "all-too-many" worshippers of the state as foul-smelling, "swift monkeys" who "clamber over" and devour one another in their greed for wealth and power. In the market place, petty, uncreative people are "poisonous flies," vengefully buzzing around and stinging inventors of new values. "Small people" with pretensions to greatness are puffed-up, "swollen and straining" frogs, doomed to burst. "Preachers of equality" are envious, impotent tarantulas, biting those whom they cannot emulate. Zarathustra is like the new rooster whom the hens peck but who remains unruffled by such "small annoyances."[3] Only readers lacking a sense of humor will fail to appreciate the wit conveyed in these and the above cited images that describe philosophers and scholars in general. This animal imagery is undeniably colorful; and each image immediately conveys Zarathustra's/Nietzsche's strong feeling. We instantly grasp Zarathustra's/Nietzsche's loathing for conventional philosophers, self-serving nationalists, vengeful conformists, pretentious braggarts, and jealous preachers of equality. The rooster image unequivocally conveys the firm determination to dismiss the attacks of such inconsequential people.

Thus Spoke Zarathustra is subtitled "A Book for All and None." Nietzsche thereby invited everyone to undertake a radical questioning of all accepted truths and values, while at the same time he indicated that no one was yet ready to embark on such a disturbing inquiry. The animal imagery helps to make the book accessible to all. For example, the comparisons to poisonous spiders suggest that philosophers and preachers of equality are life-negating. Their appeals to truth and justice respectively are as insubstantial and entrapping as the spiders' webs. The image of poisonous flies then suggests that the most likely victims of such webs are small-minded, uncreative people who harass creators.

Such animal imagery paradoxically fails precisely insofar as it succeeds. It helps to make the text witty, colorful, passionate, and accessible; but it does this by reinforcing the accepted perception of the animals. Such tacit support for the common view of the animals is completely at odds with the radical questioning that the text advocates. We might interpret this as a flaw that Nietzsche intentionally gave his protagonist, Zarathustra. The failure then would be Zarathustra's instead of Nietzsche's—a deliberate tactic instead of a shortcoming in Nietzsche's philosophy. This interpretation is not viable. None of Nietzsche's other works has a dramatic narrative; and the philosophy articulated in those works is entirely consistent with Zarathustra's teachings. Zarathustra's understanding of his mission deepens in the course of the narrative, but his portrayal of animals remains unchanged. Nothing in Nietzsche's other works suggests any disagreement with Zarathustra's perception of animals. Instead, his other works indicate that Nietzsche identified Zarathustra with himself.[4]

Several critics have warned against identifying Zarathustra with Nietzsche. Gary Shapiro, for instance, has argued that *Thus Spoke Zarathustra* is "a book which deliberately questions our expectation of finding a single view, an authoritative voice, or a systematic teaching."[5] Shapiro questions whether we even know the meaning of a unitary author consciously directing texts bearing that author's name. He considers it erroneous to think that Nietzsche always consciously controls the narrative of *Thus Spoke Zarathustra*. In his discussion of this text Shapiro contends that many readers and commentators have unhesitatingly identified Zarathustra with Nietzsche because they failed to distinguish between the animals' exposition of the thought of eternal recurrence and Zarathustra's comprehension of it. According to Shapiro the animals explain that thought prosaically, whereas Zarathustra comprehends the metaphilosophical problems of communicating it. The dissolution of the integral individual intensifies as agents and voices double and pluralize in the fourth part of the text. The identity of the individual self becomes radically indeterminate—thus thwarting the tendency to hypostatize "the individual consciousness as center of activity."[6]

Daniel Conway has likewise argued that Nietzsche deconstructs his own textual authority in *Thus Spoke Zarathustra*, thereby encouraging his readers to reconstruct the text on their own similarly partial, fragile, and contingent authority.[7] Conway examines the discontinuity between the close of part one and the start of part two, and contends that "we must resist the temptation to identify Zarathustra strictly with Nietzsche."[8] According to Conway, Zarathustra at first needs to deceive himself because he originally operates under a flawed model of self-understanding. As his experiences collectively invalidate that model, he acquires self-knowledge and abandons his project of teaching the *Übermensch* discursively. Instead he becomes the *Übermensch*—"an *exemplar* of Nietzsche's ideal."[9] Conway argues that Zarathustra "'grows into' the role reserved for him as Nietzsche's 'official' proxy and spokesman."[10]

Shapiro and Conway rightly note that *Thus Spoke Zarathustra* challenges philosophers' penchant for categorizing, systematizing, and absolutizing. The text indeed counteracts the traditional pretension to philosophize impersonally and impartially from some point beyond the world of everyday concerns. It questions the traditional assumption that philosophers are unitary, self-transparent individuals having a privileged insight into "the essence of things." Yet in giving us the fictional character Zarathustra, Nietzsche does not make his own authority "ultimately irrelevant" as Conway claims.[11] Zarathustra develops in the course of the narrative; but in becoming "the ideal that Nietzsche recommends," he embodies values—which readers are free to accept or reject.[12] Zarathustra deceives and excuses himself at several points in the narrative—perhaps most evidently in refusing to recognize his own face as the devil's grimace in the mirror proffered him by the child, or again in making excuses for his reluctance to respond to the demand made by the voiceless speaking of his "stillest hour." As Conway suggests, Zarathustra's understanding of himself and of his teachings develops as the story unfolds.

When speaking to him of eternal recurrence, Zarathustra's eagle and snake present two quite distinct versions. One version, which they explicitly designate as Zarathustra's, is atomistically detailed and leads to nausea. The other version—which the animals present as their own thinking about the matter—dissolves the atomistic boundaries and celebrates the intermingling of self and world in an eternal ring of becoming. Zarathustra eventually learns to sing this second version.[13] As Conway concludes, Zarathustra does become Nietzsche's spokesperson. To establish this, we ultimately need to compare *Thus Spoke Zarathustra* with Nietzsche's other works—a task which lies beyond the scope of this chapter. It is noteworthy, however, that the eagle and snake are not the protagonists of the story. They remain mere companions to Zarathustra who strides forth at the conclusion of the story "glowing and strong as a morning sun."[14]

Zarathustra's first teaching affirms the widely accepted hierarchy which ranks human beings above plants and animals. Belief in this hierarchy goes back at least as far as Aristotle's philosophy. Christianity incorporated and popularized the Aristotelian hierarchy, but it replaced Aristotle's Prime Mover with God the Father at the pinnacle. Nietzsche upheld the hierarchy and replaced God the Father with the *Übermensch* (literally translated as "Overperson"). In his first teaching, Zarathustra locates human beings between the "beast" and the *Übermensch*. He encourages the people to prepare plants and animals for the *Übermensch*, exhorting them not to regress to "the beasts." Zarathustra declares that apes are "a laughingstock or a painful embarrassment" for human beings because human beings have made their way to their present status from worms and apes. Thus, Zarathustra urges the people to overcome what is still worm and ape in themselves.[15] In his subsequent teachings, Zarathustra reaffirms this long-standing devaluation and subordination of animals, stressing, for example, that the lust to rule makes human beings become "lower than snake and swine," and that people must conquer their "savage beasts."[16]

We might extend our defense of Nietzsche by arguing that his perpetuation of the traditional hierarchy deliberately parodied the Bible. Both the Old and New Testaments contain a profusion of animal imagery involving many of the same animals that appear in *Thus Spoke Zarathustra*. Both Testaments unequivocally rank human beings above animals—although animals occasionally symbolize superior beings such as angels, Christ, the Holy Ghost, or God the Father. *Thus Spoke Zarathustra* makes numerous playful references to Scripture and several passages involving animals parody the Bible. For example, Zarathustra's copious references to shepherds and their sheep parody the New Testament's portrayal of Jesus as The Good Shepherd leading his flock and retrieving straying sheep. When Jesus bids his disciples to become fishers of human beings who would fill God's Kingdom, Nietzsche parodies this by having Zarathustra fish on high mountains for human fish to fill his human kingdom. In The New Testament, the Holy Ghost descends like a dove on the head of Jesus when he is baptized as an adult by John The Baptist. At the conclusion of *Thus Spoke Zarathustra*, Nietzsche humorously mimics this by having an entire flock of doves descend on Zarathustra. Surrounded by his disciples, Jesus sits on a hill and delivers his Sermon on the Mount to the crowds below. In *Thus Spoke Zarathustra*, Nietzsche portrays the voluntary beggar as a "sermonizer on the mount" sitting on a knoll among cows. At the Last Supper, Jesus distributes bread and wine which he declares to be his body and blood, and asks his disciples to do this in remembrance of him in the future. Nietzsche parodies this Last Supper in the section bearing that title and in the festival of the ass, during which Zarathustra asks the "higher human beings" to celebrate this festival in remembrance of him in the future. The ass festival also mimics the late medieval ass festivals and the Israelites' blasphemous worship of a golden calf while Moses conversed with God on Mount Sinai.

Such parodies, however, do not demonstrate that Nietzsche's continuation of the customary ranking of animals was a deliberate strategy. Nothing in these or similar examples suggests that the ranking *itself* was the object of parody. Moreover, most instances of animal imagery in *Thus Spoke Zarathustra* do not parody the Bible at all.

Still intent on defending Nietzsche, we might argue that—upon closer inspection—the text does not uphold the accepted hierarchy. Some of the animal imagery *favors* animals, and Zarathustra's wish that his animals lead him suggests a certain faith in, and respect for, these animals. Although it is persuasive, this argument also falls short. Eagles and birds in general, lions and lionesses, snakes, bees, and fish appear in a positive light for the most part. However, Nietzsche usually presents all the other animals negatively. In either case, the text continually reinforces the habitual, positive or negative stereotype of the animal in question. It also maintains the ranking of human beings above animals, even where Zarathustra's animals are concerned.

We might contend that the ass, which stands in for God in the ass festival, constitutes an exception. Zarathustra's initial anger parallels that of Moses; but Zarathustra's anger changes to commendation. Laurence Lampert argues that the "higher human beings'" worship of the ass is a deliberate mockery on their part to kill any remaining desire for religiosity. It shows an astute recognition that their democratic age reveres what is slowest, dumbest, spiritually grayest, and least discriminating—the ass. Zarathustra's belated comprehension of their derision prompts him to praise their wry buffoonery and finally call them his strange "new friends."[17] Lampert's interpretation here is questionable. The tenor and tone of the "higher human beings'" answers to Zarathustra's angry questions suggest that their ass festival was earnest worship that they are now attempting to excuse. Their frightened disappearance when the laughing lion roars in the closing scene also suggests that they have not genuinely learned gaiety. When commending the celebration, Zarathustra remarks that the "higher human beings" need him to blow their souls bright. Zarathustra's commendation would then be a deliberate endeavor to encourage the "higher human beings" to become truly gay by taking their excuses at face value and heeding the ugliest human being's clever reminder that a wrathful response defeats the purpose.

We might still claim that Zarathustra's call for further ass festivals implies that there are no foolish values and thus no stereotypical rankings of animal-human-God. However, the text does not support such a claim, because Zarathustra's commendation describes new festivals as "a little brave nonsense" that the "higher human beings" require for their own sakes. Zarathustra implies that having recognized—through his intervention—the foolishness of their devout worship of the ass, the "higher human beings" need further ass festivals that they can now celebrate in true buffoonery. A key element in such mockery, the ass retains its traditional status as an animal epitomizing foolishness. Both the common image of the ass and the usual ranking of animals below human beings thus remain intact.

Zarathustra's famous parable about the spirit's three metamorphoses contains an intriguing mixture of animal and human imagery. The German text uses the word *Geist*, which means "mind," "intellect," "spirit," or "ghost." These multiple meanings all connote non-corporeality and a certain solemnity. Through its metamorphoses, mind/spirit develops a sense of embodiment and playfulness. First it becomes a camel loaded with all the traditional values that make life seem arid. In this desert, the camel mind/spirit becomes a lion who refuses to revere the traditional values any longer. Instead, the lion mind/spirit fights the dragon of time-honored morality and imposes his will in place of the dragon's commands. Having achieved freedom from traditional values, the preying lion mind/spirit becomes a life-affirming, playful child for whom the old mind/body dichotomy does not exist. This animal imagery maintains the stereotypical view of the camel as only a docile beast of burden and the lion as solely a fearless, destructive hunter. The human being is the beginning and end of the parable. Although the animals supersede the human being in its initial form, the human being as innocent child replaces the animals and does what they cannot do. As a creative child, the human being ranks above both camel and lion, thus signifying a fresh start. Yet that new start perpetuates the old hierarchy of human beings ranked above animals.

In the Prologue an old hermit remarks that Zarathustra years ago carried his ashes to the mountains, but that he has since awakened and become a child. Robert Gooding-Williams has rightly noted that this suggests Zarathustra has already been a camel and a lion; moreover, he subsequently repeats these metamorphoses on his journey to becoming a child at the end of the book.[18] Since the three metamorphoses thus describe a cyclical pattern, we might argue that this pattern is not hierarchical—and hence not oppressive to animals. A careful study of the text shows the argument to be untenable. Hierarchy does not require linearity, although historically the placing of animals below human beings has usually been linear. The ranking is the essential feature of the traditional hierarchy, and the cyclical pattern of the metamorphoses retains that ranking. There are several different meanings of childhood in the text, and eternal recurrence suggests that the child which Zarathustra becomes as an old man at the end of the story is not a stage achieved once and for all. It is also questionable whether the old man/child at the story's conclusion is the child described in the metamorphoses parable. There the child is a wheel-like (activity of) willing that affirmatively wills itself as a playful creating of new values. This game of creation is an "innocence and forgetting" that presupposes the destruction of all reifications—including that of the ego—by the lion. In contrast, at the end of the story the self as ego arguably remains intact as memory comes to Zarathustra and he laughs "angrily." He becomes "absorbed in himself" and declares that he is concerned with his work.

The lion at this point is a laughing lion whose arrival Zarathustra interprets as the sign that his children are near.[19] Perhaps these children—instead of Zarathustra as old man/child—have achieved the third stage described in the parable of the three metamorphoses. However, in either case the child's rank is superior to that of the camel or lion. The lion's importance consists in bringing about the requisite conditions for the emergence of the child and in heralding the arrival of the children at the end of the story. Zarathustra nowhere suggests that the child's importance consists in ushering in the lion or any other animal. In the parable, Zarathustra says the lion must become a child—not the reverse. As Gooding-Williams has pointed out, "Zarathustra identifies neither the camel nor the lion as innocent."[20] We might still wonder whether the critique of the camel is a critique only of the domesticated camel—not of the camel as such. However, in the metamorphoses parable Zarathustra implies that the camel's desire to be well loaded is also at issue, and so, presumably, the camel's suitability for domestication. Despite their nonlinearity, the three metamorphoses thus maintain the traditional ranking.

Zarathustra's relationship with his two animals is more complex. Both the eagle and the snake have held great mythological significance since ancient times. Sky gods such as Zeus and Jupiter considered the eagle sacred; and the Romans regarded it as the incarnation of the emperor's soul. According to the Bible, God transported the Israelites out of Egyptian captivity on the wings of eagles. Over the centuries, the eagle came to symbolize majesty, military might, courage, and male power in general. The snake embodied the power of life; and pre-classic Aegean civilization considered it sacred. As the Earth Goddess Gaia, the snake was the mother of all gods and one of the most ancient symbols of female power. Since she created life, she understood its mysteries and therefore embodied wisdom. In the Bible, the snake represents both good and evil. The snake symbolizes the authority of Moses and is an emblem of healing; but the snake is also an embodiment of Satan and a symbol of death.[21] In choosing the eagle and snake as his animals of honor, Zarathustra by extension appropriates the ancient symbols of male and female power.

Shapiro has claimed that the eagle and snake should be interpreted as aspects of Zarathustra—an embodiment of some of his virtues. In this interpretation Zarathustra's remarks and rebukes to his animals would be internal dialogues and self-critiques. Similarly, Shapiro has argued that the figures who arrive in the fourth part of the text "are partial selves and that Zarathustra's distancing himself from the higher men is also a way of refusing to be tied down to any determinate, atomic identity."[22] Though interesting, this line of interpretation is ultimately not persuasive. Nothing in Nietzsche's text suggests such a radical interiorization. Even Shapiro at one point attenuates his interpretation when he declares in his discussion of part four that Zarathustra's "animals are *in some sense* an extension of himself."[23] In any event, the question would still be why Zarathustra chooses, and thus perpetuates, the stereotypical views of the snake as signifying cleverness and the eagle as signifying pride, to represent these qualities in himself. Why not choose a toad and a crow, for example?

The manner in which Zarathustra's animals first appear in the story suggests the affirmation of eternal recurrence, the integration of male and female power, and the combination of pride with wisdom. The animals' movements describe circles, symbolizing eternal recurrence. The eagle soars in wide circles, while the snake keeps herself wound companionably around his neck. Zarathustra remarks that they are respectively the proudest and wisest of all animals. Noting that he will never be wise through and through like his snake, Zarathustra expresses the wish that his animals lead him—a clear acknowledgment of their superiority. He further declares that he found life less dangerous among animals than among people, and that he is happy to see his animals. We might contend that Zarathustra's acknowledgment of his animals' superiority reverses the traditional ranking of animals and human beings. Yet Zarathustra's fleeting acknowledgment is not entirely convincing. When the animals tentatively attempt to assume a leadership role in part three of the text, Zarathustra belittles and rebukes their approach—and eventually stops listening to them. His attitude fails to dislodge the time-honored privileging of human beings over animals.

We will need to consider Zarathustra's relationships with people if we are to understand fully the role and status of animals in *Thus Spoke Zarathustra*. First, however, let us examine how Zarathustra relates to his eagle and snake. Following their initial appearance in the Prologue, the eagle and snake figure little in the first half of the story. Zarathustra asks them a series of rhetorical questions when he wakes from his dream of the child with the mirror; but the story does not indicate any reaction from his animals.

In the third of the book's four parts, the snake and eagle look after Zarathustra while he is ill from the thought of eternal recurrence. After seven days, when they speak to him to encourage him to get up, Zarathustra refers to their speaking as "chattering" (*schwätzt*). When they offer him their interpretation of eternal recurrence, Zarathustra acknowledges that his animals understand what he had to go through in falling ill and recovering from the thought of eternal recurrence. Yet he further belittles them by repeatedly calling them "buffoons and barrel organs" (*Schalks-Narren und Drehorgeln*) and by dismissing their interpretation as "a hurdy-gurdy song" (*ein Leier-Lied*).[24] Zarathustra demands that his animals be silent. He rejects their advice to sing as another "hurdy-gurdy song" even while he admits that he had considered doing the same himself. Moreover, Zarathustra misconstrues his animals' loving attention during his illness as cruel curiosity and lasciviousness. Declaring that the human being "is the cruelest animal," he likens his eagle and snake to the "small" person who revels in the great person's pain. This analogy does not reverse the traditional hierarchy, though, since Zarathustra has already devalued "small" people by referring to them as parasites, maggots, vermin, winged worms, and poisonous flies. When his animals, undaunted, repeat their advice and articulate their perfect comprehension of his destiny and teaching, Zarathustra ignores them in favor of conversing with himself. Realizing this, his animals respectfully disappear.

Shapiro has argued that Zarathustra's understanding of eternal recurrence is superior to that of his animals, and that these animals have a flawed comprehension of his destiny. According to Shapiro, the problem lies in the animals' inability to reflect on their own speech. This makes it difficult for them to grasp the problem of private language; and Zarathustra is right to rebuke them as he does.[25] Shapiro's linking of eternal recurrence with a reflection on the problem of private language is both interesting and questionable. In any case, such an interpretation maintains the traditional ranking of animals as inferior to human beings. Shapiro's—and Graham Parkes'—emphasis on the importance of singing the thought of eternal recurrence is well taken.[26] Singing is far more fluid than speaking; hence, it better conveys the dissolution of reifications (such as the ego) and their replacement by a ceaseless, dynamic becoming (instead of being). Zarathustra's animals encourage him to stop speaking and start singing. Yet since it is Zarathustra who subsequently sings the eternal recurrence—whereas the animals only speak it—the traditional ranking of animals below human beings again remains intact.

His animals reappear and address Zarathustra at the beginning of part four. This time, he applauds and accepts their advice (to climb a high mountain), but again calls them "buffoons." Worse, Zarathustra now deliberately deceives his snake and eagle so as to be rid of them for the day. We also discover that he is generally not forthright with his animals, since he states that he can speak more freely alone than in their presence. Zarathustra subsequently claims that animals like his are presently nowhere to be found on earth. He recommends their counsel to the "queer fish" whose cry of distress unnerved him, and says his animals will serve them. After dining with "these higher human beings" (*diese höheren Menschen*), Zarathustra escapes their company and calls for his animals. He asks them rhetorically whether the "higher human beings" have a bad odor; and he tells his animals that only now does he know and feel how much he loves them. In response, the animals press close to Zarathustra and look up at him.

When Zarathustra soon thereafter is overcome by an aversion and contempt for the "higher human beings" in his cave, he again slips out and talks to his animals. This time, he does not ask them even a rhetorical question. As before, his eagle and snake press close to him and say nothing. At the conclusion of part four, Zarathustra is displeased that the "higher human beings" in his cave continue to slumber while he is already awake. Hearing his eagle's distinctive cry, he is delighted that his animals are awake when he is awake. Zarathustra declares that they are the proper animals for him and that he loves them, but that he still lacks the right human beings.

Zarathustra's preference for his animals' company does not signify a reversal of the usual ranking that locates animals beneath
human beings. Instead, the eagle and snake presented in the story
are products of anthropomorphism and function as substitute
"human beings." Already in the Prologue, the old hermit cautions
Zarathustra not to go to human beings with his gift of wisdom, but
to go to the animals. As the hermit knows, given their traditionally
inferior status, the animals would not dare to mock a human being.
Disregarding this warning, Zarathustra subsequently finds life more
dangerous among human beings than among animals. The people in
the market place misunderstand and mock him when he holds forth
to them about overcoming themselves and recognizing that they are
solely bridges to the *Übermensch*.[27]

Zarathustra resolves never to speak to the people again, but to
cultivate companions who follow him wherever he wants. He envisages that such companions would be creators; yet he clings to the
desire for followers. This contradiction accounts for the unsatisfac-
tory nature of Zarathustra's relations with human beings. He considers all past and present people as only "fragments of the future,"
and rejects the vast majority as nauseating, foul-smelling, and
superfluous rabble. Zarathustra claims that he could endure living
among human beings solely by holding his nose, closing his ears and
eyes, sealing his lips, and disguising himself. The few who are willing to listen to his teachings become his disciples. These Zarathustra
seeks to sculpt with the hammer of his will into his image of the
Übermensch's precursors. He urges his disciples to leave him and
find themselves; yet he continues to regard them as the "living plan-
tation of [his] thoughts." Ultimately, the absence of reciprocity in
this relation makes Zarathustra feel wretched and homeless.[28]

Having disparaged women and excluded them from becoming
companions and co-creators, Zarathustra personifies life, wisdom,
and eternity as ideal women with whom he can engage. He appropriates women's childbearing capability and feels himself to be pregnant with the companions and children he sought but failed to find
anywhere. After a dream prompts him to leave his disciples and
return to his cave, Zarathustra rejoices that his nose is finally "deliv-
ered from the smell of everything human." When the "higher human
beings" arrive, he declares that they are failures, that they do not

understand him, and that they are not his proper companions. He insists that he needs "warriors" who are "clean, smooth mirrors for [his] doctrines." Only now, when the "higher human beings" have also proven to be a disappointment, Zarathustra feels and knows how much he loves his eagle and snake. He slips out to them for a respite from the company of the "higher human beings" who are frightened away the next morning by the laughing lion's roar. At the conclusion, Zarathustra finds himself all alone.[29]

Shapiro has cautioned against ascribing individualism to Zarathustra or making "slighting references to Nietzsche's supposed misogyny."[30] For Shapiro, the death of God spells the death of the individual. The thought of eternal recurrence involves the dissolution of the ego's boundaries; and such a dissolution is traditionally celebrated in erotic love. Shapiro therefore argues that the celebration of life, wisdom, and eternity as women adds an appropriate erotic dimension to the text.[31] Shapiro's attempt to place eternal recurrence within the private language debate is, again, intriguing but questionable; although the connecting of eternal recurrence to the ego's dissolution is entirely warranted. Yet even if we accept Shapiro's interpretation of life, wisdom, and eternity as women, the question remains why Zarathustra/Nietzsche presents such a stereotypical (heterosexual) image of erotic love—and, more generally, why nonstereotypical images of women are totally absent from *Thus Spoke Zarathustra*.

Throughout the story, Zarathustra's view of human beings as they are, is negative. He deems them flawed, contemptible, and of value only as steppingstones to the future. In vain he seeks companions who are creators and go their own ways, but who mirror his teachings and follow him wherever he wants. Zarathustra's relations with the sundry human beings he encounters are singularly devoid of reciprocity, genuine dialogue, and fruitful interchanges of ideas. At the end of the narrative, he strides forth in anticipation of meeting his "children"; but he has not renounced his desire that they simultaneously go their own ways and follow him wherever he wants. We can therefore assume that Zarathustra will again be disappointed.

Given Zarathustra's dissatisfaction with human beings as they are, it is understandable that he personifies abstractions (such as eternity) and anthropomorphizes his animals. Both strategies provide him with substitute "human beings" whom he can more readily endow with the qualities he wishes. Moreover, unlike real human beings, Zarathustra's eagle and snake remain loving and respectful, despite how he treats them. In his teachings, Zarathustra emphasizes the wisdom, pride, and courage of creators. He likens creators to eagles; and stresses their incorporation of male and female capabilities. Having chosen as his companions two animals that traditionally symbolize these qualities, Zarathustra can regard his animals as consoling substitutes for the creators he fails to find among real human beings. Since his eagle and snake are ready to follow him wherever he wishes, Zarathustra can believe that his animals embody the contradictory combination of creator and mirror. Nonetheless, Zarathustra relates to his animals in much the same way as to his disciples. Neither relationship involves dialogue, a positive exchange of ideas, or reciprocity. Yet his two animals combined are better integrated and wiser than Zarathustra, as their speeches and manner of first appearance indicate.

Several commentators have interpreted Zarathustra's character and teachings more favorably. For example, Conway has argued that in the second half of the book Zarathustra abandons his negative view of human beings as they are, renounces "his claim to an autarkic privilege," and "consciously embraces the ideal of reciprocal community."[32] Such a reading is appealing—but questionable. In the fourth part of the book, Zarathustra resorts to shouting at other human beings and beating two of them. He then rejects the "higher human beings" as failures and insists that he needs perfect mirrors for his teachings. At the Last Supper, Zarathustra resumes his preacherly mode and lectures the "higher human beings" on what it means to be a "higher human being." As the story draws to a close, Zarathustra repeatedly echoes Satan's temptation to Jesus and then declares that the purest, strongest souls "shall be the lords of the earth."[33] These passages—and several others in the same vein—suggest that Zarathustra has not renounced his autarkic stance.

Throughout the story, Zarathustra uses animal imagery—in its conventional sense—to describe the human beings he encounters, as well as those whom he envisages for the future. Since his view of people in their present form is extremely negative, it is not surprising that the majority of this imagery is unflattering to human beings. For example, spider imagery abounds and is among the most derogatory. This is perhaps because the spider has traditionally been a symbol of female power; and Zarathustra consistently devalues women. Much of the text's animal imagery makes Zarathustra's pronouncements and relationships appear unquestionable. This strategy tacitly undermines the story's overt call for a thorough questioning. Describing people in the market place as "poisonous flies," or preachers of equality as "tarantulas," for example, serves to make shunning them appear self-evidently appropriate.

Nietzsche considered *Thus Spoke Zarathustra* his best work and he identified Zarathustra with himself.[34] His other writings indicate no disagreement with Zarathustra's perception of animals. Nowhere does Zarathustra attempt to understand the being of any animal for its own sake—animals are not of interest purely in themselves. Using *Thus Spoke Zarathustra* as a touchstone, I suggest that Nietzsche employed animal imagery to help dissociate his writings from traditional philosophy, and to make some of his claims tacitly appear unquestionable. This strategy paradoxically perpetuated the old stereotypes of animals and reinforced the traditional hierarchical ranking of human beings above animals. Nietzsche's use of animal imagery is thus incompatible with his call for a comprehensive questioning of traditional views. In unfortunately supporting the longstanding devaluation of animals, Nietzsche's philosophy proves to be less radical than he supposed.

Notes

1. Friedrich Nietzsche, "Twilight of the Idols," *The Portable Nietzsche*, transl. and ed. Walter Kaufmann (New York: Viking Press, 1968), pp. 479, 482.

2. Friedrich Nietzsche, "Thus Spoke Zarathustra," *The Portable Nietzsche*, transl. and ed. Walter Kaufmann (New York: Viking Press, 1968), pp. 402, 237, 217, 215, 237.

3. Ibid., pp. 160–166, 298, 370, 211–214, 280.

4. See, for example, Friedrich Nietzsche, *The Gay Science*, transl. Walter Kaufmann (New York: Random House, 1974), pp. 274–275, 345, 371; and Friedrich Nietzsche, "Ecce Homo," *On the Genealogy of Morals and Ecce Homo*, transl. and ed. Walter Kaufmann (New York: Random House, 1969), pp. 219–220, 327–335, 340.

5. Gary Shapiro, *Nietzschean Narratives* (Bloomington: Indiana University Press, 1989), p. 42.

6. Ibid., pp. 36, 80. See also pp. 97–123.

7. Daniel W. Conway, "Nietzsche contra Nietzsche: The Deconstruction of Zarathustra," *Nietzsche as Postmodernist: Essays Pro and Contra*, ed. Clayton Koelb (Albany: State University of New York Press, 1990), pp. 91–110.

8. Ibid., p. 94.

9. Ibid., p. 109.

10. Ibid., p. 94.

11. Ibid., p. 110.

12. Ibid.

13. Nietzsche, "Thus Spoke Zarathustra," pp. 329–333, 432–436.

14. Ibid., p. 439.

15. Nietzsche, "Thus Spoke Zarathustra," pp. 124–127.

16. Ibid., pp. 301, 229.

17. Laurence Lampert, *Nietzsche's Teaching: An Interpretation of Thus Spoke Zarathustra* (New Haven: Yale University Press, 1986), p. 308.

18. Robert Gooding-Williams, "Zarathustra's Three Metamorphoses," *Nietzsche as Postmodernist: Essays Pro and Contra*, p. 233.

19. See Nietzsche, "Thus Spoke Zarathustra," pp. 137–139, 146, 438–439.

20. Gooding-Williams, "Zarathustra's Three Metamorphoses," p. 242.

21. Barbara G. Walker, *The Woman's Dictionary of Symbols and Sacred Objects* (San Francisco: Harper & Row, 1988), pp. 400–401, 387–389; and J.D. Douglas and Merrill C. Tenney, *NIV Compact Dictionary of the Bible* (Michigan: Zondervan Publishing House, 1989), pp. 91, 35–36, 526.

22. Shapiro, *Nietzschean Narratives*, pp. 80, 102, 85.

23. Ibid., p.101. Emphasis added.

24. Nietzsche, "Thus Spoke Zarathustra," pp. 195, 328–330; and Friedrich Nietzsche, *Also Sprach Zarathustra*, eds. Giorgio Colli and Mazzino Montinari (Berlin/New York: Walter de Gruyter, 1980), pp. 106, 271–273.

25. Shapiro, *Nietzschean Narratives*, pp. 80–82, 93.

26. Ibid., pp. 80, 94; and Graham Parkes, "The Dance from Mouth to Hand: (Speaking Zarathustra's Write Foot ForeWord)," *Nietzsche as Postmodernist*, pp. 133–136.

27. Nietzsche, "Thus Spoke Zarathustra," pp. 123, 124–130.

28. Ibid., pp. 135, 136, 250, 251, 291, 294, 209, 256, 296–298, 401, 199, 216, 190, 273, 217–218, 233.

29. Ibid., pp. 169, 177–179, 303, 338, 399, 403, 423, 433, 219–220, 336–343, 257–259, 394, 407, 408, 434, 437, 438.

30. Shapiro, *Nietzschean Narratives*, pp. 91, 95.

31. Ibid., pp. 91–96.

32. Conway, "Nietzsche contra Nietzsche: The Deconstruction of Zarathustra," pp. 109, 106–107.

33. Nietzsche, "Thus Spoke Zarathustra," pp. 360, 367, 394, 432.

34. Nietzsche, "Ecce Homo," pp. 219, 327–335, 340; and *The Gay Science*, pp. 274–275, 345, 371.

FIVE

From Merleau-Ponty's Concept of
Nature to an Interspecies Practice of Peace

Elizabeth A. Behnke
In Memoriam B.C.

Between 1956 and 1960, Maurice Merleau-Ponty offered three
courses at the Collège de France concerning Nature: "Le concept de
Nature" (1956–1957); "Le concept de Nature. L'animalité, le corps
humain, passage à la culture" (1957–1958); and "Le concept de
Nature. Nature et Logos: le corps humain" (1959–1960). Until
recently, this material was only available in summary form,[1] with
the exception of a short segment drawn from lectures of 14 and 25
March 1957.[2] Now, however, traces and inceptions of these lectures
have been published in a volume called *La Nature*,[3] which provides
transcriptions of student notes for the first two courses and offers
the third in a reconstruction based on notes that Merleau-Ponty
himself used in preparing his lectures.

Merleau-Ponty's lectures are rich and wide-ranging; he not
only presents a survey of the treatment of Nature in the Western
philosophical tradition, but engages in detailed expositions of scientific theory and research—much of it concerning living beings.
Here, however, I propose neither to show how this material builds
upon his earlier work on human and animal behavior,[4] nor to elaborate the ontology of Nature outlined in the lectures by relating it

to his reflections in other texts.[5] I shall also set aside the task of linking the themes of the lectures to the treatment of similar topics in more recent scholarship.[6] Instead, my response to the lectures on Nature is guided by a project that is akin to, but other than, Merleau-Ponty's own—namely, the exploration of an intercorporeal/ interspecies practice of peace. Thus although I am taking up such Merleau-Pontyan themes as intercorporeity, interanimality, *Ineinander*, and flesh, I am not answering a question posed within the framework of the lectures, but am allowing these themes to move forward in a different way.

I should also acknowledge that although I am not framing my investigations in terms of the texts of Emmanuel Levinas, the practice described in the second part of this chapter emerged in the context of an encounter with alterity in his sense of the term. But recognizing the claim that was thereby ineradicably laid upon me by the Other—not only by his predicament as a whole, but also, and most poignantly, by the look on his face on the evening of 26 June 1996—happened in this case to entail recognizing and responding to the appeal of a nonhuman Other. Here I make no attempt to justify extending Levinasian concepts in this way, but report instead on what happened when I found myself already responsible for this Other prior to any philosophical reflection, already honoring his appeal prior to any justification.

Finally, although my approach derives from the work of Edmund Husserl, I must reserve for other occasions any account of Husserl's own discussions of nonhuman animals.[7] Instead, I follow his commitment to proceed by going back to the "phenomena themselves" rather than by relying on what others have said about the matters in question.[8] Thus although my research report will begin with some remarks on Merleau-Ponty's *La Nature*, the research project itself began with a particular type of interspecies interaction—and it is the lived experience of interspecies encounter that remains the final court of appeal for all of my theoretical reflections "about" it.

1. In Light of the Lectures on Nature

My aim here is neither to summarize nor to comment upon the lectures gathered in *La Nature*, but to draw upon them while diverging from them. Accordingly, I shall confine myself to sketching four interrelated "figures" in whose field of gravity the present investigation moves: the figure of frontality, the figure of a determinate world, the figure of genesis, and the figure of the animal.

A. *The Figure of Frontality*

Throughout the lectures on Nature—as in much of his other later work—Merleau-Ponty is deeply suspicious of what may be termed a "frontal" relation with Nature (N 20, 117), Being (N 119, 282), space (N 49), duration (N 87), etc., in which these are posited as an object over-against a subject contemplating them from the outside, whether from "above" (*survolé*—N 271) or directly "opposite" (*face contre face*—N 282). Linked with such a "frontal" attitude are themes of the "*kosmos théoros*" ("*contemplateur du monde*"—N 141, 181, 182, 279) confronting Nature as a totality of "sheer things" (*bloße Sachen*) spread out before it (N 104–106), as a determinate realm of *partes extra partes* not only known by, but dominated by, a theorizing spectator (N 153) in such a way that being-known (or being-object) becomes the measure of Being (N 264). For Merleau-Ponty, however, Nature itself—wild, savage, primordial, pre-reflective Nature— "resists" such a maneuver (N 117). A way must thus be found to speak from "within" (N 279, 282, 332) this Nature that is not in front of us but is behind us (N 119) or beneath our feet, supporting us (N 20). In other words, we must learn to speak from within this Nature that surrounds and includes us (N 118), this Nature with which we are intermingled (N 164), this natural being that we are (N 267).

Now Merleau-Ponty's concerns in the lectures are ultimately ontological (N 149, 180, 265, 309), and his way of proceeding relies heavily on "reading" the ontology assumed by the sciences (N 267, 309), applying his customary strategy of refusing to take either side of the familiar Cartesian dichotomy and seeking instead an alternative to the entire Cartesian framework (N 272, 275). Hence although he does make reference to the need for reflection upon the pre-reflective (N 66, 103–104), the main type of experience he will have recourse to will be that of the scientist (N 122), and his chief task is to understand the ontological import of scientific investigations better than the scientists do themselves (N 121, 149). In contrast, my own interests are not ontological, but practical and ethical, albeit in a specific way: I am not concerned with the philosophical construction of ethical systems, but with identifying, studying, fostering, and teaching bodily practices that can contribute to the development of an "embodied ethics."[9] And the kind of embodied ethical conduct I want to focus on is not a matter of applying some pre-existing "norm" or "value," or of carrying out an already established moral "rule"; instead, it is a "responsive ethics" attuned to a "situative claim" that emerges within a particular context as an obligation *"in statu nascendi"*[10] and demands a genuine, and often innovative, response.

Moreover, even though Merleau-Ponty points to the dangers of turning the world into a noema (N 102), my own working methods are phenomenological: I turn to experiential evidence, trace correlations, note invariant structures, and investigate genetic relationships. A truly responsive phenomenology, however, need not be oriented solely toward the experience of a status quo in which everything is already pre-understood and unfolds as anticipated, but can remain open to— or even invite and provoke—emerging phenomena and the alternative orders they imply.[11] Accordingly, just as Merleau-Ponty wants to move beyond a Cartesian ontological framework, I propose a descriptive phenomenology that does not assume a "Cartesian" way of experiencing, but speaks from a style of improvisational comportment characterized by a thoroughly bodily reflexivity.[12] In other words, just as Merleau-Ponty wants to move from a "frontal" ontology to an ontology explicated from within a shared flesh (N 273), I want to move, within lived experiencing itself, from a separative, subject-facing-object type of experiencing to a more inclusive, connective mode—indeed, the ability to perform such a shift is crucial for the phenomena with which I am concerned. Thus in the second part of this chapter I will be discussing a type of situation in which a particular shift in bodily comportment simultaneously transforms this situation from a spectacle I confront (and attempt to dominate from the outside) to a co-situatedness, a situation of which I myself am a part and in whose dynamics I am always already participating, whether I realize it or not.

B. The Figure of a Determinate World

In a 1960 interview, Merleau-Ponty tells us that philosophy "must necessarily be a philosophy of *brute being* and not one of docile being which would have us believe the world can be fully explained."[13] He accordingly rejects a deterministic Cartesian or Laplacean ontology for which the present state of the universe is the effect of its previous state and the cause of its following state, so that the future course of natural being is necessarily and irrevocably preordained by inviolable and all-encompassing causal laws (N 28, 49–50, 55, 118, 123–24, 153, 173, 203, 265–66, 301). Yet he is also critical of the equally exhaustive "finalisms" proposed as rival explanatory schemes (N 26, 184, 200–201, 269). Instead, he sees both finalism (whether theological or secular) and mechanistic causality as stemming from a shared constellation of presuppositions (for example, thinking Being as "positive" and constructing external governing principles to account for its order) and seeks a genuine alternative to this entire entrenched debate (N 119, 176, 177, 202, 238, 299, 332, 333). Thus he turns to such concepts as behavior, field, statistical being, and whole-part, global-local, and macro-micro distinctions. Moreover, he seizes upon the notions of "theme," "norm," and "level," along with those of "sketch," "absence," and "interrogative being" (N 207), in order to articulate how an organism can develop, deploy, and display its typical patterns of comportment. And all this is undertaken in service of an ontology of wild Being that can do justice both to natural productivity and to natural regularities, yet without subjecting Nature to a dominating theoretical gaze that "de-natures" it (N 118) by attempting to contain it in a pre-formed mold (N 58).

Along with Merleau-Ponty, I too am critical of the model of a determinate world and a preordained future. But while Merleau-Ponty addresses the issue ontologically, I want to take it up experientially. It can be shown that even the operative bodily intentionalities of passive synthesis function as a "striving" geared toward ongoing further determination and enrichment of the object of interest,[14] and that in the course of this process, the past "casts a shadow" over the future,[15] so that protentional anticipations strongly tend to establish the experiential presumption[16] of a determinate world— one that "is" already "this way," in itself, prior to my experiencing it—by ordering the "new" in terms of the already known:

> Ahead of what I see and perceive, there is, it is true, nothing more actually visible, but my world is carried forward by lines of intentionality which trace out in advance at least the style of what is to come (although we are always on the watch, perhaps to the day of our death, for the appearance of *something else*).[17]

My question, then, is what sort of shift in our sedimented bodily habitus might allow a style of genuinely improvisational comportment to emerge—one in which productive action, rather than solely reproductive action,[18] is possible. But this already leads to the next figure.

C. The Figure of Genesis

On the basis of what has already been outlined, albeit briefly, it can be suggested that Merleau-Ponty is motivated to turn to questions of genesis by his desire to defend wild Being from the frontal subjugation that would make of it a deterministic universe to be explained by a theorizing spectator. Although in other works he is concerned with the genesis of truth,[19] his approach to genesis in the lectures involves studying the genesis of individual organisms (embryology) and of entire species (theory of evolution), as well as considering questions of regeneration of lost organs or after sectioning. In contrast, I am concerned—as already indicated—with the genesis of new styles of comportment. More specifically, however, I am interested not in the arbitrarily novel, but in a responsive, co-participatory comportment that allows not just anything, but "what is needed next here" to emerge, even if it has never occurred before—a process that involves a receptive, interrogative attitude rather than one that imposes and posits. Elsewhere, I have addressed similar questions in relation to musical improvisation and transformative somatic practice; here I am concerned with the shift from routinized comportment in a familiar world of recognizable situations and typical outcomes to improvisational comportment in local and fluid situations, yielding a *Stiftung* of an entirely different set of possibilities that redefine the situation itself. But since my co-participants in the kind of situation I want to describe happened to be nonhuman sentient beings, I shall turn to a final figure in Merleau-Ponty's lectures before embarking upon my description.

D. The Figure of the Animal

It can readily be demonstrated that for Merleau-Ponty, the body is an ontological emblem that refutes, in its very being, the entire framework of Cartesian dualism (N 106–108, 266, 269–70, 271, 278, 287). What the lectures on Nature now also make clear is that the animal, too, is a "loophole" through which to escape from explanatory schemes that want to assign everything either to the realm of pure "mind" or to the realm of pure "matter," or at the very least to maintain these categories unscathed when they are applied to those stubborn and disquieting cases in which they appear to be mingled (N 269, 275, 277). Merleau-Ponty poses the question of animal consciousness (N 259); refers to animal culture, animal institutions, and animal communications (N 254, 258, 269, 276); alludes to his key notion of intercorporeity by insisting that a species is not a sum of separate individuals, but must be described in terms of interanimality (N 247), a term he also applies to relations among species (N 227); and rejects the Cartesian concept of the animal as machine. Instead, for Merleau-Ponty the human-animal relation is not a "hierarchic" one characterized by the "addition" of rationality to a mechanistically conceived animal body, but a lateral relation of kinship, *Einfühlung*, and *Ineinander* among living beings (N 269–70, 271, 276–77, 318, 335, 339). The human animal is simply another way of being a body (N 269, 276–77), another variant of sensing/sensible sentience within the sensible (N 277, 338).

Yet despite this promising recognition of our kinship with animals in the flesh of the world, there are major lacunae in Merleau-Ponty's lectures. Many animals are referred to, from axolotl to zebra, but the working or companion animals we share our *Umwelt* with on an everyday basis are seldom mentioned, and then only in passing—typically, in contexts significantly different from those of our everyday commerce with them. Similarly, the question of the human-animal "relation" is treated only ontologically, and there is only fleeting reference to human-animal sociality. More seriously, however, the unthematized relation between human beings and animals that undergirds many pages of this volume is a frontal relation of contemplation, objectification, intervention, and domination; the animals are not only observed from the outside and theorized about, but interfered with—removed from their native *Umwelt*, experimented upon, severed, grafted, dissected, etc. Thus when Merleau-Ponty speaks of "interrogating the axolotl" (N 202), it resembles the type of "interrogation" perpetrated by a police state: something may indeed be learned by someone, but the one under interrogation may not survive the experience. Here it is not possible to pursue the wealth of ethical issues (and further philosophical implications) raised by animal experimentation. Instead, my point is a more modest one—namely, that if Merleau-Ponty truly wishes to develop a concept of Nature from within wild Being as a field of shared flesh, he is looking in the wrong place, so to speak, if he turns only to scientific investigations of animals for evidence of our lateral kinship with them. Such evidence is even more abundant if we speak from within our life among animals—from shared situations in which we and the animals co-participate, from the lived experience of interspecies sociality where it is not just I who looks at the animal, but the animal who looks at me. I will approach this question by considering a particular type of fluid situation that calls not only for a shift from a "frontal" attitude attempting to dominate the situation from outside to becoming a part of a shared situation among fellow sentient beings, but also for a shift from "knowing in advance" what is likely to happen (and reacting accordingly) to relinquishing the project of "knowing" and allowing "something else" to emerge among us instead.

2. With the Animals on the Earth

Let me begin by describing the initial situation in the natural attitude. The principal characters are two male cats: my own neutered male cat JoJo, roughly three years old at the time, and an older, homeless male named B.C., whose status in the neighborhood can be gauged when one learns that "B.C." stood for "Bad Cat." At the time I am describing, B.C. had recently been neutered (though he had not yet fully undergone the behavior-altering hormonal changes this usually entails), and temporary housing had been found for him. But he had fled that location under traumatic circumstances, and had returned—confused, shocked, and desperate—to his original neighborhood, where the only place he was tolerated was on my landlord's property, near the studio cabin I rented. Unfortunately, this coincided with what JoJo regarded as his own territory, and confrontations between them were even more frequent than they had been before. Prior to getting involved in an effort to save B.C. and find a home for him, I had attempted to break up their confrontations by rushing out as soon as I heard the typical yowling and chasing B.C. away; when he reappeared, traumatized and in need, I would run

out and try to calm the cats down by speaking softly and sooth-
ingly (a practice sometimes called "toning"[20]) in the hopes of keeping the situation from escalating into actual violence. But whether
I attempted to intervene by threatening or by toning, I was reacting,
as an outsider, to a situation I perceived as dangerous: as soon as I
heard the howls that typically precede a cat fight, I experienced the
situation as "a potential cat fight," and even if I succeeded in avert-
ing an actual fight, I still experienced the situation precisely as "an
averted cat fight." In other words, I experienced it throughout as one
of inevitable aggression and conflict (after all, I reminded myself,
male cats are "naturally" territorial); to borrow (and perhaps stretch)
a Merleau-Pontyan term, the "level" did not change, and the very
horizon of my everyday world was pervaded by its tone. (Note, inci-
dentally, that this brief summary of everyday events in the natural
attitude already incorporates some elements from a naturalistic
attitude as well—for example, references to territoriality, hormone-
driven behavior, and even post-traumatic shock syndrome).

But a working phenomenologist is, I think, occupationally pre-
disposed to bring a phenomenological attitude and an awareness of
the results of previous phenomenological work to bear in his or her
personal predicaments as well as in his or her professional reflections. Thus although I had initially had no plans whatsoever to do a
phenomenological description of the "incipient cat fight" problem,
the experiential structure of the situation began to stand out for me
as the number of cat confrontation episodes mounted. I began to
notice, for example, not only that my own dominant response to
these episodes was fear, but that what I was reacting to was something that had not yet happened (in other words, I was afraid that
they "would" fight). In addition, I was able to see that underlying or
pervading what I had taken to be the cats' aggression, there was also
a strong component of fear on their part. And it suddenly dawned on
me that there was a kind of intercorporeal circulation and contagion
of this fear among us, so that by rushing out, full of anxiety about
what I thought was going to happen, I was only making matters
worse. But once I realized, with the help of Merleau-Ponty's technical term, that the situation was an "intercorporeal" one, I began to
develop what I found myself calling the practice of peace (though I
should more properly say "a" practice of peace, since the practice discussed here is certainly not the only or even necessarily the best

such practice). In what follows, I shall describe this practice and discuss its various elements. But first I must at least mention that the more peaceful mode of intercorporeal comportment that was able to emerge among us not only effected a local, practical transformation, offering us an alternative to assuming and maintaining a framework of conflict and aggression, but functioned as a *Stiftung* (N 88), inaugurating and instituting a new style that was now available for other interspecies interactions as well.

To put it as simply as possible, the practice of peace that emerged in collaboration with the cats involves my literally assuming—taking up and exemplifying *leibhaft*—a particular way of being bodily that is not necessarily confined to me alone, but can radiate across an interkinaesthetic/intercorporeal field. More specifically, this practice involves my performing four interrelated steps (usually, but not always, in this order): letting my weight settle; experientially "inhabiting" the kinaesthesias of my gaze; opening my heart; and not-knowing what is going to happen next. I shall comment upon each of these in turn and then upon the process as a whole.

A. Letting Weight Settle (Grounding)

As Merleau-Ponty tells us (N 110–11), Husserl's later work offers us a notion of Earth not as one natural object among others in the solar system (and the universe at large), but as "ground," "soil," or "basis" (*Boden*).[21] And according to Merleau-Ponty, this "pre-object," this "weighty mass," is "always at the margin of my perception like a frame or a level"—a "first level" to which I am linked in an "umbilical relation," an "original tie."[22] However, previous phenomenological thematization of our lived relation to this Earth-ground tends to emphasize that in waking up and assuming upright posture, we effect an oppositional counterposition to the supporting ground as well as a connection with it: we "resist" that "heaviness" or "heft" usually called "gravity" and establish a particular sort of "I-Allon" relation that sets us over-against the world, although at the same time we remain in "active exchange" with it in a dialectical tension of "opposition" and "attachment."[23] The evolutionary acquisition of upright posture not only liberates the anterior members to become "arms" with "hands," and thus articulates an oriented space of action where the eyes can fix what the hands grasp (N 334, 339, 340), but also opens up a space of "beholding," of contemplation at a distance.[24] Thus in the human animal we find not only the individuating act of rising above the force of gravity and winning a sphere of primordial motility,[25] but also the inauguration of a style of separative seeing[26] and its correlative establishment of a distance from ground, things, and fellow beings.[27] These themes have been explored in detail by Erwin Straus, and both the advantages and the problems attending the hegemony of a distanced, predominantly visual mode of experiencing have been amply discussed in the phenomenological and continental traditions as well.

What I want to suggest here, however, is that bringing into play the lived, felt experience of letting weight "settle"[28] can actually shift us out of this entire frontally/visually organized paradigm of subject-facing-object and into a proprioceptive "*Selbstung*" (reflexivity, self-awareness) without epistemological "subject" (N 335, 340).[29] Yet this is not at all a matter of a ray of attention that is now directed "interoceptively" rather than "exteroceptively"—as though I now make my own bodily sensations, rather than what I am looking at, the focus of my experience—for this maintains a subject-facing-object paradigm. Instead, letting weight settle can be a lucidly lived "act" or "gesture"[30] that moves through me as a whole and grounds me more fully in the situation rather than withdrawing me from it and shunting me into the status of a spectator. And with this, my body is neither a mere point of view on things nor an objective mass over-against "me" (N 287), but a situated reflexivity, a "sensing sensible" (N 286). For to sense myself bodily in this way is simultaneously to be related to something other than my own mass (N 270): it is to have a position in the world (N 287), on the Earth-ground, with my fellow creatures in a shared field.

Moreover, as Merleau-Ponty points out, there is no precise boundary between "posture" and "action," so that any bodily attitude I may take up is already a preparation for action (N 195). In my initial reaction to the cats' behavior, not only was my attention riveted solely on the scene before me, but my muscles were tensed in a posture that could explode into action at any second. Grounding, however, alters the "motor intentionality"[31] of the situation, for letting weight settle interrupts the bodily "being on the brink of" reacting in a particular way. And when I begin to "become body" in this grounded way, rather than functioning as a pair of staring eyes mounted on a precarious pedestal poised for sudden movement, this shift ripples through the interkinaesthetic field as well. The cats' bodies subtly alter; although neither cat is giving his weight as completely to the earth as, for example, a sleeping cat in a safe place, they too are no longer so thoroughly tensed to spring forward at any moment. But this is not solely a one-way communication of calmness from mediator to potential combatants. Instead, as they begin to relax ever so slightly (while maintaining exquisite alertness), this in turn is intercorporeally circulated among us, and I find myself renewing and deepening my own settling into our shared ground. The tensions vibrating between us and permeating each of our bodies gradually begin to ease, and we can begin to see our shared situation in a different way.

B. Inhabiting Visual Kinaesthesias (Cotentive Practice)

As I have already indicated, there is a structural relationship between upright posture and the frontal relation of a subject to a world of objects over-against, and separated from, the subject. But as Merleau-Ponty notes, there are further connections between our bodily position with respect to gravity on the one hand and the movements of the eyes on the other. For not only does this "prospective activity" of the eye organize the *Umwelt* as a perceptual world (N 284), but it is the movements of the eyes that guide the movements of the body as a whole in such a way that clear and distinct vision is obtained (N 226).[32] Thus the way in which the eyes are used plays a key role in shaping our habitual postural style and habitual patterns of movement. As Trigant Burrow has pointed out, however, our usual manner of using our eyes is "ditentive," that is, it is a divisive, "partitive" way of being attentive to our surroundings and to our fellow beings, seeing the latter not only as separate from us, but all too often as hostile to the self-interest of our own "I." To this he contrasts a "cotentive" mode of feeling, which is a more primary, inclusive mode in which one senses organismic connectedness and solidarity rather than separateness, competitiveness, and potential conflict.[33] The cotentive practice Burrow developed consists of steadying the gaze, not by fixing it upon some external object, but through a kinaesthetic awareness that inhabits, from within, the usually anonymous and automatic patterns of balance and tension behind the eyes.[34] My experience of this practice has been, again, one of "*Selbstung*" without "subject" (N 335), as though the visual field now surveys itself without implying a vantage point outside the field (N 218). Perhaps some sense of this can be conveyed by referring to the Eighth of Rainer Maria Rilke's *Duino Elegies*, where he contrasts the human being—who is always a spectator over-against the world—with the animal, whose gaze sees an open world from within. Or, as Rilke put it in a 1926 letter, "The animal is *in* the world; we stand *in front* of the world. . . ."[35] Cotentive practice, however, disrupts this frontal, separative style and allows me to reclaim a sense of being a part of, rather than a spectator of, the open field of the visible.[36]

Moreover, as Merleau-Ponty also points out, the animals themselves are visible to one another, not only mirroring one another in a "specular" intercorporeity (N 247), but attuned to the communicative dimension of their mutual visibility (N 254, 256). And ethologists emphasize the communicative import of different types of gaze in particular. (For example, in a remarkable session many years ago, my cat Sheba taught me to return a blink when she blinked at me and to initiate a blink for her to return. Subsequently I learned that an exchange of blinks is a well-documented greeting ritual between cats, with the interruption of the gaze by the blink indicating a willingness to establish and maintain friendly relations and mutual respect.) Thus if I impale the cats with anxious, pinpointed staring, I am contributing to the aggressive tone of the situation; if I soften my eyes and heighten proprioceptive, kinaesthetic awareness from within, I am not only relieving some of the tension within the inter-kinaesthetic field, but am displaying a less confrontational style of intercorporeal comportment within our shared communicative field.

C. Opening the Heart

Though this aspect of the practice I am describing undoubtedly has many precedents and parallels in other practices, I was motivated to adopt it by noticing that my initial, anxious reaction to the incipient cat fights was characterized by a kind of bodily narrowing or tightening around the vertical line of the breastbone. I cannot claim, however, to have hit upon a specific way of "doing" something to reverse this configuration; I just remind myself to allow my heart to open, and the shape of my upper body shifts of its own accord in response (sometimes subtly, sometimes more noticeably). At the same time, my breathing typically changes: I am no longer holding my breath (or breathing shallowly), but more fully join the shared field of air moving among us in reciprocal interpenetration and exchange. And this shift too appears to be intercorporeally "contagious" among creatures that breathe, even—indeed, perhaps especially—among members of different species.[37]

Moreover, if we turn, as Merleau-Ponty so often does in the lectures on Nature, to the field of scientific investigation, we can note a surprisingly rich constellation of issues connecting the heart as a metaphorical center of emotion, the heart as central organ of blood circulation, and styles of communicative interaction not only between human beings but between human beings and animals. In a series of studies, James J. Lynch found that our blood pressure fluctuates during conversation: it rises when we speak and falls when we listen,[38] as though a shared tide ebbs and flows across the communal body of the speakers. Even babies had higher blood pressure when crying than when quiet.[39] Furthermore, persons with "Type A personality," who are apparently at greater risk for heart disease, typically speak rapidly, loudly, aggressively, and "with a certain breathless intensity," often interrupting and speaking over others.[40] "Rather than listening," Lynch tells us, "our hypertensive patients appeared to be preoccupied, thinking about what they wanted to say next, almost as if they were continuously engaged in a contest or fight rather than in a comfortable dialogue."[41] And whereas a normal person's blood pressure falls, sometimes even below the baseline level, when attentively listening, the hypertensive person's blood pressure may fail to fall back to the baseline level, and may then rise even higher the next time he or she speaks.[42] In contrast, people talking to their pets—typically, talking softly, gently, and slowly while stroking them—did not display the usual rise of blood pressure while speaking.[43] And the heart rate and blood pressure of dogs varies significantly with the presence of a human being and the quality of the interaction.[44] All of this leads Lynch to challenge the Cartesian physiology of irrevocably separate bodies and to propose that we are linked in a larger, "communal" body.[45] Or to put it in Merleau-Ponty's own words, we are "like organs of one single intercorporeality,"[46] "co-functioning" as one body,[47] participating in a shared flesh. To bring this back to the context of the cats, I can report that as I let my heart open—silently, without either threatening or toning, sensing my body from within rather than letting words run angrily or anxiously "through my mind"—the frequency and intensity of the cats' howls diminished, until they too were silent. Of course, there was no apparatus present recording my heart rate and blood pressure, or JoJo's, or B.C.'s. But my point is that the "physiological" state of each organism, the quality of communication among them, and the overall tone of the situation as a whole are inextricably intertwined: "opening my heart" is not a merely "symbolic" gesture, but can have a genuine intercorporeal effect.

D. Not-knowing

It is outside the scope of this chapter to discuss in detail how not-knowing—adopting an interrogative attitude that relinquishes the project of knowing in favor of a responsive comportment[48] that can allow "what is needed next here" to emerge—contributes to improvisational comportment in general and to the practice of peace in particular. Perhaps the key practical point to make here is that neither an attitude of "Oh my God, the cats are going to fight!" nor one of "Aha, they're starting to relax—they are not going to fight after all!" was helpful in allowing the situation to shift from one of conflict to one of peace. Instead, I not only had to assume a genuine attitude of not-knowing what was going to happen next, but maintain and renew this attitude along the full span of the process.

Moreover, the kind of not-knowing that is at stake here (which is not at all a matter of a lack within a pre-assumed scheme—see N 60) is not just cognitive, but incorporates a not-doing as well. Yet this is not inaction, but a way of putting out of play the sedimented, habituated bodily-kinaesthetic reactions to a situation we have already recognized as "this kind of situation."[49] In other words, what is required is a kind of "bodily epoché"[50] that suspends our "developed readinesses"[51] in favor of a style of corporeal comportment that is characterized by a "readiness for improvisation."[52] Thus the not-doing proper to the improvisational body cannot be equated with my assuming, for example, a customary position of repose as the "null-posture" (*Nullhaltung*)[53] from which habitual movements can unfold in the context of familiar tasks and types of interaction. Instead, the improvisational body in the sense meant here is a body of "wild kinaestheses,"[54] a primordial motility that is not already geared

toward (and limited to) a particular repertoire of movement possibilities geared in with a familiar world of typical things and situations.
Such an improvisational body would then be a "wild body" (*corps
sauvage*)[55] beyond the sedimented patterns of personal history or cultural habitus, a "protean body"[56] whose social shaping is thus never
total or final. Yet it is not a question here of abandoning all routinized behavior and replacing it with some sort of continual improvisation; the point is that where existing modes of comportment are
no longer adequate, the improvisational "moment" may help us to
act freshly, allowing "what is needed next here"—what is implied by
the situation but not possible within the current local order, level, or
framework—to emerge,[57] along with its own new order, measure,
and possibilities.[58] And in this case, what emerged from the moment
of not-knowing/not-doing was a more open, responsive attitude, a
new way of embodying the possibility of peace—one that was word-
lessly communicated to the cats, reverberating across our shared situation and shifting it accordingly.

E. Connections and Questions

I shall bring this research report to a close by commenting, as promised, on the practice as a whole, understood as a practice undertaken
by a human peacemaker in response to an encounter with nonhuman Others. Seen from the outside, it is at the very least a way for
the human spectator of an animal encounter to undo the physiological "startle reaction" that was my initial postural response to the
sounds of an incipient cat fight. For Merleau-Ponty, however, the
body is not one thing among other things, but "*chose-étalon*" (N
287)—it is the level, the standard, the canon, the norm around
which my sensible insertion in the perceived world is ordered.[59] But
what happens when this bodily level itself shifts?

In the first place, the kinaesthetic awareness that is swung into
play by the practice offers, as already indicated, a radical alternative
to the pervasive style of separative seeing that makes Being,
Nature, Others, etc., into objects over-against a subject; instead, it
opens a kinaesthetic "dimension" that is neither an appearance of an
object-body nor a sensation making a subject-body present to an
experiencing "consciousness," but the inauguration of a lucidly lived
style of comportment that situates us in an englobing field lived

from within as a whole. In other words, the "frontality" entailed in assuming a primarily visual mode undergoes a profound transformation, a penetration or permeation of the visible by an invisible depth that "exists only as tactile or kinesthetically,"[60] so that the relation of my weight to the ground "beneath" me, the kinaesthetic activity "behind" my eyes, and the sense of my heart "within" me are as palpable as what I see "before" me—which is no longer a spectacle, but a situation in which I myself am implicated. Thus the shift from a "seeing from outside" to a "sensing from within" mode is simultaneously a shift from a "separative" to a "connective" sociality. Yet whereas Merleau-Ponty either emphasizes a visual, specular intercorporeity (N 247, 340) or turns to Freudian language and concepts to elucidate a libidinal intercorporeity (N 272, 281, 287, 335, 346–47), the key feature I find at work in such a sociality is a shared interkinaesthetic field.[61] Here the phenomenon of "tonus imitation" may be mentioned—the intercorporeal "contagion" of muscular tension.[62] But release of tension can be contagious too: if one "member" of the communal body is able to let weight settle, with steadied eyes and open heart, this will almost inevitably affect the other "members" of the local communal body as well, for "nothing is more contagious than genuine tranquillity."[63] Note, however, that the shift from a "separative" to a more "connective" experiential style does not thereby "create" an intercorporeal "unity" where before there were only atomistic "bodies." Instead, everything happens as though we are always already interkinaesthetically linked, and what the practice I am describing does is to lift this connectivity from blind anonymity to lucidly lived awareness: now that I realize that I am caught up in a shared field of tension, I can use my own ability for proprioceptive awareness to recognize what is going on and actively allow it to change.

Moreover, as Merleau-Ponty points out, organisms lacking proprioceptive feedback act explosively, at the mercy of whatever instinctive reaction is triggered (N 226). In contrast, both practitioners in the field of somatics (body work and body awareness practices) and persons working closely with animals have found that heightened proprioceptivity is linked with the ability to move beyond entrenched motor patterns, be they deep-seated "habits" or "instinctual" responses.[64] But here it is not a question of replacing these familiar "kinetic melodies" with an "improvisation," remaining, so to speak, within a certain "key" or "tonality" that sets the "level" or framework around or within which the entire melody will play and prefigures a certain style of resolution from the very beginning (N 228, 303). Rather, what I have elsewhere termed "deep change"[65] occurs, for there is a qualitative shift in the "level" of the communal habitus itself—and with this, a shift in the "level" of the situation as a whole: it is no longer a question of either "actual" or "averted" violence, no longer an occasion for "potential" violence, but an occasion for the practice of peace. And I am no longer the observer of what I have instantly, pre-reflectively perceived and reacted to as an "incipient cat fight," but a co-participant, along with my fellow sentient beings, in a fluid situation—not only one in which "what will happen next" is not determined in advance, but one in which "what kind of situation this is" is open in principle to transformation. In this way a local, situated moment of openness allows "something else" to emerge, inaugurating a "new dimensionality" (N 268), a new style of intercorporeal comportment, with attendant new sensibilities, new "readinesses," new interests, and a new sense of the "kinship of all life."[66]

Questions of many sorts remain at this point in the investigation. For example, this report is presented from the point of view of the human participant's experience. Can a parallel phenomenological description be reconstructed from the side of the cats?[67] We might inquire, for instance, into their typical modes of experienced relation with the earth upon which they rest in repose and against which they push off as they spring forward (or as they leap up to a new surface, where they may find that they have to balance precariously, perhaps exploring the area gingerly, testing its stability by entrusting part of their weight to the advancing front paw before discovering a suitable place to settle luxuriously). Or we might study how cats form and maintain peaceful intercorporeal relations, not only with other cats (I think immediately of a tangle of sleeping kittens, touching and being touched in myriad ways, each adjusting as another stirs), but with their human companions. What, in other words, is cat peace like before it is interrupted by moments of crisis and confrontation?

Moreover, I have assumed a shared sociality in general between cats and human beings, so that, for example, the cats and I are capable of distinguishing many different types of situations and activities, experiencing them together even though the cats do not use the words and phrases that human beings do to describe and differentiate these experiences.[68] Yet the very assumption of such community has been problematic for many human beings, and this entire question not only invites further philosophical clarification, but needs further phenomenological research as well.[69]

Finally, numerous practical matters remain to be studied. For instance, will letting weight settle, steadying the gaze, opening the heart, and not-knowing work in encounters involving wild animals? domestic animals other than companion animals? other human beings? Is this practice only effective when it is undertaken by a third-party mediator, or is it helpful when I myself am involved in a confrontation? What happens when I try it out in situations that were not conflictual to begin with? How and where can and should it be taught? How does it relate to other ways of making peace among nonhuman animals, among human beings, and between human and nonhuman animals? And how might the lived experience of such a practice of peace affect our concept of Nature itself?

My investigation of an intercorporeal/interspecies body of peace began in the backyard, in lived reversibility and *Ineinander* with the cats, not in the library with the literature on animal ethics and peace studies spread out before me. Undoubtedly, studying such literature will help me develop this practice more fully. But perhaps what a phenomenological investigation of these matters can teach us is that such peace is not to be observed, analyzed, and discussed from the outside, but is to be embodied from within in an ongoing carnal intertwining that surrounds and supports us even as it moves through us and among us.

Notes

1. Maurice Merleau-Ponty, *Résumés de cours, Collège de France 1952–1960* (Paris: Gallimard, 1968), pp. 91–121, 125–37, 171–80; *Themes from the Lectures at the Collège de France 1952–1960*, transl. John O'Neill (Evanston: Northwestern University Press, 1970), pp. 62–87, 88–98, 124–31.

2. Xavier Tilliette, "Husserl et la notion de Nature. Notes prises aux cours de M. Merleau-Ponty," *Revue de métaphysique et de morale*, 70 (1965), pp. 257–69; Merleau-Ponty, "Husserl's Concept of Nature (Merleau-Ponty's [1956–57] Lectures)," *Texts and Dialogues: Maurice Merleau-Ponty*, eds.

Hugh J. Silverman and James Barry, Jr. (Atlantic Highlands: Humanities Press, 1992), pp. 162–68, 183–88.

3. Maurice Merleau-Ponty, *La Nature: Notes, Cours du Collège de France*, ed. Dominique Séglard (Paris: Editions du Seuil, 1995). Subsequently cited by the abbreviation N followed by the page numbers.

4. Maurice Merleau-Ponty, *La structure du comportement* (Paris: Presses Universitaires de France, 1942); *The Structure of Behavior*, transl. Alden L. Fisher (Boston: Beacon Press, 1963).

5. See esp. Maurice Merleau-Ponty, *Le visible et l'invisible*, ed. Claude Lefort (Paris: Gallimard, 1964); *The Visible and the Invisible*, transl. Alphonso Lingis (Evanston: Northwestern University Press, 1968); see also "Le philosophe et son ombre," *Signes* (Paris: Gallimard, 1960), pp. 201–28; "The Philosopher and His Shadow," *Signs*, transl. Richard C. McCleary (Evanston: Northwestern University Press, 1964), pp. 159–81. Subsequent references to these sources will cite French/English page numbers.

6. See, for example, Monika Langer, "Merleau-Ponty and Deep Ecology," *Ontology and Alterity in Merleau-Ponty*, eds. Galen A. Johnson and Michael B. Smith (Evanston: Northwestern University Press, 1990), pp. 115–29, 192–97; *Alter*, 3 (1995) (special issue on "L'Animal"); *Études Phénoménologiques*, 23–24 (1996) (special issue on "Phénoménologie et philosophie de la nature").

7. Edmund Husserl, *Ding und Raum. Vorlesungen 1907*, ed. Ulrich Claesges (Den Haag: Martinus Nijhoff, 1973), p. 9.

8. See, for example, Edmund Husserl, *Zur Phänomenologie der Intersubjektivität. Texte aus dem Nachlass*, ed. Iso Kern (Den Haag: Martinus Nijhoff, 1973), *Erster Teil: 1905–1920*, Beilage XV; *Zweiter Teil: 1921–1928*, Text Nr. 6, Beilage XII, Beilage XIII, Beilage XIV; *Dritter Teil: 1929–1935*, Text Nr. 11, Beilage IX, Beilage X, Beilage XLVII, Text Nr. 35.

9. Elizabeth A. Behnke, "Ghost Gestures: Phenomenological Investigations of Bodily Micromovements and their Intercorporeal Implications," *Study Project in Phenomenology of the Body Newsletter* 7:2 (fall 1994), p. 36; "Edmund Husserl's Contribution to Phenomenology of the Body in *Ideas II*," *Issues in Husserl's Ideas II*, eds. Thomas Nenon and Lester Embree (Dordrecht: Kluwer Academic Publishers, 1996), pp. 155–56.

10. Bernhard Waldenfels, "Die Responsivität des Philosophierens. Ein Gesprach mit Dimitri Genev und Dimitar Saschev," *Studia Culturologica*, 4 (1996), pp. 100–101.

11. Ibid., pp. 104, 110.

12. Elizabeth A. Behnke, "World without Opposite/Flesh of the World: A Carnal Introduction" (Felton, CA: California Center for Jean Gebser Studies, 1984), esp. pp. 9–22, 37–39.

13. Maurice Merleau-Ponty, "Merleau-Ponty in Person (An Interview with Madeleine Chapsal, 1960)," transl. James Barry, Jr., *Texts and Dialogues*, p. 12.

14. See, for example, Edmund Husserl, *Analysen zur passiven Synthesis. Aus Vorlesungs- und Forschungsmanuskripten 1918–1926*, ed. Margot Fleischer (Den Haag: Martinus Nijhoff, 1966), pp. 83–87.

15. Ibid., pp. 289, 323.

16. Ibid., pp. 211–17; see also pp. 101–109.

17. Maurice Merleau-Ponty, *Phénoménologie de la perception* (Paris: Gallimard, 1945), p. 476; *Phenomenology of Perception*, transl. Colin Smith (London: Routledge & Kegan Paul, 1962 [1976]) [rpt. with translation revisions by Forrest Williams], p. 416 (subsequently cited with French/English page numbers).

18. Bernhard Waldenfels, *Ordnung im Zwielicht* (Frankfurt am Main: Suhrkamp, 1987), pp. 144–45; *Order in the Twilight*, transl. David J. Parent (Athens: Ohio University Press, 1996), pp. 90–91 (subsequently cited with German/English page numbers).

19. See, for example, Bernhard Waldenfels, "Vérité à Faire: Merleau-Ponty's Question Concerning Truth," *Philosophy Today*, 35:2 (1991), transl. Mark Basil Tanzer, pp. 185–94; "Vérité à Faire. Zur Herkunft der Wahrheit," *Deutsch-Französische Gedankengänge* (Frankfurt am Main: Suhrkamp, 1995), pp. 124–39.

20. Linda Tellington-Jones, with Sybil Taylor, *The Tellington TTouch* (New York: Viking Penguin, 1992) [rpt. Penguin Books, 1995], pp. 36, 134, 270.

21. Edmund Husserl, "Grundlegende Untersuchungen zum phänomenologischen Ursprung der Räumlichkeit der Natur," *Philosophical Essays in Memory of Edmund Husserl*, ed. Marvin Farber (Cambridge: Harvard University Press, 1940), pp. 307–25; "Foundational Investigations of the Phenomenological Origins of the Spatiality of Nature," transl. Fred Kersten, *Husserl: Shorter Works*, eds. Peter McCormick and Frederick A. Elliston (Notre Dame: University of Notre Dame Press, 1981), pp. 222–33.

22. Tilliette, "Husserl's Concept of Nature," p. 167.

23. Erwin W. Straus, "Psychiatry and Philosophy," transl. Erling Eng, *Psychiatry and Philosophy*, ed. Maurice Natanson (New York: Springer-Verlag, 1969), pp. 34–35, 45–47.

24. Erwin W. Straus, "Born to See, Bound to Behold: Reflections on the Function of Upright Posture in the Esthetic Attitude," transl. Erling Eng, *The Philosophy of the Body*, ed. Stuart F. Spicker (Chicago: Quadrangle Books, 1970), esp. pp. 339–43, 353–54.

25. Straus, "Psychiatry and Philosophy," p. 34.

26. Behnke, "World without Opposite," pp. 4-9.

27. Erwin W. Straus, *Phenomenological Psychology*, transl., in part, Erling Eng (New York: Basic Books, 1966), pp. 144–45.

28. Mary Alice Roche, "Sensory Awareness, Phyloanalysis, and the Desire to Express," *Lifwynn Correspondence*, 3:2 (1994), pp. 13–14.

29. See also Behnke, "World without Opposite," pp. 21–25.

30. Behnke, "Ghost Gestures," p. 21.

31. Merleau-Ponty, *Phenomenology of Perception*, pp. 160–64/137–40; compare Edmund Husserl, *Phänomenologische Psychologie. Vorlesungen Sommersemester 1925*, ed. Walter Biemel (Den Haag: Martinus Nijhoff, 1962), pp. 197–98; *Phenomenological Psychology: Lectures, Summer Semester 1925*, transl. John Scanlon (The Hague: Martinus Nijhoff, 1977), pp. 151–52.

32. See also Husserl, *Ding und Raum*, esp. chs. 9–13.

33. See Trigant Burrow, *Toward Social Sanity and Human Survival*, ed. Alfreda S. Galt (New York: Horizon Press, 1984), ch. 4; Alfreda S. Galt, "Trigant Burrow and the Phylobiological Perspective," *Somatics*, 5:1 (1984–85), pp. 58–60; Alfreda S. Galt, "Trigant Burrow and the Laboratory of the 'I,'" *The Humanistic Psychologist*, 23 (1995), pp. 28–34.

34. Burrow, *Toward Social Sanity*, pp. 87–88, 96, 114; see also Alfreda S. Galt, "A Report of Proprioceptive Experimentation in Social Self-Inquiry," *Lifwynn Correspondence*, 4:1 (1995), pp. 6–12.

35. Rainer Maria Rilke, *The Selected Poetry of Rainer Maria Rilke*, ed. and transl. Stephen Mitchell (New York: Random House, 1982) [rpt. Vintage Books, 1984], p. 329.

36. See also Merleau-Ponty, *The Visible and the Invisible*, pp. 135–36, 152–53/99–100, 113–14.

37. See, for example, Tellington-Jones, *TTouch*, pp. 25, 36, 134, 167, 221.

38. James J. Lynch, *The Language of the Heart: The Human Body in Dialogue* (New York: Basic Books, 1985), p. 114 and ch. 6.

39. Ibid., p. 116.

40. Ibid., pp. 140–41.

41. Ibid., p. 161.

42. Ibid., pp. 160–61.

43. Ibid., pp. 153–55.

44. Ibid., pp. 62–64, 158.

45. Ibid., p. 179.

46. Merleau-Ponty, "The Philosopher and His Shadow," pp. 213/168.

47. Merleau-Ponty, *The Visible and the Invisible*, pp. 268/215.

48. Bernhard Waldenfels, *Antwortregister* (Frankfurt am Main: Suhrkamp, 1994), esp. pp. 320–36, 437–63.

49. Compare ibid., pp. 459-61.

50. Elizabeth A. Behnke, "Practical Intercorporeity: Toward a Phenomenological Account of Transformative Somatic Practice," presented at the Japanese/North American Phenomenology Conference, Seattle, 1991, pp. 10–12.

51. Husserl, *Analysen zur passiven Synthesis*, p. 217.

52. Heinrich Jacoby, *Jenseits von "Begabt" und "Unbegabt." Zweckmässige Fragestellung und zweckmässiges Verhalten. Schlüssel für die Entfaltung des Menschen*, ed. Sophie Ludwig (Hamburg: Christians Verlag, 3rd ed., 1987), esp. pp. 376–77.

53. Husserl, *Ding und Raum*, p. 314; compare *Zur Phänomenologie der Intersubjektivität, Erster Teil*, p. 284.

54. Husserl, *Zur Phänomenologie der Intersubjektivität, Dritter Teil*, pp. 660–61.

55. Bernhard Waldenfels, "Nähe und Ferne des Leibes," *Menschengestalten. Zur Kodierung des Kreatürlichen im modernen Roman*, eds. Rudolf Behrens and Roland Galle (Würzburg: Königshausen & Neumann, 1995), p. 22.

56. Don Johnson, *The Protean Body* (New York: Harper Colophon, 1977).

57. Eugene T. Gendlin, "Three Assertions About the Body," *The Folio: A Journal for Focusing and Experiential Therapy*, 12:1 (1993), pp. 31–32.

58. See Waldenfels, *Order in the Twilight*, pp. 146–53/91–97; compare Eugene T. Gendlin, *Focusing-Oriented Psychotherapy: A Manual of the Experiential Method* (New York: The Guilford Press, 1996), p. 245.

59. Tilliette, "Husserl's Concept of Nature," p. 165.

60. Merleau-Ponty, *The Visible and the Invisible*, pp. 311/257.

61. Behnke, "Ghost Gestures," pp. 32–33.

62. Gerda Alexander, *Eutony* (Great Neck, NY: Felix Morrow, 1985), esp. pp. 21–22, 48, 55, 57–58, 61–62.

63. Heinrich Jacoby, as quoted by Edith Matter, in Rudolf Weber, "Interview with Margaret Locher, Dr. Ruth Matter, Edith Matter, Dr. Maya Rauch, Dr. Senta Frauchiger," transl. *Sensory Awareness Foundation, Sensory Awareness Foundation Bulletin*, No. 13 (1986), p. 31.

64. Tellington-Jones, *TTouch*, esp. pp. 35, 68, 73, 111–12; see also pp. 11–18.

65. Elizabeth A. Behnke, "The Philosopher's Body," *Somatics*, 3:4 (1982), p. 46.

66. J. Allen Boone, *Kinship with All Life* (New York: Harper, 1954) [rpt. HarperCollins, 1976].

67. See, for example, H. Peter Steeves, "Deep Community: Phenomenology's Disclosure of the Common Good," *Between the Species*, 10:3/4 (summer 1994), pp. 99–100.

68. Eugene T. Gendlin, "Experiential Phenomenology," *Phenomenology and the Social Sciences*, vol. 1, ed. Maurice Natanson (Evanston: Northwestern University Press, 1973), p. 292.

69. See H. Peter Steeves, "The Boundaries of the Phenomenological Community: Non-Human Life and the Extent of our Moral Enmeshment," *Becoming Persons*, ed. Robert N. Fisher (Oxford: Applied Theology Press, 1995), pp. 777–97.

SIX

Bodily Being and Animal World:
Toward a Somatology of Cross-Species Community

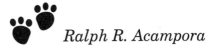 *Ralph R. Acampora*

1. Initial Issues

Thomas Nagel's question—"What is it like to be a bat?"—is the critical fulcrum of his now classic article against physicalist reductionism in philosophical psychology.[1] In the course of his argument— aimed at demonstrating that it is impossible for a reductively materialistic theory to provide a phenomenology of conscious subjectivity—Nagel claims that the phenomenon of "mind" (what some European philosophers would call "world") is widespread throughout the animal realm. About animate individuals, including many non-human ones, he says "there is something that it is like to be that organism—something it is like for the organism."[2] We may believe that the singular experiential viewpoint of another (especially nonhuman) individual is unyielding to description, and hence unintelligible. "The fact that we cannot expect ever to accommodate in our language a detailed description of bat phenomenology," counters Nagel, "should not lead us to dismiss as meaningless the claim that bats . . . have experiences fully comparable in richness of detail to our own."[3] Still, we must confess that doing cross-species phenomenology—studying what it is like to be a bat, for example—"may be permanently denied to us by the limits of our [human] nature."[4]

Nagel's agnostic warning on this point is not absolute—he allows two possible avenues of inquiry: (1) partial understanding might be had by "transcend[ing] inter-species barriers with the aid of the imagination";[5] (2) an "objective phenomenology not dependent on empathy or the imagination" may forge new concepts applicable across species boundaries.[6] Paul Taylor furnishes an illustration of the former route. He argues that if we shed the stereotypes imposed by human purposes and adopt the unique existential standpoint of another (nonhuman) organism, then

> our consciousness of the life of an individual organism is character-
> ized by both objectivity and wholeness of vision; we have reached
> the most complete realization, cognitively and imaginatively, of
> what it is like to be that particular individual. We have let the real-
> ity of another's life enter the world of our own consciousness. We
> know it as fully and intensely as it can be known.[7]

The question raised by this position is: just how fully can another organism's lifeworld be known thus? Because he is pessimistic about such an imaginative mode of cognition, Nagel lays open the second option. What this would amount to is left unclear. Therefore, let us creatively take up Nagel's phenomenological challenge and explore its potential.

Before we can proceed there are a couple of conceptual hurdles to clear. First, we must acknowledge the importance of realizing the exact nature of our task. We want to come to understand more about another animal's world, if there is such a "thing." In order to accomplish this, there is no need to conduct fanciful thought-experiments or to attempt supernatural exercises in identity-shifting. I do not actually have to become someone else in order to be familiar with that Other. Further, it is not necessary even to know precisely what it is like (hypothetically, in thought) to be that other subject-of-a-life in its own right.[8] For our present purposes, it will suffice "merely" to arrive at some sort of comprehension of what it means to be-with other individuals of different yet related species. Hence our mission is to articulate a transpecific form of the mode of being Martin Heidegger called *Mitsein*. What we seek is familiarity with cross-species conviviality.[9]

Second, we need to ask what dimension of reality is to be explored in our search for transpecific conviviality. Typically, phenomenologies of intersubjectivity are humanly intellectualized and thus limited to the level of interpersonal mentality. As a result, personhood becomes something only humans can have, and mind is characterized as Cartesian (that is, something separate or separable from the body). Beyond and against this anthropocentrism, I will instead pursue the matter on the level of bodiment. Thus, because it will not be constricted in advance to a homo-exclusive horizon, my somatic domain of description should be broad enough to allow—at least in principle—for some measure of cross-species traffic.

Do we have any reason to think that such traffic exists in actuality? One promising thread of organismic ontology suggests that existential residency might be a primordial world-relation ubiquitous throughout the biotic (or at least animal) realm.[10] Building on this clue, we will see if a phenomenology of bodily being can establish lifeworldly residence as a similitude sufficient to cross speciated differences.

Several students of animal and environmental relationship have supplied accounts of transpecific conviviality that effectively respond in the affirmative. With respect to cultural settings, Vicki Hearne's Wittgensteinian/Cavellean treatment of training work animals and Kenneth Shapiro's psychosomatic kinesiology of companion animality both furnish compelling testimony of bodily cohabitation between the species.[11] Likewise, from the perspective of wilderness experience, David Abram and Danne Polk convincingly bear deeply ecological witness to an earth-home replete with interspecifically commingled bodiment (in what Maurice Merleau-Ponty called "flesh-of-the-world").[12]

Yet the planet's phenomenal range of vital reality is not composed according to a dichotomy of lifeworlds: civilization versus wilderness (as mutually exclusive monoliths). Much biotic community occurs along a continuum of place between the extremities of technotopia and the utterly wild. Even to say this much, however, is to beg our previous question—(how) do we know that there is "biotic community" here? Perhaps we might have the intuition that there is, for instance,

> because lives open to one another in a continuum of existence,
> [O]thers live in our depths, participating in our sentient and

> motivating processes. . . . [Maybe] this communion of existence, in
> which barriers disintegrate, reveals . . . the overlapping processes
> of life as a whole. In-between is a realm of movements, with no
> fixed hierarchy.[13]

Still, to discharge more discursively this kind of intuitive assumption or suspicion, we will reconsider our original query with reference to the interzones between (or even the interstices within) comparatively civilized and wild regions of life: we ask, extending the vocabulary of ecology and phenomenology, do these ecotonal biotopes support a somatic society of species?

Answers to this question might be sought on two levels. On one, we would inquire into the global character of "world-flesh" as an existentially universal element for the totality of earthbound life: "In that middle region where the natural and the cultural are co-implicatory and com-present," one commentator claims, "we recognize the situation of sympathy where all of nature is akin: . . . naturo-cultural density is not human alone."[14] To avoid misplacing phenomenological concreteness, it is important not to overemphasize this totalizing conception. On another level, then, the perceptive somatologist returns to bodily things themselves and thus finds it proper to "reassert the experience of the earth as a heterogeneous mosaic of places and of subjects as place-limited participants in the planet."[15] Following this last commentator's salutary move to reconnect somatology with the lived reality of bioregion, it would appear that an important, perhaps primary, part of what it means to share a convivial context with another animal is to belong, at least temporarily, to some common, relatively localized environment which would serve as the milieu of any putatively transpecific "somatic society."

2. Natural History and Existential Climaticity

Now it should be stressed that our surroundings will not be described truly if we perpetuate the Heideggerian overemphasis on the temporalizing historicity of human being. Here I should like to make extended reference to Japanese philosopher Watsuji Tetsuro who, as one of the first and most astute readers of *Being and Time*, forcefully criticizes Heideggerian temporality and highlights the significance of "climaticity."

It was in the early summer of 1927 when I was reading Heidegger's *Sein und Zeit* in Berlin that I first came to reflect on the problem of climate. I found myself intrigued by the attempt to treat the structure of [human] existence in terms of time but I found it hard to see why, when time had thus been made to play a part in the structure of subjective existence, at the same juncture space also was not postulated as part of the basic structure of existence. Indeed it would be a mistake to allege that space is never taken into account in Heidegger's thinking . . . yet even so it tended to be almost obscured in the face of the strong glare to which time was exposed. I perceived that herein lay the limitations of Heidegger's work, for time not linked with space is not time in the true sense. . . .[16]

Climate, as Watsuji defines it, is the primordial dimension of our experience of nature which is "internal" to intentional being-in-a-world (or *Dasein*) and which is sensed most strongly when we stress the spatial character of such being.[17] It incorporates awareness of weather and landscape, but is not limited to meteorology or topology. According to Watsuji's ontological articulation, "the space-and-time structure of human existence is revealed as climate and history: the inseparability of time and space is the basis of the inseparability of history and climate."[18] Returning to our primary path of inquiry, if we can entertain a robustly biocentric sense of natural history, we can understand climaticity as that dimension of transhuman existence which opens up lived experience to the common convivial context shared by somatically animate organisms occupying the same eco-regional environs.

The reason why climate cannot properly be eliminated from an ontological account of humanity is because human beings are terrestrial animals embedded in evolutionary reality. Consciousness of evolution has existential consequences in that it leads us to the self-knowledge that we are earthbound organisms—and, as such, we conduct our lives in climatic conviviality with other animals. At this juncture somatic phenomena become particularly pronounced in their felt presence, for it is through the live body that we are most especially aware of climaticity. As Watsuji notes, "it will no doubt be evident that there are certain points of similarity between the problem of climate and that of 'body'. . . . The self-active nature of climate must be retrieved in the same sense that the self-active nature of the [live] body has to be retrieved."[19] As ontologists, we transcend neither the earthy nor the carnal phenomena of physical living. Quite to the contrary, "transcendence also 'stands outside' climatically. In other words, [we discover ourselves] in climate . . . [and] this becomes consciousness of the body."[20]

Without hesitation, we must admit certain speciated distinctions across the spectrum of existentially embodied environmentality. As one ethologist has put it:

> Every animal perceives the external environment only through what its senses can find out about it. It lives in a world of its own, which is more or less distinct from that of other animals and that of human beings. Such distinctions are partly based on differences in construction of the sense organs; but they are primarily evoked by different modes of life.[21]

We must not lose sight, however, of the basic bio-commonality which serves as the necessary context of similarity for intelligibly making whatever distinctions are warranted. Different species' varying sensory modalities are embodied in lifeworlds: they all subserve some form of living incarnation. Furthermore, as we will see, live bodiment can function as a conduit for interspecific conviviality.

One experiential and conceptual context for seeing this has already been mentioned—namely, Merleau-Ponty's flesh-of-the-world.[22] To deepen our comprehension of this reality we need to understand that it is a world of holistic carnality that immerses (surrounds and permeates) the individual's lived body. Thus, in the words of commentator David Abram, Merleau-Ponty "dissolves the traditional division between the human animal and all other organisms of the Earth."[23] The flesh-of-the-world is organismic consanguinity writ ecosystemically large, and, as Abram remarks,

> no thinker can really move from his/her bodily self-awareness to the intersubjectivity of human culture, and thence to the global transcendence that is "the flesh of the world," without coming upon myriad experiences of otherness, other subjectivities that are not human, and other intersubjectivities.[24]

World-flesh, then, constitutes a thoughtscape and lifeworld broad enough to incorporate conceptually and experientially transpecific intercarnality.[25] In its midst, disclosures of "organic history" and "a description of . . . [hu]man-animality intertwining" become possible.[26]

It is revealing to interpret the phenomenological lifescape of world-flesh through the thematic lens of residence, thus placing it on a hermeneutic plane. Consequently, the ·flesh-of-the-world becomes manifestly earth-as-home. The danger in such an interpretation is that the diversity of world-flesh might be oversimplified (that is, overdomesticated by the earth-home concept) and thus made into a romantic vision of naturally harmonious, domesticated bodies. Jane Bennett has argued persuasively against this sort of worldview; in its stead she proposes a multivalent mosaic or plurivocal sense of "fractious holism."[27] In terms of the present discussion, endorsing fractious holism would mean giving weight to the phenomenal fact that terrestrial carnality (world-flesh/earth-home) is not experienced as an undifferentiated or placid whole. Rather, it is fraught with all the existential tensions arising out of its spatio-temporal division into relatively individualized organisms and biomes. Human beings, then, can be envisioned materially as epidermal encapsulates of corporeality. The convivial challenge is to interpret the skin-boundary not as an impermeable barrier but as a surface of contact.[28] In meeting this challenge it becomes possible to transcend our strictly *körperlich* limitations and thus to define more broadly the *modus vivendi* of flesh-and-blood being-in-a-world as *"Leibesheim(welt)"* (that is, as the home-world or territory of the living body).[29]

Continuing in this vein of a residentially hermeneutic phenomenology of body, interpretations could be articulated indefinitely. I shall therefore focus the present discussion within a certain setting. In choosing a site to do ontology, thematizing embodiment of residence is no arbitrary affair. It flows rather from a fundamental recognition of the situational constitution of "worldhood"; for, as Bernd Jager reminds us, "the house, body, and city do not so much occupy space and time as generate them. It is only as inhabiting, embodied beings that we find access to a world."[30] Given this insight, it is appropriate to ecophilosophize in the context of the city—to do environmental phenomenology, more specifically, from the perspective of urban parkland.

3. Phenomenology of the Park

Why the park? Because, as Joseph Grange observes, "the human body in such a place is fleshed thought seeking the identity of the difference between city and nature"; thus "to wonder about place through fleshly thought is to seek our home."[31] In the midst of the urban setting, parkland clears an open space that enables a residential dialectic between nature and culture (instead of perpetuating their dubious dichotomy). Moreover, the urban park is a quintessentially interspecific site: it is the cityscape's prime setting for cross-species conviviality (including interactions with a wide variety of nonhuman animals—from the thoroughly domesticated to the relatively wild). As biocultural environments, parks present a promising and especially ecotonal locale for transpecific phenomenology.

Allow me to begin this illustration or excursion into the ontology of parkscape's *Leibesheim* by citing at length an introductory passage of phenomenology from Grange:

> A [man] sits in a park. He sees and feels the contrast between city and nature. In experiencing this contrast, he does not so much understand the differences as sense in a relaxed, dim way the fundamental unity of all reality. It is not a question of causal explanation or, for that matter, rational effort. His body recognizes the organic rhythms of nature and at the same time the powerful thrust towards order and symmetry which characterizes human building. These dimensions of human experience are different; the natural is not the urban, but the two connect because the body is able to inhere in both regions of value. What unifies these experiences is the active presence of the body. By being there in a fleshly way, the human body is one in the presence of a soaring skyscraper glimpsed through the leafy vista of summer foliage. This unification of experience is achieved through the somatic act of being in place. That is why city and nature are not opposed entities warring for our allegiance. The human body in its generosity can experience both contexts as real and laden with value.[32]

This piece of hermeneutic phenomenology draws to our attention at least two significant aspects of park experience. Ecotonally, it illuminates the way in which the park is a site of paradoxically urbanized wilderness—wherein the city and the wild interpenetrate, qualifying but not annihilating each other. Somatically, it suggests that what permits such interpenetration is the carnal character of bodily being-in-a-park. Building on these insights, and specifying their scope to deal with interspecific conviviality, we can now articulate an experience of the park, highlighting how it presents a situation of cross-species encounter mediated by the somatic mode of bodiment.

"By being there in a fleshly way, the human body is one in the presence of a soaring skyscraper glimpsed through the leafy vista of summer foliage." So writes Grange of park-experience's embodied, seasonal sense of the built and arboreal environment. Sensitivity to the cycle or dialectic of changing seasons tunes us into the phenomena of weather basic to climaticity (in Watsuji's sense of the word). There is a park in New York City's outer borough of Queens in and from which a scenario such as the one described above can be experienced: Kissena Park, in the summertime, affords a greenly tree-framed vision of the World Trade Center's twin towers on the horizon. Late in the season of heat and humidity, this sight—to further flesh out the scene—is accompanied by the sound of cicadas drumming their abdomens. The insectiphonic concert begins with maybe only one or two individuals rattling their bellies in the rising temperature of mid-morning. Through the sweaty hours of afternoon the day drips hot moisture that throbs acoustically with the pulsing crescendo and decrescendo of a cicada chorus grown now to collectively huge proportions. You do not merely notice or register this biopercussive phenomenon, as by some attenuated audition—you feel it fully and resonate with its intensity.

In such a context the "hermeneutic hearing" of David Michael Levin becomes phenomenologically pregnant. "If we listen well to ourselves," Levin suggests, "we can hear within our embodiment resonances and echoes that confirm the interconnectedness of all beings and already bring us into communication with all other mortals, gathering us together for the making of a more thoughtful history."[33] As we continue our park phenomenology, we must seek to maintain such a sense of somatic thoughtfulness.

In the scene above a life's story is given testimony through certain manifest signs of emergence and metamorphosis: at its base there are little, cylindrical holes in the ground around the tree trunk; on its bark there cling small, empty shells skeletally shaped in bug-form, cracked open along the back-line. Digging scientifically deeper, dropping the strict "bracketing" of pure phenomenology, we discover that the cicadan cycle of life is here in evidence: the tiny animals begin living below the parkland's surface, larvally burrowed into the earthy depths of some tree's root system; literally radical sapsuckers, they remain submerged for years; when the time is right (as long as seventeen years after birth), the bloated bugs belly up into the air-world above ground; there they slowly climb their arboreal hosts, wriggle out of their dirty skins, dry their winged bodies in summer heat, and finally fly off to crowd the branches of available street-trees and parks' copses; then cicadas of the city sing. If we are lucky enough, we will spot an individual splitting and shedding its old crusty flesh or another drumming its tummy under a leaf. And if we care to, we might look and listen long enough to learn of the insects' chthonic chronicle, which is sensorily present before our eyes and becomes (re)constituted within earshot's temporal range.

Now as the summer draws to a close, so too do the lives of the sonic insects. Not only its trees, but also the park's bushes and shrubs start to become empty choirs, "where late cicadas sang." Yet the passage of seasons does not strip a parkland of its corporally channeled encounters between the species. In Kissena Park, for instance, autumn is signaled in the sky by the honking flight pattern of Canadian geese. The geese alight upon the park's pond, becoming themselves avian observers of the observing human traffic that rings the water. When winter comes they will have gone, leaving the watery scene before it freezes over; then, when it has hardened, the skaters and squirrels will share ice-time. Eventually, the thickly fecund aroma of fall's decomposition will yield atmospherically to a crisp, wintry clarity of sight and smell. Warmer weather at last returns in the springtime, of course; and this warmth, though similar in objective temperature to the "coolth" of fall, is palpably different in terms of lived climaticity. Spring is alive with a felt sense of thaw and reinvigoration absent in autumn. In this season the park's faunal and floral environment alternates in tempo and tone between peppy action and pleasant calm; and it is also pregnant with the promise of another summer. Thus do this parkscape's phenomenal seasons turn.[34]

Such an account bears witness to how existentially interpenetrating are the phenomena of climate and (civilized) culture, (wild) nature and history. These phenomena form the context of interspecific conviviality. Against this backdrop experiences of transpecific bodiment come into greater relief. Examples include the sensately intertwined "haptic hearing" of cicadas by people in the park (and vice versa), as well as the reversibly observatory encounter between human beings and geese. On the level of what I dub municipal ontology, such interanimalic instances of "metropolitan *Mitsein*" phenomenally display the bodily and cross-species nature of flesh-and-blood being-in-a-world. Here, then, is an interspecies instance of "somatic society."

The last of the examples mentioned above may seem innocuously quotidian, lacking any special significance. What is at stake here? What is important about two different animals noticing each other? My point, stepping beyond rigid description, is that between the geese and the human beings there passes a perceptual process laden with pragmatic potency, an experience not reducible to the mere visual event: human-sees-bird/bird-sees-human. Perhaps a contrasting illustration will help clarify. Commenting on the zoo's milieu, John Berger observes:

> The visibility through the glass, the spaces between the bars, or the empty air above the moat, are not what they seem—if they were, then everything would be changed. Thus visibility, space, air, have been reduced to tokens. . . . All this is what makes [zoo animals] marginal. The space which they inhabit is artificial. Hence their tendency to bundle towards the edge of it. (Beyond its edges there may be real space.) In some cages the light is equally artificial. In all cases the environment is illusory.[35]

We might wonder here just what "real space" is or could be. Berger's hint is the suggestion that the circumstances would change if irreality did not mark or taint the observational media. The real space of encounter, as I would elaborate this clue, is live space—that "living room" which permits genuine con-frontation complete with all its motile possibilities of adversity, avoidance, and free association. Of course, the zoo annihilates or interrupts these possibilities (that is why it is a site of illusion, one which marginalizes its inhabitants). Yet all those potencies for activity—of fight or flight, of becoming foe or friend, of leaving off or moving in—remain in place in the wild and even at the park such as I have described it. This, then, is the existential import and philosophic upshot of watching animals watching you "in the field": here interspecific perception is charged with pragmatic concern or regard, at-tention becomes con-tention, and thus it is difficult to behold simply (neutrally, reductively) because survival vision and social sight must be literally respectful of another living being—taking care, through fear or love, to deal with the Other in a phenomenally physical dimension of vital exchange and intercourse.

4. Conclusion: Cross-Species Community

In this chapter I have posited existential residence as a transpecific "family resemblance" of being—a feature, that is, which crisscrosses various organisms' overlapping worlds. I have tried to establish the somatic or carnal nature of that residency, and thereby come to certain implicit insights: living bodiment, *qua* animation, is what makes residing possible; live flesh, *qua* vulnerability, is what makes sheltering necessary. Furthermore, by means of localized "park phenomenology" I have arrived at the suggestion that even city-dwelling human beings (can) have experiential access to a multi-species *Leibesheim* or "livebody-homesite." This suggestion responds positively to the central question of my discussion; namely, whether or not biocultural ecotones (such as parkland) serve as sites of somatic society. From the existential evidence articulated here, this question is to be answered affirmatively on two levels: (1) human beings can and do experience states of bodily being having a somatically transpecific horizon (including, for example, cicadan pulsions within our sensory and activity world); (2) some nonhumans seem also to have (capability for) such experience, so that interspecific overlay of somatic horizon is possible (and apparently actualized, for instance, when geese and humans become aware of each other's presence and behavior). These levels of experience are dimensions of somatic society both perceptually and pragmatically conceived. They usually register to differing degrees of intensity: existentially, the second tends to impart a greater sense of sociality than the first. Both, however, have axiological and moral ramifications. Indeed the line of study pursued here ends by echoing, on an explicitly interspecies level, the exhortation of somatologist Elizabeth Behnke that we "cultivate a body of compassion, an ethics of empathy, a culture of peace, in which a genuine 'coexistence in the flesh' would be possible."[36]

Notes

1. Thomas Nagel, "What Is It Like to Be a Bat?," *Philosophical Review* 83 (Oct. 1974), pp. 435–50.

2. Ibid., p. 436.

3. Ibid., p. 440.

4. Ibid.

5. Ibid., p. 442n.

6. Ibid., p. 449.

7. Paul Taylor, *Respect for Nature* (Princeton: Princeton University Press, 1986), pp. 127–128. Compare Jakob Johann von Uexküll's 1934 essay, "A Stroll Through the Worlds of Animals and Men," *Instinctive Behavior*, transl. and ed. Claire H. Schiller (New York: International Universities Press, 1957), and Kenneth J. Shapiro's "Understanding Dogs Through Kinesthetic Empathy, Social Construction, and History," *Anthrozoos* 3:3 (1990), pp. 184–195.

8. Here I borrow the term "subject-of-a-life" from Tom Regan. See *The Case for Animal Rights* (Berkeley: University of California Press, 1983).

9. This last term is taken from—but not used as in—Ivan Illich's *Tools for Conviviality* (New York: Harper and Row, 1973).

10. Compare my "Human and Nonhuman Lifeworlds," *Environmental and Architectural Phenomenology* 3:2 (spring 1992) and Allen Hance's "Dasein's Animality," paper presented at Central Division Meeting of the American Philosophical Association (Chicago: April 1996).

11. See, respectively, Vicki Hearne's *Adam's Task* (New York: Random House, 1987) and Kenneth Shapiro's "Understanding Dogs through Kinesthetic Empathy."

12. See, respectively, David Abrams, "Merleau-Ponty and the Voice of the Earth," *Environmental Ethics* 10 (1988), pp. 101–120; and Danne Polk's "Un-Cartesian Nature," *Skepteon* 1 (fall 1993), pp. 27–56. Compare Abrams, *The Spell of the Sensuous* (New York: Pantheon, 1996), esp. ch. 3.

13. F. G. Asenjo, *In-Between* (Washington, D.C.: University Press of America, 1988), p. 52.

14. Edward Casey, *Getting Back into Place* (Bloomington: Indiana University Press, 1993), pp. 255–256.

15. Neil Evernden, *The Natural Alien* (Toronto: University of Toronto Press, 2nd ed., 1993), p. 152.

16. Watsuji Tetsuro, *Climate and Culture*, transl. Geoffrey Bownas (Japan: Hokuseido Press, 1961), p. v.

17. Compare John Pickles, *Phenomenology, Science, and Geography: Spatiality and the Human Sciences* (Cambridge: Cambridge University Press, 1985), esp. ch. 9.

18. Watsuji, *Climate and Culture*, p. 9.

19. Ibid., pp. 11–12.

20. Ibid., p. 12.

21. Sven Dijkgraaf, "An Excursion through the Sensory World of Animals," in *Man and Animal*, transl. Mechthild Nawiasky (London: MacGibbon & Kee, 1972), p. 58.

22. See Merleau-Ponty's *The Visible and the Invisible*, transl. Alphonso Lingis (Evanston: Northwestern University Press, 1969).

23. Abram, "Voice of the Earth," p. 139, n. 12.

24. Ibid., pp. 114–115. Cf. Novalis, *The Novices of Sais* (New York: Curt Valentin, 1949), p. 77.

25. Again, see Abram, "Voice of the Earth," p. 113.

26. See Merleau-Ponty, *The Visible and the Invisible*, pp. 167, 274. Compare Abram, "Voice of Earth," p. 119.

27. Jane Bennet, *Unthinking Faith and Enlightenment* (New York: New York University Press, 1987).

28. See Angelika Fischer's M.A. thesis, "Bodies, Selves and Boundaries" (Nedlands: University of Western Australia, 1984).

29. See Douwe Tiemersma, *Body Schema and Body Image* (Amsterdam/ Lisse: Swets and Zeitlinger, 1989). Compare also Evernden, *The Natural Alien*, p. 151.

30. Bernd Jager, "Body, House, and City," *Dwelling, Place, and Environment*, eds. David Seamon and Robert Mugerauer (New York: Columbia University Press, 1989), p. 215. Compare Immanuel Kant, excerpts in Stuart Spicker, *The Philosophy of the Body* (Chicago: Quadrangle Books, 1970), esp. "What is Orientation in Thinking?"

31. Joseph Grange, "Place, Body, and Situation," *Dwelling, Place and Environment*, pp. 81–82.

32. Ibid., p. 82.

33. David Michael Levin, *The Listening Self* (New York: Routledge, 1989), p. 272. Compare Michel Haar, *The Song of the Earth*, transl. Reginald Lilly (Bloomington: Indiana University Press, 1993), esp. preface.

34. Compare Alan Devoe, *Lives Around Us: A Book of Creaturely Biographies* (New York: Creative Age, 1942), chapter on cicadas.

35. John Berger, "Why Look at Animals?," *About Looking* (New York: Pantheon, 1980), pp. 22–23.

36. Elizabeth A. Behnke, "On Edmund Husserl," *Lifwynn Correspondence* 4:2 (spring 1996), p. 29; originally appeared in "Edmund Husserl's Contribution to Phenomenology of the Body in *Ideas II*," *Study Project in Phenomenology of the Body* 2:2 (fall 1989). Compare my "The Problematic Situation of Post-Humanism and the Task of Recreating a Symphysical Ethos," *Between the Species: A Journal of Ethics* 11:1/2 (winter/spring 1995).

SEVEN

They Say Animals Can Smell Fear

 *H. Peter Steeves*

1. Introduction: In Preparation

"[Hunting] is a relationship that certain animals impose on man, to the point where not trying to hunt them demands the intervention of our deliberate will. . . . Before any particular hunter pursues them they feel themselves to be possible prey, and they model their whole existence in terms of this condition. Thus they automatically convert any normal man who comes upon them into a hunter. The only adequate response to a being that lives obsessed with avoiding capture is to try to catch it."

—José Ortega y Gasset

One case of gin would not be sufficient. Neither would ten thousand bullets. Gordon Cumming doubled the gin order and added a request for gunpowder and shell casings so as to make more ammunition as needed. The safari could drag on for months, possibly a year, and there was no sense embarking ill-prepared into the African interior. Traveling with three hundred pounds of rice, the same amount of sugar, plus several hundred more pounds of eating and cooking supplies would slow the group, but it could not be avoided. The continent promised plenty of trophies but little hope for food. What did the natives eat? "300 lbs colored beads," wrote Cumming, reminded of the likely need to pacify human natives. More bullets and more beads. And if all goes well, more trophies, more money, more safaris.

In 1838, Gordon Cumming had left Scotland to join the East India Company's Madras Cavalry. Deer hunting in the homeland was no longer the thrill it had been, and imperial service had offered the chance to encounter elephants that could take a bullet like a mosquito bite and tigers that may very well be hunting you right back. But the climate had been unbearable, and thus he had quickly resigned. The Canadian regiment provided a cooler camp, but there were so few truly dangerous animals in North America that Cumming again had requested permission to leave, this time turning to the Cape Mounted Rifles. There were wonderfully dangerous animals to kill in Africa, but military duty proved so demanding that there had been little personal time to hunt. Thus came a final resignation of commission. Afterwards, he was on his own, a gentleman hunter, and he would need to bring in sufficient ivory to support himself and his habit. The decision to bring too much or not enough rice, for instance, could doom the safari. And certainly the question of the appropriate amount of gin and bullets was even more pressing. It was a lot like the hunt itself—planning, thinking, instinctually choosing. But the managerial duties of the safari held no thrill of the chase, of the encounter.

Cumming's decisions proved personally profitable. Throughout the 1840s he terrorized interior Africa, making a name and a fortune for himself as a courageous hunter and an ivory dealer. In 1849, he retired from the ritual. Not because he was "in the slightest degree satiated," he announced, but because he was tired. Returning to England he would become a local hero, publishing a book about his adventures, overseeing a museum stuffed with the bodies of his conquests, and lecturing each evening at eight o'clock (Saturday matinee at three) under the title: "The Lion-Slayer at Home."[1]

Cumming's stories differ little from the familiar hunting narratives of the nineteenth century. They ooze with imperialistic, sexist, Freudian imagery. And it is perhaps since they are so typical that they deserve special attention. Could we speak in necrophilous tones of Cumming's friend, who remembers Gordon killing a "beautiful cow" gemsbok and then stroking the corpse, "milk[ing] her into [his] mouth, . . . [thus] obtain[ing] a drink of the sweetest beverage . . . ever tasted"?[2] Could we question Cumming's hesitance to shoot wild dogs—generally considered the most dangerous and ferocious predators of the plains—because the "jolly hounds" reminded him too much of his own "noble" canines?[3] Could we wonder at the contradictions in a man who respects and murders, who once "came upon an extremely old and noble black rhinoceros lying fast asleep . . . [so he quickly] fired from the saddle"?[4] Indeed. But I do not wish to dwell on the hunter and his neuroses. Instead, I want to consider a multitude of relationships between, on a larger scale, human beings and animals as they involve fear. Cumming's stories speak of the terror of the confrontation; the "intense and maddening excitement of the chase"; the "extraordinary perils" of the hunt; the moment of fear and exhilaration of coming upon five bull elephants, knowing that they can kill you, feeling the confidence that presses you forward, assuring you that you "can ride up and vanquish whichever one you fancy," the whole anxious moment evolving into something "so overpoweringly exciting that it almost takes a man's breath away."[5] Here there is a sexual fear, a fear of eating and being eaten, a fear and awareness of being-with. There is an interplay between animals—human and other—rich with moral meaning. There is much that needs to be said.

2. Encountering the Other in Fear

"Fear is not, then, reduced to a mere and occasional moment of weakness. Fear is rather an important revelation of the truth that to be is, for *Dasein*, an issue. . . . Fear is not learned; it is discovered. The point is this: How can we be threatened by anything unless we exist in such a way that we are intimately connected with the world . . . ?"

—Michael Gelven

It is surprising to note that the typical hunting narrative does not involve boasts of fearlessness. Autobiographical accounts such as Cumming's tend to admit the "terror of the confrontation" and often attribute the kill to good skill in equal measure with good fortune. The tactic, however, is not born of humility. The man who faces a deadly opponent without fear is a fool; the man who presses forward through his fear is a hero. Courage cannot exist without fear, and thus the hunter who admits his fear accentuates his accomplishment.

When we are afraid of animals there are outward manifestations of our supposed interior life. The body reacts. Charles Darwin writes:

> The frightened man first stands like a statue, motionless and breathless . . . the heart beats quickly and violently . . . the skin instantly becomes pale . . . the hairs also on the skin stand erect . . . the mouth becomes dry. . . .[6]

Fear lives in the body—in "tendons and cartilage," writes Alphonso Lingis.[7] How amazing, in fact, it is to realize that tendons and cartilage and bodies in general share ways of being in fear: the frightened dolphin's teeth chatter; the gorilla, too, goes weak in the knees. Yet it would be wrong to think that emotions are bodily changes—that they can be reduced to their manifestations. William James comes close to this, but ultimately avoids it. "Common sense," he argues, "says we lose our fortune, are sorry and weep; we meet a bear, are frightened and run . . . but the more rational statement is that we feel sorry because we cry, . . . [that] we feel frightened because we are running away."[8] A lot rests on this "because." For James, fear is a *recognition* of bodily changes—recognition *causes* the emotion, which is a lot like saying that the emotion *is* the recognition since there is no difference between "fearing the bear" and "recognizing that I am running away from the bear."

The intentional element of this recognition is often overlooked by James' critics. Such recognition requires a contextual horizon, and thus cannot be explained fully by biophysical states. Psychologists critical of James' notion of emotion typically appealed to tests run on subjects for whom "it was discovered that the direct and artificial stimulation (e.g., by drugs) of the organs and systems responsible for mediating the bodily changes involved did not produce the expected emotional reactions."[9] Massive shots of adrenaline, for example, made the subjects edgy but not afraid; and the majority of test subjects could distinguish true emotional states from the drug-induced states.

The problem here, however, is the bad philosophical model of the tests. It is akin to adopting a sense-data model of perception in order to study phenomenological theories. In his best-selling, dystopic, pied-piped ad jingle, *The Road Ahead*, Bill Gates imagines, among other things, a virtual reality bodysuit "lined with tiny sensors and force feedback devices that could be in contact with the whole surface of your skin; . . . [a] full bodysuit . . . lined with little touch sensor points—each of which could poke one specific tiny spot . . . [such that] if they were controlled finely enough, any touch sensation could be duplicated."[10] This, of course, will never happen. "Virtual movies" may someday exist as movies that are three dimensional and involve more than sight and sound; but they will never stand in for worldly experience in the same way that seeing photos of Bill Gates' "house of the future" cannot stand in for actually dropping by. Anyone who has brushed a dog and a sweater; anyone who has felt what must be the wind on her leg only to discover an ant scout making his way up; anyone who has reached out to stroke a cat and later felt that cat rub against his leg, squeeze between an arm and a side, rise to meet his unexpecting hand, filling it all at once with fur and flesh in a reciprocating arching stroke; anyone who has lived in the world knows that all tactile experience cannot be reduced to bits of sense data, and thus cannot be reproduced by zapping the appropriate nerve endings. The same thing goes wrong when a psychologist injects adrenaline and stimulates organs. Fear does not result, but this says nothing about James' theory. His is not a "sense-data" theory of emotion. Instead, it is a suggestion that fear necessarily manifests itself in the body, and our recognition of this (within the manifold horizons of the context of living) we call "fear."

Yet to say that fear resides in the body is not to say everything that can be said about fear. Fear is a mode of state-of-mind. The dog experienced through fear is not frightening; our relationship, our proximity, our way of being-with the dog is *as frightened*. Fear is spatial. Is it not proof enough we share an intersubjective world with animals that we can fear them? Where the dog sits snarling—Here for him, There for me—can quickly become Here for us both. Martin Heidegger knows: *"That in the face of which* we fear . . . is not yet within striking distance, but it is coming close."[11] Heidegger knows, too, that fear is temporal. And although what draws close is feared as something that will be here in the future, fear is essentially backwards looking for it is what I have been that I fear I may not be. Not-near-the-snarling-dog is what I have been in the past, and fearing the dog is a way of clinging to this past way of being. To fear is to be threatened as having-been, to desire what *was* over what *is* and what *can/will* be. As a result, we turn our attention away from Being and focus, instead, on what has been. In this shifting of attention we forget ourselves, we lose ourselves, we are bewildered. Aristotle defines fear as bewilderment. And Heidegger adds:

> The bewilderment is based upon a forgetting. When one forgets and backs away in the face of a factical potentiality-for-Being which is resolute, one clings to those possibilities of self-preservation and evasion which one has already discovered circumspectively beforehand. When concern is afraid, it leaps from next to next, because it forgets itself and therefore does not *take hold of* any *definite* possibility. Every "possible" possibility offers itself, and this means that the impossible ones do so too. The man who fears, does not stop with any of these; his "environment" does not disappear, but it is encountered without his knowing his way about in *it* any longer.[12]

When Douglas Adams hitchhiked a ride to Zaïre with the BBC in order to report on the state of endangered animals, he encountered a mountain gorilla and was struck with a "kind of humming mental paralysis."[13] Iconoclastic zoo owner John Aspinall once "felt an almost trance-like numbness steal upon" him when playtime with a tiger turned into a full-fledged assault.[14] And David Livingstone lived to write about being taken up in the mouth of a lion and shaken "as a terrier-dog does a rat." He reports:

> The shock produced a stupor similar to that which seems to be felt by a mouse after the first shake of the cat. It caused a sort of dreaminess, in which there was no sense of pain or feeling of terror, though I was quite conscious of all that was happening. It was like what patients, partially under the influence of chloroform, describe, who see all the operation, but feel not the knife.[15]

Adams, Aspinall, and Livingstone were bewildered. Their bodies registered it and made it manifest. Their environments did not disappear, but were encountered without their knowing their way about in them. They retreated in the face of the spatial-temporal nearness of the Other. They were afraid.

Fear is one of the few emotions which scientists are unafraid to attribute to animals without concern for anthropomorphizing. A great deal of empirical evidence exists attesting to the fact that animals fear. Their bodies manifest the emotion in familiar ways. This is not speciest; this is not to say that the only real fear is human-like fear. It is, rather, to admit the depth of our relation to the living world: a tendon is a tendon is a tendon, each holding fear the same. Doubtless, animal bodies without such structures manifest fear in different ways. But it is not for such reasons that scientists tend to accept animal fear. In the grand evolutionary scheme, fear is seen to serve a purpose; it is a friend to self-preservation, a tool to keep the fittest surviving. The buck that fears the hunter lives longer and produces more offspring. And it is the same for the mouse that fears the cat, the cat that fears the dog, and so on. Theoretically, fear makes sense.

This is assuming, though, that fear properly resides in the weak. It would not be beneficial for a lion to fear a gazelle. But what of the proverbial elephant's fear of the mouse? What purpose could this serve? Why do some bears fear humans while others act indifferently or attack fearlessly? Because the picture is much more complicated than a theory of evolutionary hard-wiring suggests. Fear, in fact, can prove life threatening rather than life sustaining. Caught in the humming mental paralysis which manifests itself in weak knees, the animal can freeze, thus securing her doom, or run wildly (becoming wilder, be-wild-ered) into the path of certain danger. We will consider below the case of a young boy whose fear caused him to panic and run into oncoming traffic in order to avoid a single bee. And animals in the grip of fear certainly can freeze rather than fight back. Believing such paralysis to be a state "probably produced in all animals killed by the carnivora . . . [and thus] a merciful provision by our benevolent Creator for lessening the pain of death," as Dr. Livingstone presumes, does not solve the problem.[16] A peaceful death is an evolutionary disadvantage, if anything. Those who go gentle into the good night of death have need neither to rage nor to fear.

As essentially backwards looking, fear, though, is less about death than it is about life. And the ways in which it makes its appearance in our life with animals affects our Being. Not only the hunter encounters the animal with fear.

There are some who argue that to be with animals in a respectful and knowledgeable way may require fear. Lynn Rogers, a wildlife biologist specializing in black bears, learned when it was appropriate to lunge at angry bears and when it was appropriate to run away: "Once I started looking at bears in terms of their fear, and interpreted all the things that used to scare me and interpreted those in terms of the bear's fear, it was easy to gain their trust and begin walking with them very closely, sleeping with them—doing all the things that you have to do to see how an animal really lives in its world."[17] Aspinall, too, believes that fear is a necessary element of any loving relationship with nondomesticated animals—especially if that relationship is to be a personal, physically close one:

> Mood watching and mood interpretation are the secrets of survival if one is to retain any tactile relationship with a four-hundred-pound adult gorilla. . . . [F]ear is the magical ingredient. . . . Fear is probably born of the race memory from that great reach of time when the mammals were our competitors. Nascent in this fear is respect, and from a fusion of them both is distilled a pure love and understanding. A love . . . [in] which you risk everything and expect nothing back except the stake.[18]

Lingis reminds us that Immanuel Kant saw a strong relationship between respect and fear—respect for and fear of the moral law, to be sure, and not gorillas, but then Kant never left Königsberg much. What is surprising here is the sense in which fear is characterized as good—morally, intellectually, physically. As a disintegrating of Being and a backwards-looking longing for what was, fear is inauthentic for Heidegger. To encounter the animal in fear is to forget ourselves and evade *Dasein*. But it is possible that bewilderment can be beneficial—for wildlife biologists, for international playboy zoo keepers, for recluse philosophers, and for normal human beings. Possible, indeed, but not probable. For our fears turn typically abusive.

How often we assume fear to be the standard relation between human beings and other animals. Armed with such a model, we strike terror in the world. We see the deer as frightened, and we live up to the expectation—we constitute the buck as fearful so that we can hunt it. We test the laboratory rat by shocking it when it fails to perform—what does the rat fear? the shock? the past? the researcher? the being-with the researcher? We manipulate animals with our models of their fear. We shoo away the fly, run through the flock of foraging pigeons, scream (perhaps bark) at the neighbor's dog. Roger Fouts, the trainer of a chimpanzee named Washoe who learned to communicate with sign language, grew to know Washoe so well that he created a fictional monster to keep her in line. Looking out into the night through a window in Washoe's trailer, Fouts once told Washoe that he feared he had spied the "bogey dog." He signed to her that he saw "a big black dog with long teeth that ate baby chimpanzees."[19] From that day on whenever Washoe was enjoying herself outside and refused to go in, Fouts or his research assistants would sign that they saw the bogey dog, thus causing Washoe to scramble inside in fear. How many bogey dogs have we created? How many have we become?

Zoos, institutions which embody traditions which in turn embody values and a view of the Good, stand among us as testaments to our fear. They exist to offer encounters with animal Others without fear, but they cannot succeed. They announce our fear of being-with animals, a fear of our own captivity, the fear of losing a comfortable past notion of ourselves as at large and in charge. They sublimate and repress our fears even as they bear witness to them, brick by brick, bar by bar.

If fear is related to respect, so too is it related to disrespect. The architecture of the zoo makes the point: we are in control; we look down on you. The orderly structure of the paths seeks to impose the force of our presence by means of contrast with the "wild" animals we encounter. The London Zoological Society, for instance, once practiced little subtlety, allowing the "physical relation of the menagerie to the rest of Regents' Park [to] symbolically [reiterate] the association between its zoological riches and human privilege. . . . Immediately inside the segregated precincts, a terrace offered early patrons a chance to look down on those outside . . . before beginning their promenade past the animals."[20] The peasants in their slums and the animals in their cages at once conjure up pride, guilt, and fear. Historian James Turner argues that we need to view our relationships with animals through the lens of capitalism, especially early capitalism which caused a spiritual crisis for those unaccustomed to prospering while in the midst of great suffering. Finding it "difficult to reconcile the exploitation of the working class with their consciences," the upper-class turned to performing "good deeds" now and then, and "being kind to animals gave most satisfaction, . . . [since among] animals there were no socialists, who would sooner or later bite the hand that stroked them."[21] Of course, fear of the bite perpetuates slums and zoos. Those who live in neither need both—to remind them of their place; to motivate them through a fear of the Other; to comfort them and refocus the gnawing fear that the whole system, the whole organizational worldview, may be to blame. Cleaning up the inner-city and starting another soup kitchen are acts of kindness—pseudo acts of redemption—that do not question the larger picture, the larger fear, but instead work within the system, ultimately supporting it. So, too, do zoos go about their business. The local paper asks us to become "zoo partners" by means of a charitable donation; the national news praises our intelligence and compassion as another cute endangered animal is born in captivity (a triumph! we are saving the world!); the scholarly literature speaks of the good life we are providing the animals—free meals, no predators. By the sounds of it, we should capture all of the animals for our zoos—out of compassion—if we could only afford it; we should lower the minimum wage so that we can then bring a soup kitchen to every neighborhood. The happy prisons of our zoos and our cities we could then visit and attend, our fears repressed, our hearts filled with compassion. It is in such a spirit that Gerald Durrell implores us to remember that releasing animals from zoos is not necessarily best for the animal. "It would be the same as taking a millionaire of long standing out of the Ritz and making him sleep on a park bench covered with newspapers and forage for his food in dust-bins."[22]

There are zoos with an open history of terror. Read Betsy Swart's account of her visit to Noell's Ark—a simian "Midnight Express" populated by broken, desolate, often insane chimpanzees.[23] And there are zoos with a "noble" history, the patrons of which bristle at the mention of abolishing the institution. No fear here, cry the supporters. In fact, with its basis in sound science, the zoo is declared rational—its detractors are the emotional ones. David Hancocks writes:

> There are sentimental extremists who regard even the best zoological gardens as the worst kind of prison and plead for the liberty of the animal. Their emotions ignore the fact that zoo animals can be healthier and better fed than in the wild; that zoo animals live a longer average life; that their illnesses are treated scientifically and that old animals, which could not compete in the wild, are cared for and protected.[24]

But the imprisonment issue will not go away—regardless of the free food and health care. Substitute "working class humans" for "zoo animals" in Hancocks' argument and the prejudice becomes apparent. Though we may seek to imprison both, we have separate institutions to do the job. And we would be right to point out: who but a capitalist would think a free meal is important for an animal? The free lunch ideal stands behind all that Hancocks is saying: healthier food, longer life, high-tech medicine—all for free! Thinking that a prepared bucket of Tiger Chow is good because the animal need not work, speaks only to our cultural devaluation of work. Thinking that zoo food is healthier is testament to a culture that fears dirt, death, and all that is unprocessed. Tigers, no doubt, see hunting as enjoyable and gazelle flesh as delicious. But part of the meaning of their incarceration is that they are kept from these things. According to Stephen St. C. Bostock though, "[t]hey don't necessarily 'experience' any deprivation; they just fail to have experiences which would give them satisfaction."[25] This dubious bit of phenomenology fails to allow nonhumans the same intentional structures which we know are necessary for our own consciousness. Certainly, tigers—animals—experience presence and absence. Certainly, a tiger presences the hunt-as-absent—to assume otherwise is to adopt a false model of the Being of objects and creatures. The play of presence and absence must be at work. Aspinall, speaking in nonphenomenological terms about tigers, suggests that such structures are necessary for normal life: "[h]unger followed by satiation, cold by warmth, solitude by company, these provide a backdrop that alone can make life bearable for a mammal."[26] To say that a tiger can experience the absence of the hunt is to say that she can miss it.

Aspinall's zoo is, perhaps, an exception to the rule of the menagerie of disrespect. Perhaps. His approach is different for a variety of reasons. He acknowledges fear. He allows groups of animals to form on their own—tiger families develop, gorillas set up bands. Fruits and nuts are scattered in the deep straw allowing gorillas to forage for hours for their food—something close to what they would do in the wild. Aspinall dreams of friendship with animals, of becoming an "honorary member of another species," and of learning to be-with animals. He has spent hundreds of hours acknowledging his fear and respect for animals by being in their midst: wrestling and grooming gorillas, chasing and being chased by tigers. He has known honest tigers and treacherous ones, gorillas that have been altruistic and gorillas that have been self-absorbed. And he has called for the end of all zoos, including his own, with the eventual release of each animal into a world that does not threaten their environment and their lives each day. For these reasons, Aspinall refers

to the animals as his guests—as if they were just stopping by for a
bit before moving on—and laments the fate of the animal who is "an
'inmate,' an object of curiosity or, to use the word so sadly popular
with many zoos, an 'exhibit.' [For the animal knows,] [j]ust as a
human knows whether he is a prisoner or a guest."[27]

The distinction between a prisoner and a guest is not founded
solely on the freedom to leave, although this has been promoted as
one test for determining what zoo inhabitants really are. Bostock
suggests that "if you opened the door" and the animal chose to stay,
then you have a good zoo.[28] Surely this test would find most zoos
empty, but even if this were not the case nothing would be proven.
Consider Durrell's approach:

> Our first attempt to return the Pink pigeon to the wild in Mauritius
> was an example of how easily things can go wrong. . . . The pigeons
> behaved beautifully and flew out and sat on top of the aviaries. We
> then expected them to take advantage of their freedom and fly off
> into the trees. They sat stolidly on top of the aviaries without blink-
> ing an eye, looking like mentally retarded examples of an amateur
> taxidermist's work. How I wish all the idiotic people who prate
> about the cruelty of captivity and the joys of freedom could have
> seen those birds.[29]

Durrell is in charge of the Jersey Wildlife Preservation Trust
at the Jersey Zoological Park in the Channel Islands. He is a self-
proclaimed lover of animals—has been since the age of six when he
began a miniature zoo in a matchbox. But his love masks a fear. It is
a fear of being-with intelligent and free Others—a fear, perhaps, of
human freedom as well. Why the repetition of the Others' mental
inadequacies? The animals are retarded; the other humans are idi-
otic. Why the insistence on the failure of choice to inspire freedom?
Is it not obvious that the prison *creates* the zoo animal? Molding,
constructing their bodies into docile objects, we cannot help but envi-
sion them in taxidermists' metaphors.

The body is at stake. Here is the path where lion feet will pace;
here is the slope where penguin bottoms will slide. Here, then, are
feet and bottoms newly created—a body, ordered and structured, for
consumption. The colorful ones sell best—mocking what it is to be a
drab human being—unless the albino body can be coaxed into birth.

Mr. Jiggs wears a tuxedo and drinks liquor. He roller-skates
around the audience in New Jersey, entertaining the crowd. He looks

like an old vaudeville veteran with his gray hair, wrinkled face, and slipping suspenders—except for the fact that he is a chimpanzee. He is happy, says his trainer, Ron Winters. Actually, *she* is happy, since Mr. Jiggs is really a female—her sexuality reconstructed through clothes and mannerisms. "She's happy and good because she's never in a cage," says Winters, though her front teeth have been permanently pulled and her molars are locked shut before each show. She is happy. And good. She never misbehaves. Although she continues to wear a radio-controlled electric shock device on her back, Winters reports: "I never have to use it anymore." The absence of shock is like an open cage door. Does Jiggs perform because she chooses to perform? After twenty-seven years, does she choose to stay in the business?[30]

In the end, I do not wish to focus on animal choice. Choice is a modern, human, Liberal notion which cannot adequately address the question of freedom. It is not (just) choice that separates the guest from the prisoner. It is not (just) choice which we must allow animals. Neither do I wish to argue that what is natural is good—such commitments lead Aspinall to bad politics,[31] and philosophers in general to dubious distinctions. But we must admit that something has gone wrong in our living-with Mr. Jiggs, the Pink pigeons, and the Purina Chow eating tiger. It is exhibited in our exhibiting them. It is at the heart of Hancocks' claim that captivity is not wrong, since no animal is truly free—all "are prisoners in space and time, confined not only by their geographical distribution but also by their relationship with other animals."[32] As invitingly and depressingly existential as this may sound, it speaks only to our fear. Time may hold us all—green and dying—but it makes the living possible. And our relationships found our being, they do not diminish and threaten it.[33] Only the misguided Liberal Self sees hell as other creatures, sees relations as chains. Being is being-with. Consequently, we may not appeal to the "prison of life" as a legitimation for our imprisonment of Others. We must tell the full story—the story of the fears of our inadequacies and the fear of freedom—that founds our institutions.

Attempting to do away with our fears, though, does not guarantee redemption. We can miss the point. In the case of the seven-year-old boy who was so afraid of bees that he would run, bewildered, into traffic upon encountering one, the treatment for the fear was a form of behavior therapy called desensitization. Stanley Rachman explains:

> At first the boy was shown small photographs of bees and then he
> was assisted through the following stages: large photographs, dead
> bees in the bottle at the far end of the room, dead bee in bottle
> brought gradually closer, dead bee out of the bottle, dead bee on
> coat, gradually increasing manipulation of the dead bee, introduc-
> tion of several dead bees, playing imaginative games with the dead
> bees. The boy made gradual and systematic progress and after
> eight sessions he and his mother both reported a considerable
> improvement. His mother stated that he was "very much improved
> . . . he no longer had the physical reaction. He used to go white,
> sweaty, cold and trembling, and his legs were like jelly. He can now
> play alone in the garden quite comfortably."[34]

What does it mean that such therapy works? Why, we might
wonder, does the boy lose his fear of living bees through successive
treatment with dead bees? Because it is *being in the world with bees*
that has become problematic—a world with bees rich in agency and
body.

Often it is the case that behavior therapy is thought to be a
process of rational growth: the patient has irrational beliefs about
the world and the therapist must replace those beliefs with rational
ones. Perhaps it is thought to be bad induction ("one bee stung me,
therefore all bees will sting me"). With a larger inductive sample—
more exposure to nonstinging bees—the bad logic will be evident
and the patient will alter his behavior accordingly. But again, why
does exposure to *dead* bees do the trick here? The boy is being shown
how dead bees cannot harm him, but he never was afraid of dead
bees. The problem here is that the therapy is not correcting an irra-
tionally held false belief. Quite the opposite takes place, in fact—a
phenomenology is being shaped, a falsehood is being presented for
the truth, a fear is being quenched with a lie that masks a larger fear.
Through therapy, the boy is learning to presence bees as objects, bee
bodies as things to be manipulated. His horizon of possible experience is being molded and he is beginning to suppress partially the
publicity of the world. His sense of self changes as well. He used to
constitute himself as being at the mercy of the agency of bees; but
rather than discover that the relationship is multidimensional, he
begins to remove bees from the world. He no longer will see himself
in relation to them. He will become a manipulator—not of Others,
but of things. He will manipulate bees out of his experience of the
world. The fear subsides, but the phenomenological lie which does

the job is a sign of an even greater fear. To live a "normal" life, the boy is molded into what we recognize as human: he will be alone, isolated, apart; he will be a destroyer of life, or, if his sentiments persuade him, a protector of life (he will be a courageous hunter or a compassionate steward), but he will be separate. The therapy is a success, cries his mother, he can now play alone in the garden quite comfortably. He can *be alone*.

Children have fears. It is part of life to sort them out, to see relationships from different angles and discover that fear is one way of being-with, one profile of a shared world, that cannot stand in or substitute for the whole. If a child were to fear clowns instead of bees, no doubt it would never cross the therapist's mind to treat the fear by exposing the child to clown corpses ("There is a dead clown at the far end of the room; Here is a dead clown touching your coat"). Such images themselves are frightening. And this is an important point: dead humans conjure fear; dead animals supposedly belay it. This is why we learn to whistle while passing through graveyards and to boast about our prowess with a fly swatter.

So fear can found our general encounter—in a variety of ways—with the deer in the hunt, the tiger in his cage, the chimpanzee in her tuxedo. Still, our analysis has not said all that needs to be said about specific types of encounters, particular ways of being-with. We have approached Pink pigeons and frightened boys, but let us say more about the birds and the bees.

3. Sex, Self, and Animal Others

"If this ark's a-rockin', don't come a-knockin'"

—Noah's bumper sticker

One hundred bullets would not be sufficient. More soldiers would have to be called in to bring down the "stupendous Animal." But discretion and care were called for; the Exeter Change Menagerie was on the second floor, and beneath it were shops owned by various anxious businessmen. If Chunee were to break free of his cage during the execution, he could easily collapse the second story. Only the floor directly beneath his cage had been reinforced (by a carpenter who had come to admire Chunee, remarking that the elephant "accommodated himself to his wishes in every respect").

In 1826 Chunee was the most famous and beloved Indian elephant in captivity. And he was huge. His disposition was praised by all who met him, and for nearly two decades he had entertained the citizens of London without incident. But for the past few years, he had been experiencing "annual attacks" during which he became excited, agitated, and aggressive. Large doses of laxatives were administered during these "fits" so that he would be occupied, distracted, and weakened. But Chunee was getting wise to the "medicine" and became increasingly ingenious at determining which of his foods had been spiked. The experts finally figured out the problem—it was linked to a primal cycle, a deep and forbidden urge. At certain times of the year, Chunee was suffering from "sexual excitability." Isolated though those days may have been, and still loved by all (in the way that a community can turn an exhibited animal into a social symbol, a local spiritual mascot), fears soon developed. Might he break free? Might he cause the entire second story menagerie to collapse? What might he do, running wild in a sexual frenzy? Chunee was sentenced to death.

Arsenic was prepared, but the elephant refused it. Three executioners fired round after round, but the musket balls merely stung his hide and hid in his flesh. Bleeding and betrayed, Chunee was growing angry. More soldiers were called in. But one hundred bullets would not be sufficient. Blood flowed steadily to the floor, dripping from the hundred wounds. They reloaded and fired, reloaded and fired. More than an hour later—with the elephant screams drowning out the sound of the rifles discharging—Chunee weakened and dropped. His old keeper approached him cautiously and finished the job with a sword. The slow death was done, the fears put to rest.[35]

What is it about animal sexuality that both titillates and disgusts, fascinates and frightens us? What is the source of our nervous laughter when the neighborhood dogs discover each other? Zoos—especially large, urban zoos—have long known the importance of sex for their survival. Breeding, of course, is fundamental; it is a legitimating factor. But zoo sex is deeper. It involves an ambiguous response from the public—a secret desire to witness strange couplings, and an outward contempt for the indecency of it all. Masturbating monkeys have long been a problem. With their actions, their bodies, their passions so familiar, monkeys and chimps have shared a dirty little secret with their visiting cousins since the days of the first zoos. Modern keepers discovered that boredom played a role in such behavior, and with richer surroundings—trees and grass instead of bars and cement—the animals tend to spend more of their time in less self-absorbed pastimes. But they still seem to enjoy the activity now and then.

Few of us handle animal sex comfortably. And we have invented a variety of ways to prevent unexpectedly encountering it in all of its phases and manifestations.

Keeping the dog and cat population low enough such that no pet goes hungry and homeless is a good idea. How best to accomplish this, though, is highly debated. The government of Los Angeles spends two million dollars every year to kill thousands of unwanted animals. As a result of pressure from animal rights groups and taxpayers, the city is considering a new "spay or pay" program designed to impose a fee on those who do not spay or neuter their dogs. Show dogs, purebreds, the best-of-the-best will be exempt. But there is opposition. To some, this is a sort of pet eugenics. What right do we have, such critics ask, to impose our will on canine sexual practices? What right do we have to separate the show dog from the mutt, promoting reproduction for the one and genocide for the other? Surely, having fewer hungry and homeless human beings is a good idea too. But enforced sterilization is not an appropriate path to such a goal— even less so when there is talk about only sterilizing some groups. Human hunger and homelessness is a political-economic problem not essentially related to population growth. It is a problem of aiming at an equitable distribution of resources, not one which needs to be addressed through sterilization programs. The pet problem, too, is political, economic, and not essentially related to population growth. Americans play the same ruthless games with their pets as they do with each other. Money determines worth; lineage determines power; the hungry must beg; the homeless are pitied yet shunned, given shelters instead of an equal shot at "the good life," and labeled "tramps," "bums," and "strays" (to become a stray is to stray from the ideal as it is socially constituted).

A recent trip to Venezuela opened my eyes to a slightly altered routine and ideal. Although some Venezuelan pets live in the upper stratas of society—a handful of them reaping the rewards of their owners' (more often than not) corruptly accumulated, petroleum-based wealth—most do not "belong" to a single family. They wander the neighborhood, napping in the steaming shade, moving from door to door. They do not come begging. They come expecting what is theirs. And they eat table scraps or, if they are lucky, specially pre-pared dishes. There is hardly a pet food industry to speak of in Venezuela—how strange, I am told, that we Americans think our pets need Alpo and Meow Mix; how indicative, I realize, pet food is of a culture of excess in which disposable income is waiting for the next phase of the commodification of life to call it into service.

Señora Nelly calls "Miso! Miso!" and a muscular, black cat named Silvestre makes his way to the porch. He moves slowly, like so many creatures adjusted to the tropics. He sniffs at a small lizard and cuts across the street to avoid the not-as-petrified-as-they-may-seem igua-nas laying thick in the bushes. On the porch there is a bit of fish from the Gulf—part of the family's dinner, part of the way in which the boundaries of the family are extended. Tonight he will meet Henrieta.

What is accomplished when we sterilize animals? It is not just popu-lation reduction. Midas Dekkers wonders:

> What possesses people to make a love-life impossible for the objects of their love? . . . The neutering of animals satisfies human needs. On the one hand, castration expunges the fear that sex inspires, and on the other, satisfies the desire for power. To castrate is to de-sex and without sex it is easier to form a friendship. . . . [Yet] if cas-tration is on the one hand prudish and pacifying, on the other it is erotic and belligerent.[36]

To castrate is to dominate—it is a political and a sexual power. In this sense it differs little from the power to kill. Both are domina-tions over the being of the Other; in both cases something is done to the body of the Other; and both are lairs for some of our darkest fears.

Round Island is a volcanic creation thirteen miles northeast of Mauritius, home of the reluctant Pink pigeon. When goats and rab-bits were brought to the island's 350 acres sometime in the 1800s, they began to change the indigenous ecosystem by eating most of the greenery, contributing to mass erosion, and thus destroying the habi-tat of the local snakes, lizards, and birds. The government decided

that restoration was in order in the late 1970s, and so they ordered
that strychnine-laced food be placed throughout the island in order
to poison and kill the goats and rabbits. They called in Gerald
Durrell to oversee the project and to capture some of the snakes and
lizards to be held in captivity "for their genes." When the press
uncovered the plan, however, the poisoning was put on hold. The
necessary slaughter, Durrell lamented, was being blocked by "animal protection societies . . . baying like hysterical hounds."[37] An
expert marksman was eventually brought in to "eliminate the goats
with the aid of a rifle"—which he did—but this still left those "insid-
ious munching rabbits."[38] The New Zealand Wildlife Service agreed
to provide a painless poison capable of only eradicating mammals;
and thus the cleansing went forward, eventually killing three thousand rabbits. For utilitarians, the problem had been that the strych-
nine was going to lead to a painful death. For some animal rights
activists, though, killing is killing, and thus alternative solutions
were sought, but to no avail. In similar situations, Maureen Duffy
has argued that birth control is the better alternative.[39] Food laced
with chemical sterilizers could have been left on Round Island, and
thus the rabbits and goats could have led full but childless lives,
eventually dying naturally. The result would have been the same—a
mammalless island—but the means would have been more humane.

Now, it is not at all clear what is meant by the "natural state" or
"indigenous ecosystem" of Round Island. The claim that rabbits and
goats have ruined the island is not actually a claim that rabbits and
goats have ruined the island. More foundationally, it is a suggestion
that rabbits and goats *brought by human beings* have ruined the
island. What makes the island unnatural is the activity of human
beings. Such thinking is as dangerous and misdirected as the thinking of strip miners and whalers who believe that the world is one big
resource meant for their consumption. The environmentalist who
calls for a return to a state untouched by human hands is separating
human beings from nature, and this is the same mentality that moti-
vates those who destroy the environment. Surely there is room left to
discriminate between living well on the earth and living poorly on it;
yet while the whaler causes more damage initially, environmentalism
which separates human beings from nature ultimately perpetuates
the misguided thinking of development and abuse. Humanity is seen
as outside of nature, usually quantifying, analyzing, and controlling

it. This, too, is the mentality that leads a government to order the round up of lizards in order to preserve their genes—as if the lizard is its genes, as if the preservation of genes preserves the lizard. There is a related point here about the mentality of killing and sterilizing, both of which are founded on a belief that it is our place to intervene. This is not to say that humanity should remove itself completely from the picture, but instead we must address the question of an appropriate way of being-in-the-world. When we make the move to alter the sexuality of animals, we make a move to "expunge the fear that sex inspires." Perhaps in the rabbit's urge to fill up an island, in the cat's urge to spend a night in passion, there is too much of a reminder of our own Being, of our own animality. The erected barrier between humans and animals is a comfortable fiction. Reminders that the boundary is not secure are met with the desperate actions of fear.

In 1679, two London residents scoffed at the boundary and paid with their lives. The woman was tried for her indiscretions and hanged on the grounds of sexual misconduct. Her lover received a trial and was met with the same sentence. Both died at Tyburn: two pendulous bodies—one human, one canine—swaying in public space, announcing their sins with their silence. Nearly a century later, and across the Channel, Jacques Ferron was smitten with a she-ass, and, having the misfortune to be discovered in the act, was tried and put to death for the crime of bestiality. The she-ass, however, had good legal representation and was acquitted in the most curious way. Character witnesses were called to testify to the ass' good character. Several persons of good standing claimed that they had known her for four years and that "both at home and outside, [she] had always behaved virtuously and carefully and had never caused trouble to anyone. . . . [Indeed,] in her whole manner of life she [had been] very law-abiding." The court ruled that the ass had been "the victim of force and had not co-operated of its own free-will with the crime of its master."[40]

Hidden—and not too deeply—in such claims is the assumption that an animal is a moral agent, capable of choosing its sexual behavior and capable of knowing that some choices are wrong. Morality aside, this is a startling claim. It is also not very modern. Contemporary scholars such as Barbara Noske and Carol Adams maintain that all bestiality is rape simply because animals are forced into the relations and are unable to choose to stop it. Adams explains:

> Silence is a major problem. Unlike most forms of sexual contact, in which either partner can report the experience, only one of the participants in bestiality can talk. . . . [N]o matter what the prevailing view of bestiality, it does not consider the animals' perspectives at all. It is always animal abuse. Relationships of unequal power cannot be consensual. In human-animal relationships, the human being has control of many—if not all—of the aspects of an animal's well being. Sexual relationships should occur between peers where consent should be possible. Consent is when one can say no, and that no is accepted. Clearly animals cannot do that.[41]

Some acts of bestiality involve pain, torture, and even death for animals. Surely such actions are immoral; but their immorality resides in the causing of pain, torturing, and killing. If there are examples of bestiality in which the animal does not seem to feel discomfort—if, in fact, there are instances of bestiality reportedly initiated by animals—where does the immorality reside? Adams suggests that the imbalance of power and the animals' inability to consent make all bestiality abuse. This is understandable. Consent, though, must not be reduced to the linguistic matter of talking; there are other paths toward consent. The strongest reading of Adams' claim would tie the two notions together: animals are incapable of consenting because their relationships with humans leave animals unempowered. The same issue arises when questions must be answered concerning sex between drill instructors and new recruits, prison guards and convicts, bosses and workers, teachers and students. The inherent imbalance of power in the initial relationship cannot help but be reflected in the development of a sexual relationship, and thus it could be said that the second party in each of these couplings cannot make a truly free decision—regardless of who made the initial move. The problem, however, is that Adams ultimately envisions a future in which human-animal relationships are based on equality. Would all acts of bestiality then be abuse? Beyond the fear of breaking a cultural taboo, perhaps there is the greater fear of admitting equality. What is, after all, so strange about a woman and a dog being hanged, or an ass being acquitted, is the assumption that animals can choose *and that we share a moral world with them.* Even if our conceptions of appropriate morality are skewed, thinking that animals may have access to moral decision-making is a wonder and a triumph. Adams rightly points out that animals live their sex lives in public rather than private spaces, and that this is part of the human attraction. But it is also a source of fear—a fear that another artificial boundary, that of public and private, will come crumbling down in the presence of the animal Other. Animals seem to have no moral concerns when it comes to their sexual behavior. Hanging them, castrating them, and "fixing" them are related actions each motivated by fear.

But what is there to fear? What is there to get so worried about? Most people don't *love* their animals. Alfred Kinsey did report that more than five percent of Americans had had a sexual experience with an animal. His data did show that eight percent of men and more than three percent of women admitted some bestiality in their past. The numbers may seem higher than we might imagine, but they are nothing compared to the statistic Kinsey offered for rural males: fifty percent, said the data, had had sex with an animal. The explanation is often one of availability: availability of the animal and the lack of availability of a human partner. For similar reasons, the Talmud forbids widows to keep pet dogs. Yet the Monks of New Skete not only keep dogs but offer a three-tape video series on how to raise dogs, in which they say, somewhat ambiguously: "How shall we respond to our aloneness? . . . [A dog's] presence, I think, does a remarkable amount of good for celibate people. We don't have a spouse to go home to and be affectionate with."[42] Availability is not just an explanation for bestiality. It is an ingredient in all sexual relationships: from Adam and Eve to the modern intra-office romance, we tend to fall for those who are readily available.

The fear that is wrapped up with sex in general can become a crippling force or it can be used as a weapon. Konrad Lorenz would not approve of the Monks of New Skete, just as he did not approve of most pet owners' love for their pets. Such human beings, claimed Lorenz, deny "love to mankind in order to transfer it to a dog or a cat . . . [and they are] definitely committing a grave sin, social sodomy so to speak, which is as disgusting as the sexual kind."[43] But just as "social sodomy" can inspire a crippling disgust based on a fear of love (and not just sex), so too can it be used to manipulate Others in an expression of a fear of being-with in general. In stories as equally tragic as Chunee's, elephants have long been persecuted for the mysteries of their sexuality. Geographies in which elephants and human beings are available for each other have created cultures in which stories of the elephants' attraction to human female breasts abound. So taken is the bull elephant with these bits of human flesh, he can be led to death with the promise of a fondle. No doubt the truth lies somewhere between the words of such stories; but scholarly accounts, even, remain. From 1372 we have the report of Bartholomew Anglicus:

> Among the Ethiopians in some countries elephants be hunted in this wise: there go into the desert two maidens all naked and bare, with open hair of the head: and one of them beareth a vessel, and the other a sword. And these maidens begin to sing alone: and the beast hath liking when he heareth the song, and liketh their teats, . . . and then the one maid striketh him in the throat with a sword, and the other taketh his blood in a vessel. . . .⁴⁴

Why breasts? Why the temptation of a *ménage à trois*? Why death? Killing an elephant lured by sex undoubtedly satiates (and feeds) a variety of fears—fears of crumbling boundaries, hidden desires, and, of course, castration. Sometimes a trunk is not just a trunk.

There are those who would claim that animal fears are always symbolic of deeper yet fully human-centered sexual fears. Psycho-analyst Melitta Sperling has argued that "most investigators seem to agree that [in cases of arachnophobia] the spider is a representa-tion of the dangerous (orally devouring and anally castrating) mother, and that the main problem of these patients seems to centre around their sexual identification and bisexuality."⁴⁵ Unsurprisingly, Sperling's analysis is indebted to Sigmund Freud, who also saw ani-mal fears as a symptom of some more latent sexual fear. One of Freud's most famous cases, that of Little Hans, involved a boy who feared horses as well as giraffes and other large mammals. Although Freud met Hans only once, he received reports from the boy's father and was able to diagnose the source of the problem: an Oedipus Complex in which the boy lusted after his mother, feared retaliation from his father (probably castration), but could not consciously accept fearing his father and so buried that fear in his subconscious only becoming consciously aware of it as it manifested itself in a more acceptable form—fear of horses. Freud's armies of supporters and detractors have been fighting over the validity of such interpre-tations for nearly a century. I choose not to be conscripted into this war. But we can acknowledge this before we move along: fears are often deeper and more complex than common sense would suggest. And fears about sex are essentially fears about being-with.

Simone de Beauvoir attributes some of this fear to confusion, which is to say *bewilderment*. The moment of the first sexual encounter between a man and a woman—for de Beauvoir, "the wedding night"—creates a tension that

> transforms the erotic act into a test that both parties fear their inability to meet, each being too worried by his or her own problems to be able to think generously of the other. . . . The difficult problem facing the husband is this: if, in Aristotle's phrase, "he titillates his wife too lasciviously," she may be scandalized and outraged. . . . But if, on the other hand, the husband "respect" his wife, he fails to awaken her sensuality. . . .[46]

The man is clearly cast in the active role here, with the woman passively waiting to respond appropriately to her lover's advances. Is it sexist to maintain such stereotypes as the proper model for human interaction? Most likely. Is it sexist to admit that models such as this have existed and have inspired bewilderment and fear in real people in the past? Most likely not. Feminists such as Carol Adams have done important work in pointing out the relationships between men-and-women-and-animals. The parallels between meat-eating and prostitution, for instance, are philosophically startling. There are times, though, that the identification of woman-as-animal is a source of fear as well as oppression. Sex becomes a hunt—in de Beauvoir's words, a woman "makes her lover in truth her prey."[47] The familiar mixing of sex and violence manifests itself in the brutal chase and inevitable capture of the male. Although it is correct to point out that a woman's power is still seen only through her ability to control sex, the fear is real. Even the romantic Friedrich Schiller worries:[48]

> Da werden Weiber zu Hyenen
> Und treiben mit Entsetzen Schertz;
> Noch Zuckend, mit des Panther's Zaehnen
> Zerreissen sie des Feindes Herz.

> (Then wenches turn into Hyenas
> And mockery of terror make;
> With panther's teeth they tear apart
> Still quivering, the enemy's heart.)

That moment of startled bewilderment before the prey is devoured—
that incarnate fear of which Darwin spoke—has become a carnal
fear. Schiller's poem is certainly from the male point of view, just as
was Gordon Cumming's hunting narrative. Whether hunter or
hunted, woman or animal, the Other inspires confusion and fear
because she is not the Self, the First Person, the agent. And yet she
is there, bodily, inhabiting the self-same world. In the public's preoccupation with show dogs, albino tigers, and the art of taxidermy,
there is a fascination and curiosity about the body that is different.
So, too, in the sexed-body of the woman lives an otherness. Surely to
admit this is to admit to the paternal foundations of society and
epistemology, to admit that what is known is human and male,
known properly by the human male. To say that a woman's body is
different is to say that it is different *from something that is known.*
But de Beauvoir, again, sees something deeper:

> The sex organ of a man is simple and neat as a finger; it is readily
> visible and often exhibited to comrades with proud rivalry; but the
> feminine sex organ is mysterious even to the woman herself, con-
> cealed, mucous, and humid, as it is; it bleeds each month, it is often
> sullied with body fluids, it has a secret and perilous life of its own.[49]

There are points to be made about the primacy of vision in our epistemology. There are points to be made about what it means—socially,
ethically—for a woman to find her own body *different.* But the point
for us to make is the reaction to the body. Hidden and complicated as
it is, a woman's sex is said to inspire bewilderment. The elephant
charges at breasts, but from the sixteenth century comes this advice
from a North African explorer: "If a woman were to meet a lion in
some lonely spot, she [has] only to expose her private parts and the
lion [will] at once lower his eyes in confusion and depart."[50] The puzzle of the Other marks unexpected boundaries.

Sex is always a matter of boundaries: the Here becomes also a
There, a kind of Being is shared. It is not only prudish societies that
acknowledge the enigma of sexual union, the fear that is bound up
with the encounter, the impropriety of bestiality. Modern science
maintains that sex creates *natural* boundaries—in a sense, created
animals.

Stephen R. L. Clark argues that species has nothing to do with
shared characteristics but rather is a function of genealogy: to be a

member of a species is to be related to past members of that species more closely than some other species, and to be able to breed successfully. "Cows are not mammals because they feed their young on milk," writes Clark. "[B]ovine mothers feed their young on milk because they are mammals. Being a mammal is being genealogically linked with a complex individual, the order Mammalia. . . ."[51] But since we are all genealogically linked if we go back far enough— since all life can claim some wet, mysterious, ancient mother—the concept of species also includes the provision of successful reproduction: "*Drosophila pseudo obsura* and *Drosophila persimilis* are sibling species, indistinguishable to naïve observers, but certainly distinct (because their members do not successfully breed together)."[52] Being a human being, then, was made possible by tens of thousands of years of appropriate sex. Sex created humanity and continues to separate it from animality. As a result, refraining from bestiality is what makes bestiality possible, and in this wonderfully circular bit of metaphysics lies the absurdity of the notion of a boundary. No, "absurdity" is too harsh. Better to call it "fictional functionality." Dekkers, then, is not quite right when he writes:

> Sex is something that by definition you have with another being, whether of the same or a different sex, someone of the same race or a more exotic choice. Every sexual encounter is a breaking of bounds, an intrusion into an alien realm, every sexual encounter retains a whiff of bestiality. What use is the other person if they are not different? You find true satisfaction only when you let yourself go.[53]

Sex, rather, is an approach toward a functional boundary only to discover that it vanishes before us. Fear resides not only in the disappearing barrier, but in the realization that we have not known the truth, that we have been hiding foolishly, that we are not alone.

Together. We are bodies with endless needs, living with each other—bodies and needs intermingled. Letting ourselves go, we discover the Other and ourselves. And if our Being is a Being-toward-death as well as a being-with, perhaps it is the case that the two are inseparably bound. This is not to excuse the massacre of Chunee and the mutilation of dogs. It is instead to see the *petite morte* and the Big Death as they truly are. Lingis has called sexless organisms— those which reproduce by schizogenesis—immortal.[54] Indeed, sexless beings break off pieces of themselves and continue to be, indefinitely.

It also follows, then, that with the development of sex comes the inevitability of death. Evolution is the ultimate black widow, setting us up on a date in order to kill us off. To be sexual is to die and become someone's dinner. Sex, death, and dinner are inevitably woven together in fear. The bedroom farce concluded, then, let us turn our attention to the eating.

4. Being Eaten

"When you die wouldn't you rather be eaten by your own kinsmen than by maggots?"

—Mayoruna native to nineteenth century English visitor

I know an epistemologist who knows a cannibal. They met several years ago on a summer trip to the Arctic. The cannibal was the pilot of the small charter plane dropping the party off up river. Evidently, he didn't like to talk about what had happened—that time he had eaten his passenger when the plane crashed.

On November 8, 1972, Martin Hartwell took off from Cambridge Bay on an errand of mercy. Two of his three passengers were in need of medical attention and the nearest facility was 535 miles away at Yellowknife. Neemee Nulliayok was eight months pregnant and experiencing premature labor. Her 14-year-old nephew, David Kootook, was in extreme pain and seemed to be suffering from acute appendicitis. The third passenger, Judy Hill, was a nurse, and her time was spent comforting the two patients and hoping that they would hold on until the plane touched down at Yellowknife. The weather was not good; the sun was going down. The plane was 180 miles off course when it crashed into a hillside.

The women died—the nurse instantly, the mother-to-be a few days later. As search parties continued looking for the missing plane, the weather grew worse. Heavy snow came with temperatures 40 to 60 degrees below zero. On the twenty-third day, the boy died. The emergency rations from the crashed plane had long run out. No one held much hope that survivors would be found. But nine days later—thirty-two days after the crash—rescue parties discovered Hartwell alive. In the crash he had broken both ankles and his left knee. He could not walk, but he could drag himself through the snow with his arms. Apparently, he could drag himself to the wrecked plane to search for an ax. He could drag himself to the body of Nurse Hill. And he could drag pieces of Nurse Hill back to his makeshift camp, where he had placed them in his sleeping bag to thaw before eating them.

"Welcome to the camp of the Cannibal," cried Hartwell as the rescue party approached. Master Corporal Bob Bisson could not accept the reality of the scene. His eyes fixed on the hump of flesh—what must be "a hind-quarter of a caribou or moose," he thought. The ax was leaning against the hump, what turned out to be the remains of the nurse's body. A rescuer reported:

> One of the nurse's legs was in two pieces. . . . Both had been severed in sort of a V at the crotch. . . . Her light blue panties were still on and so were her blue socks. . . . [Hartwell had] consumed quite a bit.[55]

On the plane ride home, the survivor ate pears, raisins, and a Hershey bar. He said that he might have lasted another month with his meat supply. "He talked about it the same way as if he had gotten a rabbit."[56]

When the truth came out about Hartwell's survival techniques, there was debate. Reverend Jean-Guy LeMarier, the Dean of Theology at St. Paul's Roman Catholic Seminary in Ottawa, declared that "there [was] no specific moral problem involved. . . . Incidental elements, like homicide or sexual perversion, have been studied and discussed, but the simple fact of eating human flesh has not been considered a moral dimension of the situation."[57] Archbishop E. W. Scott of the Anglican Church of Canada commented: "There is a sense in which society has no right to judge this particular case . . . [since] the event took place outside of society. . . ."[58] RCAF Flight Lieutenant Sheldon Coleman, however, condemned Hartwell. "All I can say is that Hartwell did not display much self-discipline . . . [and] did not uphold the tradition of the early northern pilots and crew."[59] Coleman, it turns out, had once survived about the same amount of time after crashing in the Arctic in 1936. Without injuries, though, he had picked berries and hunted squirrels to stay alive.

Hartwell went through court proceedings and public scrutiny. He was neither proud nor repentant of his actions. "You won't believe it," he declared, "but I'm a vegetarian and look at what's happened to me."[60]

Years later, he would pilot the charter plane in which my friend and his party traveled. Too respectful to mention the past yet unable to think of much else as they pressed forward together into the vast country beneath the north pole, the epistemologist kept an eye on the cockpit and attempted to sort it all out silently.

We are what we eat. Also, we are what we are in virtue of the fact that we eat: we are eaters. Also, we are picky eaters. Custom and tradition, no doubt, shape our tastes. Bill Clinton complains of having to sample moose lips on a trip to Europe; Lucy Ricardo demands ketchup for her escargots; Sitting Bull ate puppies but was horrified by sardines. How few nonhuman animals seem to have our finicky eating habits. Our family dog, Snowball, pondered the edibility and eventually partook of things I prefer not even to think about years later. And in a discussion with Judith Strasser on Public Radio, Jan Grover speaks of her admiration for birds she once saw picking through human vomit for anything useful, anything edible.[61]

Why is it that we would not eat vomit and yet those birds did? Perhaps it is because birds don't know it is vomit—just as Snowball never knew that that refreshing drink was toilet water. This is to say that animals lack a bit of knowledge human beings have, that if only birds could see vomit for what it truly is they would stop, thinking "Oh my God! What have I been doing?" Or perhaps we would not think of eating vomit because we have so many other options— McDonald's, Burger King, Veggie Burgers—but the poor animals are in a constant struggle for life and have no hope of surviving if they are picky. This, I think, is the more popular and modern answer. It is based on a general hubris, a devotion to thinking that we are superior in every way, and a faith that progress exists and has been on our side. And it is behind most modern evaluations of cannibalism. Who knows what we might have to resort to if we found our options suddenly limited? Martin Hartwell is a curiosity, but essentially understandable. Those who eat humans by choice are true enigmas—the true source of our cannibalization fears.

Choice again. It is such an important part of our self-understanding—of our misdirected thinking that we are the classical Liberal selves of Hobbes and Descartes. And it forms a large part of our fears, because we fear the freedom which we assume accompanies choice (Sartre) and we fear the wrong choice (psychoanalysis), whether we make it ourselves or it is made by some confused/evil Other. David Kootook lived twenty-three days, dying in the Arctic in part because he chose not to eat the nurse. We understand David, too. We have a mechanism to explain it—his will to live was not greater than his abhorrence of the means to the end—and we are comforted. It is, in fact, comfortably nonfalsifiable—the will to live is not strong enough if the will to live is not strong enough to force you into doing what you need to do to live—but never mind.

There are times when human beings must choose to eat strangely or not to eat—to be (something strange) or not to be—although history has provided unforeseen third options at times. Lewis and Clark, while exploring North America to make it safe for theme parks and strip-malls, traveled with dogs, knowing that their companions would eventually become food when other options diminished. Knowing in advance may seem to have made the explorers less traveling companions to the dogs than nomadic herders, but there was always the option not to eat their best friends. After weeks of canine cuisine, the human beings in the party were converts. "Having been so long accustomed to live on the flesh of dogs," wrote Meriwether Lewis, "the greater part of us have acquired a fondness for it, and our original aversion for it overcome by reflecting that while we subsisted on that food we were fatter, stronger, and in general enjoyed better health than at any period since leaving buffalo country."[62] The poet-conquistador Gaspar Villagra had a similar decision to make. Trapped in the high altitudes of Arizona during a snowy winter, Villagra's horse slipped into a crevasse and was lost. Without transportation or supplies, the warrior-artist eventually turned to his dog for food. After some hesitation, he stabbed his canine compadre; but as the dog was dying he looked at the man and licked his hand. His appetite overwhelmed by guilt, Villagra could not eat his friend, and so determined to survive by some other means.[63]

During the Gulf War, Iraqi soldiers ate the population of the Kuwait City Zoo—the collection dropped from 442 creatures to 24 in seven months. It was a decision based on circumstances, and yet, what decision is not? Peter Lund Simmonds, of British high society, loved the taste of zoo animals—especially monkeys and pumas—and declared England's "allegiance to beef" a "national weakness."[64] Darwin agreed, and met regularly with a group of friends from

Cambridge to dine on "beasts which were before unknown to the human palate."[65] In the early 1800s, London's Regents Park regularly served whatever died in the zoo, and select patrons were treated to panther steaks, elephant trunk soup, and roast giraffe.[66]

Villagra's guilt did not reside in Lewis and Clark, Darwin, or the zoo tasting club. It does not live in the majority of human beings who turn chickens, cows, and pigs into meals. Would we want to promote vegetarianism through guilt? Why not? It is a state-of-mind that has recently come under attack from a society founded on talk show confessions and prozac-inspired ways of being. Religions have long known its power. Midwesterners, I have come to believe, are the only Americans who still acknowledge that a little healthy repression and guilt go a long way toward making good neighbors. Snowball and I were from Ohio, and I still feel as if I should have closed the toilet lid more often, thus limiting her drinking options and bettering her life. But guilt, like fear, is backwards-looking. Villagra, after all, did not eat his dog, but he killed her. And I suspect that guilt is not what keeps most human beings from cannibalism, although the cannibal's lack of guilt may be part of what makes him fearful.

Most cultures have hints of cannibalism in their traditions and practices. Even if they do not eat their enemies or family members, cannibalistic symbols remind them who they are—which is to say to whom they are connected. Among the Bagesu, an animal is placed beside a human corpse, and then the animal is eaten. Sometimes the animal's skin is used to wrap the dead person while the mourners eat the animal. A Bavarian tradition calls for *Leichen-nudelh* to be baked for a funeral by first allowing the yeast dough to rise on the body of the deceased. In part of Albania, funeral cakes in the shape of the dead body are made from boiled wheat; they are carried in the funeral only to be eaten when the body is lowered into the grave. This tradition of "corpse cakes" is sometimes reversed as well, with the living offering parts of their flesh to the dead. In this spirit, the Orang Sakei of Sumatra drip blood from their heads onto the face of the corpse of a family member. In countries where Christianity has influenced death ceremonies, cannibalistic mutilation practices are seen as going against the Bible. Christian code allows for ashes to be smeared on mourners "in a symbolic sublimated mutilation," but today most funeral-goers prefer to wear dark clothing as a symbol of the symbol of such an offering.[67] Christianity, of course, makes no attempt to hide the cannibalistic ritual of the Last Supper. Faith in the reality of transubstantiation is critical, and parishioners, hungry for the truth, continually re-enact the moment that not only reminds them of the sacrifice made by the Lamb of God, but of their own identification with Christ.

The meaning is something similar to that which stands behind numerous "primitive" cannibalistic practices. Cannibalism marks the identification of the eater and the eaten. Like bestiality, cannibalism is feared in that it is perceived as a violation of boundaries; yet the truth is that it is a recognition that such boundaries do not exist. Commentators tend to get it slightly wrong, just as they did with bestiality. Eli Sagan writes:

> The cannibal eats those who are *other*—who are *not me*. Civilized society enslaves or exploits or makes war on those who are not me—those who are not human.[68]

Civilized society, too, eats the Other—this is what hamburger is all about. But some cannibalistic practices do not strengthen the distinction between Self and Other as Sagan suggests. Instead, they are ways of noting the distinction's arbitrariness. There becomes Here; You become Me. There is the inherent danger in all of this that Emmanuel Levinas' fear will be realized and the Other will be reduced to Me—or at least understood as for-me. But this is not necessarily so. "Affectionate" cannibalism, as it is still practiced among some peoples, and Christian communion are surely not meant to be understood as sublimations of radical alterity. On the contrary, *thoughtful eating* can bring the same realization that a careful reading of Husserl's fifth *Cartesian Meditation* brings: to be is to be-with; we live only in—and through—one another. Husserl, in fact, is probably tougher to chew.

So what if we eat thoughtfully? What will we eat? Philosopher and anthropologist Raymond Corbey notes, thoughtfully:

> Reflections upon how we have treated, and still do treat, other animals leads to feelings of uneasiness, if not perplexity. . . . What we eat and what we do not eat, what we kill and what we do not kill, what we define as cannibalism or murder and what falls outside this definition—here our most fundamental taboos are involved. . . . Admitting the moral equality of other animals like apes, pigs or cows seems to leave us with only two possibilities: being prepared

to rear, kill and eat humans as well, or refraining from killing and
eating equals altogether.[69]

A muscle is a muscle is a muscle. And then what? Some cultures
happily acknowledge this and happily eat themselves.

Stanley Walens and Susan Reid have studied the Kwakiutl
Indians of the Northwest Coast of North America and discovered a
system of flesh-eating that is founded on our interconnectedness.[70]
Kwakiutl culture has cannibalistic practices that do not involve
human flesh; there are Man Eater monsters that roam the forest, and
an intricate religious-ethical system ties all that is living into the
same Being. Not surprisingly, salmon are the anchor of Kwakiutl philosophy. The fish have formed the basis of the tribe's diet and success
for 5,000 years, and they form the basis of ontology as well. So interconnected are the Kwakiutl and the salmon, the idea of a boundary
between them has long ago been abandoned. Eating salmon thus not
only shows the similarity between and interdependence of human
beings and fish, it is also a form of cannibalism, recognized and celebrated as such. Other animals, too, eat salmon, and thus are man-
eaters. Mixing human flesh with their own, these animals become
human by eating humans. Ultimately, humanity is shared by all living things and thus loses cohesion as an isolating definition. When a
member of the tribe dies, his or her body is offered to ravens which
tear apart and digest the flesh. It is said that this is the only true
death: were a Kwakiutl to be buried, he would not be dead; were a
Kwakiutl to be cremated, she would never have her soul—her spirit,
her Being, her humanity—released and reborn. To die is to offer up
one's self as food, and this element of willing sacrifice is integral. A
salmon that does not want to sacrifice itself must not be eaten; a
human that does not wish to become food for ravens has some spiritual growing to do. Walens writes:

> [A]nimals that eat salmon must perform the rituals that make the
> salmon want to die, the rituals that promise them resurrection. But
> even more important, since salmon are humans, and humans eat
> salmon, by analogy humans eat humans—and are thus cannibals.
> Furthermore, crest animals that eat salmon are themselves de
> facto man eaters. In point of fact, most crest animals actually do
> eat humans, either live humans (killer whales, wolves, and bears)
> or dead humans (eagles and ravens). Thus, because these animals
> are all direct links in the cycle of resurrection for both humans and
> salmon, they are themselves by definition humans.[71]

Romanticism aside, what would it mean for a salmon to want to die? How is this essentially different from Ortega y Gasset claiming that some animals are asking to be hunted, that it would very nearly be disrespectful not to hunt and kill them?

A partial solution can be found in the Kwakiutl belief that "Those who wish to eat must become food." It is a claim that emanates from a particular people in a particular lifeworld; it must be understood as deeply philosophic. Enmeshed in the living world in a sacrificial way, it is an acknowledgment that the very act of eating is a way of preparing to become food. It should not be thought of as fattening a pig for slaughter, though there are echoes of an acknowledgment of the interconnection between eating and being-eaten here too. It is, instead, a way of saying that *Dasein* is directed toward death; that eating (living) is directed toward being-eaten (death); that sacrifice is the necessary economy of existence. In the salmon's urge to eat is its acceptance of death. The worm on the hook is less a cruel trap and trick than it is an invitation for the fish to accept its being and become food *by pursuing food*.

I say that this is a partial solution because I have a certain sympathy for it, yet I am somewhat unconvinced. It has the flavor of a likely story we must find suspect. Are fish choosing to become food when they take bait? No doubt it is my hard-to-shake Liberal bias, but I fear that the individual salmon are not willing participants in all of this. Salmon do not typically kill people; neither do ravens for that matter. While it is true that the Kwakiutl offer their corpses for the consumption of birds, these corpses were created by accident, old age, sickness, etc. Human beings are doing most of the killing and are trying to escape being killed at every turn. Interconnected though they may be, humans and the salmon are *unequally* related when one eats the other. The reply may come, though, that the power of the salmon resides in the fact that the Kwakiutl would not exist without the fish, that the Kwakiutl recognize this and appreciate the fact that they need the sacrifice of the salmon in order to continue being.

Is knowing that an animal has sacrificed so that we may eat enough to make the arrangement moral? Our large, industrial society seems to work toward the goal of obscuring the sacrifice that makes our existence possible. Capitalist competition needs losers in order to generate winners, but we do our best to hide those who come up short—we avert our eyes, evict the homeless from our city parks, and try not to think about it. Behind the products we consume stand the anonymous faces of wage-laborers who made it all possible by sacrificing their lives to the assembly line, the processing plant, the time clock. We will never know them. We can never know them, comfortably hidden behind layers of social processes and institutions. The food at our tables, in our freezers, and at our drive-thrus is the result of animal sacrifices, but how hard this is to see in a Big Mac. The animal is so far removed from our experience that we cannot begin to recognize the extent of its participation in our continued existence. And peeking behind the curtain is a frightening prospect.

But is knowing enough? If I know that a cow died to make my hamburger, is it enough to make hamburgers moral? Perhaps a first step would be to clarify what it would mean to *know* such a thing. Knowing is not to be understood as an abstract process involving "information." Such a model of knowledge as without context may fit a scientific techno-culture in which knowing the weather means having access to seeing the number of degrees a thermometer is registering (or being able to afford cable and thus the Weather Channel), but knowledge is not merely a collection of facts, nor is it fully mental. To know the origin of the hamburger is to be-with the animal and experience the sacrifice—to be aware that a cow's body is at steak. The Kwakiutl *recognize* the sacrifice of the animal, which is to say that a particular phenomenological structure exists. And this is only possible given the appropriate experience. Gene Logsdon, an Ohio farmer, has championed gardening as a first step toward bringing an urban culture into contact with the world and thus closer to knowing and recognizing. The garden, as a link to the farm, involves the whole body—it requires contact, argues Logsdon, and

> [i]f that contact is not close, it is not meaningful at all. To feel the searing heat as well as the comforting warmth of the sun, or to endure the dry wind as well as the soothing breeze; to pray for rain but not too much rain; to long for a spate of dry weather but not too long; . . . to know that life depends on eating and being eaten; to accept the decay of death as the only way to achieve the resurrection of life; to realize that diversification of species, not multiplication within species, is the responsibility of rational intelligence—nature will handle that latter activity much better than we can . . . —these are all part of an education that the industrial world hungers for but cannot name.[72]

Not all people know where hamburger comes from—it can be a traumatic moment when a child learns the truth—but most think that they know. They know that hamburger is not flour and water; they know that it is muscle. But they do not really *know* this. It is evident in their phenomenology of eating, in the way that the cow is not present in the hamburger for them. The felt sacrifice of the animal—the presenced absence—is not there. No doubt part of what people fear in cannibalism is the presence of the person, the way that Nurse Hill's leg-meat retains the echo of the woman, the way it cannot so easily be experientially reduced to food. But perhaps a reduction to food is always inappropriate, regardless of the meal. Each bit of food can make present the web of sacrifices behind it; a salad, too, can be a kind of communion.

Say we no longer commodify our meals. Say that we apperceive the whole being behind our meal as well as the sacrifice which made it possible. Even appreciating that sacrifice (and I mean "appreciating" in the sense of both giving thanks and recognizing through directed attention) does not seem enough. The serial killer may be appreciative. The serial killer may be very happy and grateful that his victim picked him up hitchhiking, that his victim is a sweet and innocent girl, that his victim chose to die by taking the bait of stopping for him along the road. Perhaps what makes this a bad parallel, though, is that there is no *mutual* sacrifice here. Surely the immorality of the serial killer lies in his killing and not in the fact that he offers no return self-sacrifice to his victims, but let us consider this further. Perhaps his lack of sacrifice is partially what made him into a killer, and the Kwakiutl tribesman's willingness for self-sacrifice is partially what excuses his salmon-eating.

We are not a culture of sacrifice. Few willingly choose to offer themselves without hope of reward and profit. And nearly all of us fear being eaten. Concrete vaults and steel caskets speak to this fear, but it runs deeper still.

Some would say that our fear of being eaten is a result of our biological memory—bits of a recollected dark past in which we were lower on the food chain. But the answer is not so simple. The Buddha is said to have offered his flesh to a starving tiger and her cubs. In the Far East during the seventeenth, eighteenth, and nineteenth centuries, Pekinese dogs were so revered that they had human wetnurses. In New Guinea, too, Hagerhai women suckle captive boars, rearing them as their own children. And purposeful leeching was a well-established medical practice in the West until modern medicine and HMOs replaced it with a more metaphorical and monetary version.

Still, we fear. At the first Olympic Games of 776 B.C.E., Milo the sprinter is said to have celebrated his victory by carrying a cow throughout the stadium and then settling down to eat her. Finishing the entire animal in one meal, he was slow and groggy and filled with meat. A pack of wolves descended on Milo and ate him alive. Many years before, Actaeon unfortunately and accidentally stumbled upon the goddess Artemis while she was nude. She turned him into a deer and he was eaten by his dogs. The carnality of sex, fear, and food are forever intertwined. Each culture tells the story slightly differently.

In the heyday of the British Empire, exotic and dangerous animals were the stuff of nightmares. Tigers, especially, burned bright in the nightmares of British citizens. Harriet Ritvo remarks:

> About the tiger there were no two ways of thinking. It epitomized what man had to fear from the animal kingdom and from restive human subordinates. . . . The ultimate measure of the tiger's unregeneracy was its fondness for human flesh. Many tigers living in the populated parts of India and Ceylon routinely preyed on domestic animals and occasionally became man-eaters. . . . The British public was both horrified and fascinated by such assaults. In 1800 the East India Company put a mechanical model of a tiger eating an Englishman, which had been captured in 1799 from a rebellious Indian potentate, on display at its London Offices, where it drew crowds for several generations. Within the body of the tiger was a kind of organ, which caused particular delight when the handle was cranked, reproducing both the cries of a person in distress and the roar of a tiger.[73]

Today we have less contact with animals and more faith in our abilities to control them. The modern becoming-food fear is less about Little Red Riding Hood and Shere Kahn than it is about flesh-eating viruses and hungry aliens. The relationship between science fiction aliens and classical animal stories—between these two types of nonhuman Others—must remain a topic for us for another day. But the move to a fear of unseen animals—that is, microscopic life in the form of insects and viruses—is worth our attention.

When I was young I experienced two traumatic events involving animals, eating, and fear. The first took place when I was six years old and was feeding a hot dog to a German Shepherd. I'm not exactly sure what happened. My own memories are spliced together with the various versions of the story I have heard from others for all of these years. But it seems that I gave the hot dog in pieces to the Shepherd, and in our mutual excitement he snapped out to get the last piece and, our being about the same height, he bit off most of my right cheek by mistake. What I remember is the fear. And the sudden equation of my cheek and the hot dog. Luckily I overcame my fear of dogs without need for a therapist placing a dead German Shepherd on my coat or inviting me to play "imaginative games" with German Shepherd corpses. The second event took place later in elementary school when we saw a film about the microscopic life all around us, in our homes and on our bodies. I was terrified for days. To think it is true! Follicle mites were living at the base of my eyelashes. They were laying eggs from which their wormlike children would be born—each one hatching onto my body, exploring my eyelids and forehead, and eventually claiming a hair follicle of its own to call home. Each hour 10,000 bacteria were entering my nose and mouth in order to start an unseen war. Every twenty minutes their number doubled through some sort of sexless self-copying. Were it not for my own unseen mercenaries, I would be overrun. The bacteria were called "micro-organisms" but they sounded like animals. Yet my own defenses—white blood cells, especially—were not animals, were they? Luckily, I was constantly shedding skin flakes (400 million cells an hour), and half a million bacteria clung to falling skin and thus were jettisoned from my body at a comforting rate. Some ended up in bed, though. There, skin cells floated down like fish flakes in an aquarium to sustain the millions of dustmites patiently waiting their nightly feeding in my mattress (dustmite numbers, I later learned, increase in the beds of sexually active couples!). At every moment in unseen ways, I was—I am, we are—being eaten alive and dead.

It does not occur to us to welcome being eaten. The sacrifice seems too great: what's in it for us? And yet it is necessary. Those who wish to eat—to be—must become food. The necessary sacrifice may not seem a true sacrifice—it may seem a taking—but it is the structure of existence, an aspect of what Lingis reminds us is a solar economy. The sun, as the source of all local life, burns itself out as fast as possible, spending the majority of its body to generate radiation into a vast abyss that cannot possibly utilize the gift. And the sun does not ask anything in return. The sacrifice is complete; its way of being is to be consumed and to make us all possible. Sun worshippers who offered sacrifices—human, even—in thanks could only have offended, were solar offense capable of being taken.

Plutarch was a vegetarian. His "On the Eating of Flesh" should be widely read. It eloquently defends vegetarianism by turning the dinner tables and asking how anyone could possibly eat meat. "[I]n what state of soul or mind [was] the first man who . . . touched his mouth to gore and brought his lips to the flesh of a dead creature," writes Plutarch, "and ventured to call food and nourishment the parts that had a little before bellowed and cried, moved and lived?"[74] Plutarch also pre-dates scientists' findings on the "unnatural" status of human carnivorousness by appealing to the shape of our teeth and the inadequacies of our gastric juices when it comes to using the bodies of animals for energy. But most importantly, Plutarch suggests that eating animals may offend the earth, for it is a way of saying that the earth is incapable of providing for us. "Why slander the earth," he cries to the human carnivores, "by implying that she cannot support you?"[75]

Farming, too, requires sacrifice. And it also requires the respectful receipt of the earth's gifts. But as a thoughtful activity, it must not take more than what is offered, nor must it be merely a form of consumption. Good farmers *know* this. Feminist hunter Mary Stange has it all wrong when she writes:

> One may argue for a vegetarian diet and abhor all meat-eating on the grounds of cruelty. But in a single sunny afternoon, a farmer plowing a field wreaks more carnage, in the form of outright killing and the destruction of nests and mating areas, not to mention the impacts of pesticides and herbicides on wildlife, than the average hunter does in a lifetime.[76]

Agribusiness fits this model, but good farming need not. Good farming can participate in a sacrificial economy rather than extort its gains from the earth. But this is not an easy task. It does not require, I think, a Jain mindset such that we continually fear doing damage to an Other. Neither does it require veganism, in which a distancing *respect* again is tantamount to *fear* (à la Kant). Knowing how much to give and take from the land, from a tree, from a cow is just the kind of knowledge we need but mostly lack. I cannot offer it here. There are times and conditions under which a cow's milk is a wonderful and appropriate gift; but I could not imagine an appropriate circumstance for torturing and killing her for food.

Yet this ethical claim rests neither on an abstract conception of rights nor a mathematical quantification of suffering. It is, instead, an implication of our being-with Others, an acknowledgment of the collapse of is and ought within a deep community.

Although it is only one mode of relation, consider friendship within this community. Developing and maintaining friendship with other human beings requires a constant balance that cannot be mapped out or calculated, but rather lived. I will not ask my friend to die for me, but I may ask him to lend me a book, listen to some of my worries, or teach a class of mine when I must be out of town. And I am prepared to do the same *and more* in return. This is not essentially reciprocation. It is not a matter of contracts.

For the same reason, I will not steal from my friend. It has nothing to do with the fact that he has a right to property or because his sadness would increase the general disutility of the world. Such obligations and concerns are not fundamental; they arise only when the ethical nexus of being-together is already established and recognized. Such is the nature of friendship without fear. Someday, I may offer my life for my friend. But day to day, the relationship is sustained by offering time, conversation, and concern.

Each relationship is unique and requires its own rhythm. And this is true as well for friendship with animals. Snowball offered her attention, her concern, her protection to me as part of a sacrificial economy. I walked and ran with her, cared for her health, and spent cumulative hours scratching her chin and ears. There were times I let her down. We are always only practicing these relationships. Snowball and I could not discuss philosophy, but I do not discuss philosophy with my next door neighbor either, and the relationship does not suffer. Snowball and I shared mutual acquaintances and dreams. We had separate interests and goals. In short, we were friends.

It is true that we cannot befriend every animal around us, but the same is true of human beings. Friendship takes work, and thus there will always be merely a small circle of close friends. Technology, cities, capitalism—the mega-machine—make true friendship difficult. The common life is ripped apart; the initial conditions for friendship are not met. The metropolis packs strangers together; the telephone, television, and the Internet offer a reduced and interpreted presence of the Other. Animals, too, get lost in the mix. And we feel alone and frightened.

How can I know what to take when I do not know what is truly being offered? How can I know what to sacrifice when I do not know what is needed? I knew these things in relation to my dog because I knew my dog. It is knowledge and proximity, not domestication, that makes such friendship possible—and thus knowledge and proximity must be our goal. I do not know what would be required to know a cow or a bear or an egret. I've never shared a life with one. I am constantly struggling to know the squirrels, the ants, the frogs outside my door. It is difficult. They have been cast in so many cultural roles that it is hard to see them differently—hard to forgive the thieving squirrel when he takes the finest seeds from the bird feeder. So many local animals have been killed off; the ones that remain have been conceptually murdered by casting them as pests, vermin, infestations, and thieves.

I'm not even sure that I can learn what I need to know under my current conditions. We may have to leave our cities and our anonymity in order to begin to be-together in meaningful ways. But in the interim, I will not eat meat, I will not support factory farming, I will not presume that something is mine for the taking (there is no room for profit in a sacrificial economy) simply because it appears before me. And I will continue to frequent the wet grass where the frogs sit, contemplating, eating ants, taking and sacrificing appropriately. I think some of them are philosophers. Perhaps we have more in common.

The human womb is a fleshy place—the most sterile of environments. With only the absent presence of Others (at best), it is a space of being, of coming-to-be, and thus potential being-with. Free even of bacteria, it can support only the life of the baby. As the birthing process begins, so does the need for present Others. Nurturing takes many forms.

Deadly clean, the child must immediately acquire the thousands of bacteria that will make outer life possible. This he does as he slides through the vaginal canal, passes near the mother's anus at birth, and is handled by those awaiting his emergence. The mouth first, gasping for air, is colonized. Hours later, the nose and throat and armpits are infected. The bacteria consume the child, stabilizing their growth to live comfortably on his skin secretions. A few days later, the mother will be able to recognize her baby by smell—the consequence of the feast of micro-animals.

Stuffed animals await the child at home; he will learn to talk and think with animals and animal representations. A dog is pensive, recognizing the absence of the woman, the break from routine. Soon he, too, will learn the new child's scent. As the child will learn the dog's.

But now there is little awareness of the community in which he has been thrown. The baby cries to continue being; he cries to eat. He will search and suck and consume his mother's milk in an act of cannibalism we would never label as such. For some time, this will be his life: eating, being eaten, sleeping—punctuated by moments of crying that are as melodious as they are shrill. Sacrificially, these weeped notes rise up in offering as a gift—a recognition of his being and his need—asking presence in return.

And it is thus that we sing. Like the child passing through the graveyard. Like the whale reaching out into a liquid world. Like the sea in its chains, the bird, the newborn—announcing the joy and renouncing the terror of our collective being.

Notes

1. See Harriet Ritvo's account of Cumming in Harriet Ritvo, *The Animal Estate* (Cambridge, Mass.: Harvard University Press, 1987), pp. 241-288.

2. Ibid., p. 267.

3. Ibid., p. 266.

4. Ibid., p. 264.

5. Ibid., p. 270.

6. Charles Darwin as quoted by Stanley Rachman, *The Meaning of Fear* (Middlesex, England: Penguin Books, 1974), p. 26.

7. Alphonso Lingis, *Excesses: Eros and Culture* (Albany: State University of New York Press, 1983), p. 14.

8. Rachman, *The Meaning of Fear*, p. 33.

9. Ibid., p. 34.

10. Bill Gates, *The Road Ahead* (New York: Viking, 1995), p. 132.

11. Martin Heidegger, *Being and Time*, transl. John Macquarrie and Edward Robinson (San Francisco: Harper & Row, 1962), pp. 179–180.

12. Ibid., p. 392.

13. Douglas Adams and Mark Carwardine, "Meeting a Gorilla," *The Great Ape Project*, ed. Paola Cavalieri and Peter Singer (New York: St. Martin's Press, 1993), p. 21.

14. John Aspinall, *The Best of Friends* (New York: Harper & Row, 1976), p. 76.

15. Ibid., pp. 76–77.

16. Ibid., p. 77.

17. Lynn Rogers as quoted by Jeffrey Moussaieff Masson, *When Elephants Weep* (New York: Delacorte Press, 1995), p. 46.

18. Aspinall, *The Best of Friends*, p. 32.

19. Masson, *When Elephants Weep*, p. 61.

20. Ritvo, *The Animal Estate*, p. 212.

21. Midas Dekkers, *Dearest Pet*, transl. Paul Vincent (London: Verso, 1994), pp. 188–189.

22. Gerald Durrell, *The Ark's Anniversary* (New York: Arcade Publishing, 1991), pp. 127–128.

23. Cf. Betsy Swart, "The Chimp Farm," *The Great Ape Project*, ed. Cavalieri and Singer, pp. 291–295.

24. David Hancocks, *Animals and Architecture* (New York: Praeger Publishers, 1971), p. 179.

25. Stephen St. C. Bostock, *Zoos and Animal Rights* (London: Routledge, 1993), p. 70.

26. Aspinall, *The Best of Friends*, p. 74.

27. Ibid., pp. 139–140.

28. Bostock, *Zoos and Animal Rights*, p. 59.

29. Durrell, *The Ark's Anniversary*, pp. 128–129.

30. Eugene Linden, "A Curious Kinship: Apes and Humans," *National Geographic*, vol. 181, no. 3 (March 1992), p. 9.

31. See, for example, Aspinall, *The Best of Friends*, pp. 139, 149, 150.

32. Hancocks, *Animals and Architecture*, p. 179.

33. I have argued this specific point in other places. See H. Peter Steeves, *Founding Community* (Dordrecht: Kluwer, 1998); "The Boundaries of the Phenomenological Community: Non-Human Life and the Extent of our Moral Enmeshment," *Becoming Persons*, ed. Robert N. Fisher (Oxford: Applied Theology Press, 1995), pp. 777–797; "Husserl, Aristotle, and the Sphere of Ownness," *Southwest Philosophy Review*, vol. 12, no. 1 (1995), pp. 141–150.

34. Rachman, *The Meaning of Fear*, pp. 63–64.

35. This account is based largely on the one found in Ritvo, *The Animal Estate*, pp. 225–226.

36. Dekkers, *Dearest Pet*, pp. 179–180.

37. Durrell, *The Ark's Anniversay*, p. 147.

38. Ibid., p. 148.

39. Cf. Maureen Duffy, *Men and Beasts* (London: Paladin, 1984).

40. Dekkers, *Dearest Pet*, p. 123.

41. Carol J. Adams, "Bestiality: The Unmentioned Abuse," *The Animal's Agenda* v. 15, n. 6 (1 November 1995), pp. 30–31.

42. "Raising Your Dog with the Monks of New Skete" quoted in *Entertainment Weekly* no. 403 (31 October 1997), p. 115.

43. Dekkers, *Dearest Pet*, p. 172.

44. Bartholomew Anglicus as quoted by Anne Clark, *Beasts and Bawdy* (New York: Taplinger Publishing Company, 1975), p. 78.

45. Melitta Sperling, "Spider Phobias and Spider Fantasies," *Journal of the American Psychoanalytic Association*, v. 19 (1971), p. 493.

46. Simone de Beauvoir, *The Second Sex* (New York: Alfred A. Knopf, 1953), p. 443.

47. Ibid., p. 164.

48. From Wolfgang Lederer, *The Fear of Women* (New York: Grune & Stratton, 1968), p. 106.

49. de Beauvoir, *The Second Sex*, p. 386.

50. Lederer, *The Fear of Women*, p. 43.

51. Cavalieri and Singer, ed. *The Great Ape Project*, p. 115.

52. Ibid.

53. Dekkers, *Dearest Pet*, p. 3.

54. Cf. Lingis, *Excesses*, p. 73.

55. This quote and the account of Hartwell's story in general comes from Peter Tadman, *The Survivor* (Alberta, Canada: German and Gorman Ltd., 1991), pp. 41-42.

56. Ibid., p. 43.

57. Ibid., p. 135.

58. Ibid., p. 136.

59. Ibid., p. 156.

60. Ibid., p. 44.

61. Jan Grover interviewed by Judith Strasser on "To The Best of Our Knowledge," Wisconsin Public Radio, Program 97-05-11-C, Airdate November 16, 1997.

62. Quoted by David Comfort, *The First Pet History of the World* (New York: Simon & Schuster, 1994), p. 185.

63. Ibid., p. 195.

64. Ritvo, *The Animal Estate*, p. 237.

65. Ibid., p. 238.

66. Ibid.

67. Cf. Eli Sagan, *Cannibalism: Human Aggression and Cultural Form* (New York: Harper & Row, 1974), esp. pp. 27–34.

68. Ibid., pp. 75-76.

69. Raymond Corbey, "Ambiguous Apes," Cavalieri and Singer, ed. *The Great Ape Project*, p. 135.

70. See Susan Reid, "The Kwakiutl Man Eater," *Anthropologica* 21 (1979), pp. 247–275; Stanley Walens, *Feasting with Cannibals* (Princeton: Princeton University Press, 1981).

71. Walens, *Feasting with Cannibals*, p. 101.

72. Gene Logsdon, *The Contrary Farmer* (White River Junction, Vermont: Chelsea Green Publishing Company, 1995), pp. 50–51.

73. Ritvo, *The Animal Estate*, p. 28.

74. Plutarch, "On the Eating of Flesh," *Moralia*, vol. 12, transl. Harold Cherniss and W.C. Helmbold (Cambridge, Mass.: Harvard University Press, 1933), p. 541.

75. Ibid., p. 545.

76. Mary Stange, *Woman the Hunter* (Boston: Beacon Press, 1997), p. 120.

EIGHT

Transcendental Phenomenology and the Eco-Community

 James G. Hart

The first part of this chapter will deal with senses in which Edmund Husserl's transcendental phenomenology is compatible with forms of eco-philosophy; the second part will deal with how phenomenological senses of community embrace ecological concerns.

1. Transcendental Phenomenology and Eco-Philosophy

Although the theme of a universal monadology in Husserl makes contact with eco-philosophy, the basic principle of "consciousness" would seem to cast Husserl's thought into the framework of hopelessly anthropocentric or speciest traditions. In such a view, the transcendental ego would be identical with human beings and therefore a part of the whole would have arrogated to it a status surpassing a mere part. Such an understanding would misinterpret what Husserl intends by the transcendental ego. Nevertheless, it raises the important issue of whether human beings have any claim to a unique status within the whole and what the eco-ethical significance of this status might be. Eco-philosophers such as Paul Taylor[1] have urged that we distinguish between claims for human superiority based on

179

merit and those based on inherent worth. As to the first, Taylor argues that only humans are moral beings and thus they alone are the ones who can have moral merits or be deficient in such merits. Although his point is clear, it must be questioned whether or not it does justice to those animals which we associate most closely with human culture. Is, for example, the courage, loyalty, prudence, sympathy, etc. of dogs to be disdained as the mere corruption of the pure feral form exemplified in the wolf? But even if we grant forms of moral consciousness in some animals the human moral record taken for the most part is not such as to merit claims to superiority.

The second claim for human superiority, inherent worth, is, according to Taylor, due to the transposition of human class structures onto relationships with animals. Or it is due to an inflation of the capacity of reason, which is a property of human beings important for human life only but not of such significance as to entitle a claim of inherent superiority over animals. Or it is tied to the notion of soul which is either an unwarranted theological residue ("God's image") or it is, again, a celebration of thinking which is valuable only to humans. Indeed consciousness itself is of no value to many living things. All of these appeals to superior inherent worth have been used at times in the feeble form represented by Taylor. But I do not think it does justice to a central contention of the tradition. This central contention is reflected in eco-philosophy itself which almost universally recognizes that willy-nilly human beings, for better or for worse, are responsible for the consequences of their agency in nonhuman nature. Some thinkers would attribute this to a kind of moral deficiency: If human beings had not arrogated to themselves a status transcending that of one member-species of the ecosystem and if they had lived within their proper natural limits, mindful of the inherent value of the other species and members, then the responsibility for others would not be an issue. It is the crisis caused by human arrogance which generates the theme of human global responsibility.

All of this is true, but it neglects another consideration. When human beings automatically and mindlessly live within their biological niche they are inauthentic, behaving improperly, etc. Thus philosophy exhorts them to their natural determination or capacity to be reasonable, and this involves taking account of the evident surroundings or of all that is evident as the context of life. And when they do not do this, it is often a result of repressing this evident context of life. Thus emerges the thesis that willy-nilly, humans live in the world and not merely a natural environment pre-determined by their genetic make-up. By "world" is meant the implicit context of all experience and the whole which comes up for consideration in both practical and theoretical matters. For this reason we have eco-philosophy—that is, descriptions, arguments, and preferred forms of evidence which point out both the human arrogance as well as the appropriate dimensions in which human beings are part of an ecosystem which is a larger whole. These considerations implicitly disclose how human beings live not only pre-programmed in an environment, analogous to the slug or deer, but also within the seemingly connected endless whole which eco-philosophy aspires to describe and make evident.

To say that arguments, evidence, truth, etc. are, in some sense, the result of the pre-programming of innate endowments is, of course, not false, but it is on the verge of saying that knowing, theory, science, etc. are not such—are not knowing, theory, science, etc.—but only the necessary constituted environment of human beings in the way that a silhouette of a hawk is an ingredient of the cognitive scheme of a chipmunk. But knowing that chipmunks have such schemata or knowing that I have similar schemata are not the same as having such schemata. Not only is there no relationship of biological necessity in knowing, but the necessity involved in knowing, for example, the necessity of evidence or logical implication is of a different kind than a biological necessity.[2] Whether some animals have a theoretic capacity is not precluded. One sign of it would be their collaboration in the pursuit of eco-philosophy.

As various philosophers have emphasized, we must distinguish between the way animals have, or exist in, a natural environment and the way the human type exists in the world. There is a capacity in higher-animals, most conspicuously in most human beings, not to be totally involved in the importunities of life's drives and the closed form of the goals of these drives. This is a capacity to be aware of myself and to be able to detach myself from the present urgencies in favor of taking up another perspective. By this ability, we can appreciate the same as other and the other as the same; this is eventually to appreciate it as named, as an object with properties, and thus as present in a way which is indifferent to its presence or absence and indifferent as well to its associative pull and to its relationship to our needs.³ This is a way of saying that humans exist in the world as the ultimate context of all there is and not merely in a natural environment.

In the Aristotelian-Thomist tradition there is a sense of "ontological dignity" which can do justice to this feature of human (and perhaps some other animal) being and yet need not be an occasion for *hybris*. Intellect as the desire and capacity to be intentionally united with the forms of all other things gives to the beings with intellect a participation in the existence and life of all other beings which is not enjoyed by beings without intellect.⁴ For Aristotle and the scholastics, therefore, humans are different from animals that are proscribed by or restricted to a single form, entelechy, or environment; human animals are by nature, rather, "in a certain respect everything." Of course we might speculate with Alfred North Whitehead that all entities ("actual occasions" and "societies of occasions") may be imagined to "prehend" the entire cosmos; but this is not a conscious participation in the entire cosmos. In so far as human beings are at least potentially intentionally "connatural" with all being they are the "shepherds of being," as Martin Heidegger once put it. Or, as the religious tradition has it, this is in part what is meant by being the image of God and having stewardship.

But this tradition also held that there were beings of infinitely greater ontological dignity than the human species/essence, namely angels, each of which was a species unto itself and, therefore, each of which was as different from one another as an elephant from a fly (St. Thomas Aquinas). Now it turns out that angels—although infinitely superior to humans in ontological dignity because of their unique intuitive intellectual/spiritual powers—were not the center of value of the universe in terms of its salvation. From the eco-philosophical viewpoint something similar might be entertained: Human beings might well be said to have a superior "ontological dignity" but they presently embody demonic forces, "powers and principalities," going about devouring the earth. The well-being of the earth might well lie in letting other species of lesser ontological dignity be more at the center of the stage of the world's salvation. Their well-being is to be fostered at the expense of human convenience, habit, material progress, and so forth. Whether contemporary humans can or ought to make room for beings of superior ontological dignity analogous to the ancient notions of angels, a proposal found in some science-fiction accounts of extra-terrestrials, remains to be seen. As it is arrogance for human beings to assume moral or biotic superiority over other species, so it would be a form of arrogance to rule out this possibility. From a purely philosophical point of view, banking on it seems silly.

But such a consideration does not get at the transcendental phenomenological issue of the transcendental ego. Part of the sense of the transcendental ego is reflected in the etymology of *Bewusst-Sein* (most often translated as "consciousness"), the manifestness or knowness of being. For Husserl, being is inseparable from manifestation and that to which the manifestation occurs. If we think of the transcendental ego as an essential, ineliminable aspect of being, as the dative of manifestation, or that to which being, as all that appears, appears, then we may see that the human being, with all its "ontological dignity," is merely one among the beings that appear. Still, it would seem fitting that there be a connection between the transcendental ego and human being as the "place" where being discloses itself (cf. Heidegger's *Da-Sein* or the shepherd of being).

Yet being discloses itself in some way to each of the all of monads. That is, every center of consciousness is itself a dative of manifestation or that to which being discloses itself. Of course the starfish does not seem aware of the world as such or being as being. Being discloses itself to the starfish within the frame of the starfish's closed environment—a closure determined by its drives and instincts, or, if one prefers, by its genes. Perhaps there is a feeble analogy in the way the world might be disclosed to someone through a picture which he took to be all there is, and not as one picture among many in a gallery. This picture might well be an exquisite rendering of the world to which the other viewers (not belonging to his family/species) had no first-person access.

The transcendental ego is not one of the perspectives within the all but that to which the all of perspectives is present, if, for the most part, only so in an empty, presumptive way. And each Other, each other monad, is present to the transcendental ego as a transcendental ego, that is, as one to whom the all of Others or perspectives is present. The moral dimension of respect, I have elsewhere argued,[5] is inherent in the empathic presentation, what Husserl calls *Einfühlung*, of Others. Whereas affixing moral respect to ecosystems

or entelechies does not seem appropriate, surely awe and wonder are.
(Here we face a problem analogous to Immanuel Kant's "respect" for
the "law.")

Part of the meaning of Husserl's monadology is: The all is comprised of datives of manifestation; the world is the all constituted by
the reciprocity of perspectives. The divine is the synthesis of actual
perspectives as well as the ideal perspective of each within the all. It
is not one of the monads, not a transcendental I, but the entelechy
and Ideal of the all of monads. In this respect, there is more affinity
between Arne Naess' deep ecology of Self-Realization and Husserl
than between Husserl and the eco-philosophies of Paul Taylor and
Holmes Rolston III for whom there would seem to be a problem of
the unity of "nature" as a unification of ecosystems, which, in turn,
are a unity of entelechies or dynamic forms.[6] These latter thinkers
have rejected monadological considerations in so far as these are
bound to consciousness as the ultimate principle. And they have
urged that their descriptions demand some sense of "respect" for
these impersonal ecosystems which are more basic than individual
organisms or even species.

Yet, Leibniz, Husserl, and Whitehead extended the notion of consciousness to include forms of what are usually regarded as unconsciousness. Rolston, instead of positing conscious centers as ultimate,
favors Aristotelian-like entelechies or morphological fields—that is,
formal and final causes, which are unconscious principles of organization and which include and transcend forms of consciousness in the
organization of nature.[7] Value, in this framework, thus is independent of intentional acts. Somewhat surreptitiously, however, the
Leibnizian/Whiteheadian theme of universal unconscious feeling or
mind is disseminated everywhere: not only conscious beings but also
genes, molecules, organisms, species-forms, and most importantly
ecosystems "strive for" and "seek" values, "promote" their ways of life,
their normative forms of existence.[8]

For Rolston (as well as, seemingly, for Taylor), the most basic,
encompassing consideration is the ecosystem. It includes within it
the various specific entelechies or dynamic forms which are more
basic and of more value than the individuals because, from an ecological point of view, the individuals are the vehicles for the realization of the values of the species. The ecosystem itself, however, is
more basic than the species. It is the community as a whole. As each

species makes more individuals of its kind, so the ecosystem makes more kinds, generating ever-richer community. Unlike the organisms that are centers of consciousness seeking their own normative form of existence, the ecosystem is a decentered and unconscious system employing conflict, competition, and chance to enrich the community. The ethical perspective therefore cannot make the category mistake of orienting the whole by what is featured in one species. Rather, all species must take their bearings from the description of the ecosystem's efforts to produce the best biotic community, that is, one which enables a maximum number of species to flourish.[9]

In the second half of this chapter I want to reflect on eco-philosophical understandings of community, but here I wish to dwell on the theme that the "perspective" of the ecosystem is the appropriate one for eco-philosophical ethics. In Rolston we have left behind all senses of consciousness and are now dealing with a "wilder, more logical because more biological" ethical perspective.[10] Yet this perspective is a result of a philosophical description—dependent on science and scientific theory—wherein the "ought" of the description is "*not so much derived from an 'is,'* as discovered simultaneously with it."[11]

Three points here:

(1) The establishment of an ethics from a description of essential states of affairs or at least prominent *Gestalts* with their own kinds of necessity or near necessity would be welcomed not only by Aristotle but also by Husserl. What is to be greeted here is an effort to establish the unity of the world and the unity of reason. But how we hold together the propositional or descriptive account of the world and the deontic realm is the great problem. What kinds of bridges are there between the "is" and the "ought"?[12]

(2) Insisting on the dependence of philosophy on the most recent developments in natural science or indeed on any natural scientific theory would seem to be the death-knell of the integrity of philosophy, certainly as phenomenology understands it. And surely Darwinism does not provide the kind of adequate evidence capable of serving as a first principle of philosophy. Natural scientific theory may inform our reflections on the phenomenon of development, the manifest surds and anomalies of biological experience, etc. But development, species fields/entelechies, surds, randomness, biological anomalies,

history, etc. may be thematized independently of natural scientific theories and Darwinian theory. Thus the eco-philosophical position need not be a handmaid of science or Darwinian speculation. It is one thing to be enriched and informed by science, but it is quite another for philosophy to derive its principles from natural science and Darwinian theory.

(3) The claim for the philosophical ultimacy of the perspective of the ecosystem does not eliminate mind or consciousness. After all, it is, as we have learned, a philosophical description informed by science. Mind or consciousness has not been eliminated; it is merely suppressed and anonymously functioning in the description. The thematization of the ecosystem merely naïvely subsumes, and regards as negligible within its frame, all senses of consciousness and animal or human mind. But from what perspective is this account of the ecosystem given? Is it an account from the ideal scientific observer who is nowhere and everywhere, at no time and all times? Does it itself aspire to be the "perspective" of the ecosystem which, properly understood, is not a perspective but The True System, Absolute Spirit/Sport, generating the optimum biotic community? Or is it merely a perspective on, indeed an interpretation of, a state of affairs, the best that a particular finite (in this case, human) mind can do at the moment? Whichever of these or other options one might choose, all are achievements of mind and manifest to mind. In what sense then has one really eliminated mind from the scene? These are some of the issues which Husserl's transcendental ego raises about the eco-philosophical elimination of mind in favor of the ecosystem. But this position is a far cry from saying that the human species transcends the biotic web of relations in such a way that it is biotically superior to all the other species and ecosystems. Rather it is an ontological determination, that is, a determination of being's inseparability from manifestation and mind.

2. "We Monads" and the Biotic Community

Aldo Leopold's now famous statement, "The land ethic simply enlarges the boundaries of the community to include soils, waters, plants, and animals, or collectively, the land," has generated a basic question in eco-philosophy. How are we to understand this community? Is it a community of quasi-persons? If so, what is our model today? The nation-state? The metropolitan center? The village? The family? Or is it the quasi-moral community of organisms in the mutually dependent web of life where there is a more or less automatic unconscious "pursuit" of the individual good in connection with the overall good of the larger organism? Or is it a sense of community defined by a non-moral random ecosystem wherein "community" gets stretched to embrace conflict, competition, forms of aggression, survival of the fittest, etc.?[13] The attempt at objective, impartial, scientific descriptions of the "biotic community" seems to oscillate, admitting considerable crossover and variation between, on the one hand, communitarian-like interpretations of a nature suffused with a motif of mutual aid, decenteredness, and altruism, and, on the other, interpretations wherein aggression, competition, and chance prevail. In both cases, the description of the way "Nature" truly is tends to serve as an exemplar for the human community, or at least it functions as a guide to human dealings with other members or ingredients of the biotic community.

One reason for the divergence in the description depends on the metaphysical understanding of nature and whether room is made for the category of spirit and, if so, how spirit and nature are to be connected. If eco-philosophy becomes a doctrinal equation with a form of naturalism that eliminates spirit or that reduces spirit to a kind of epiphenomenon of nature, matters get as oversimplified as when nature is reduced to an unfortunate accident of spirit. Using a naturalist sense of nature is "more logical because more biological" only if the elimination of senses of spirit prevail. But it is the hesitation to simplify matters that accounts in great part for the rich complexity of contemporary discussions within eco-philosophy.[14]

I propose, independent of a resolution to these important issues, that human beings can say "we" of the "biotic community" and, even more so, of nonhuman animal persons in ways analogous to how human beings say "we" with reference to one another.[15]

We must distinguish among senses of "we." The most elemental sense of "we" is derived from the presumptive "to us all" of the world's publicity. Things within the world appear to me, but they appear to me as having the feature of appearing the same to us all in spite of and through our necessarily differing perspectives. This is basically what Husserl means by the world appearing as "the same for us all." The realm of the *polis* is born out of this presumptive "us" and "we" in so far as one of its basic functions is to confirm and secure the *res publica*, the common world with its common goods, as indeed not only presumptively but actually our common affair. The sense of "we"/"us" as tied to the publicity of the world is basic to all other senses; without them the others would not be possible. It is complicated enormously with the inclusion of the biotic community because in this case it is evident that the same world appears to us all, but its sameness, how it appears, what from the human standpoint may be regarded as its categorial features, are not clear in most instances, except for the few animals with whom we are able to enter into something resembling a conversation.

This "we"/"us" is typically anonymously functioning and provides but a loose sense of community. Motorists in rush hour, bathers at the beach, or pedestrians in a crowded mall all have a sense of the world being evident to, for example, us motorists, bathers, and pedestrians; but this is not really a proper sense of community. In such instances we need not communicate, and what we have to do might well be done in the absence of Others; in such a case, we live next to one another but not with and in one another. This holds even more so for how I might vaguely be aware of the snail, butterfly, and bee also attending to the same flower. In which case "we" would all behold the flower. But would we all behold it as the same for us all? Would we all have the category of publicity? Even if we would, it would not necessarily be like the friends looking at the flower together or like the empathetic ecologist looking at the flower with his/her friends, the snail, bee, and butterfly. In the case of friends, the perspective of the Others enters into and shapes mine, and mine enters into and shapes the Others'; in the rush hour case, the presence of Others is a matter of indifference; in the ecological case, only the ecologist's perspective is clearly shaped, although we cannot rule out the possibility of a modification in the perspective of the nonhuman animals.

The notorious authoritarian or wishful senses of "we," that is, the royal or editorial usages, presume to include all the Others but with indifference to the differing perspectives. In such cases I either autocratically will that Others be subsumed under my own will or perspective or I appeal to Others in order that they may be included in my perspective or relinquish their opposition. These familiar senses of "we" call attention to the consideration that "we" is an achievement (an indexical and performative) which properly is realized when it appropriately, not willfully or merely wishfully, represents Others. Thus typically I say "we" to Others (or an Other) who for some reason are not coincident with "us" for whom I speak.

Of course to represent Others I must intend them. But when saying "we," I obviously do not intend them in the first-person. I can only say "I" in reference to me. Nor are they the second-person referent, the "you" to whom I say "we." Nor do I intend them in the third-person. I am not intending "them," that is, Peter, Paul, and Mary, when I am addressing you with the "we" which includes Peter, Paul, and Mary. I am not talking about them nor thinking of them when I say "we." Rather I apperceive them as an ingredient of what I do and say, and therefore I intend them in the way I am aware of myself in my doing and saying. (Husserl called this, following Leibniz, an "apperception"; but "appresentation," which he restricts to my awareness of Others, seems also fitting for "we.") Thus "we" is first-person reference, but plural and not singular.

Yet I may do this only if I am empowered by them through an immediate or mediate second-person agreement. You empower me to say "we." Or another person may be empowered by you to tell me that I am empowered by you.

"I" does not misfire; it has a kind of inerrancy.[16] "You" can misfire; I can be deceived thinking it is you I am perceiving when in fact I am not. Similarly, I can be mistaken in regard to my intending Others in the third person, that is, in regard to him, her, or them. Likewise, "we" can misfire. I can falsely believe that I have the right to include you when in fact I do not. The reference of "I" has a certain adequacy and apodicticity which "we" does not have. In this respect, "we" resembles second- and third-person reference.

Thus there are conditions involved in my saying "we." These are the conditions of both my apperception/appresentation and representation of the Others. I have to have appresented you, that is, become aware of you as involved in my self-consciousness and agency.

If I see you doing what I am doing but next to and independently of me, there is a non-communitarian sense of us both doing the same thing (for example, we are both riding bikes). But that is different from riding a tandem bike or riding our own bikes but riding together on an outing. The latter is more like playing music together, preparing and having a picnic, or carrying on a good conversation or discussion. I take these to be exemplary forms of community. Each person's will is part of the Other's will and wants what the Other wants as the Other wants it. There is both a unique common will and common good. This is different from the universal drives, for example, of hunger or sex. Such drives can become communitarian through the interpenetration of wills that builds on the prior overarching sameness of the drive or instinct.

You can become unified with my self-consciousness when you make known your views to me, when they agree with mine, and when you ask me to represent that fact to Others. Then I can say "'we'/'us,'" "our point of view," and "we believe. . . ."

But I can also represent our picnic or bike ride in your absence, saying, "And then we did this . . . and then we felt that . . . ," etc. Here I must appresent both your point of view and your willingness that I speak on your behalf. And I can be mistaken on both accounts. My appresentation of your point of view is clearly foundational; and being wrong about your willingness to be represented is even more grievous than a misfiring.

When dealing with most members of the biotic community I am not able to regard them (as you regard me) as one who refers to himself as I. Humans have notorious difficulty referring to other animals as "you" and as in some sense capable of a kind of self-reference. (I will return to this.) And in many cases where I do this, for example, with my cats and dogs, I have confidence that I know their intentions from observing their behavior in the third-person as well as from our mutual efforts at communication. This, of course, is what a parent of an infant would say as well as the parent of a mentally handicapped child.

A basic question here is whether a being which is incapable of self-reference and self-consciousness can experience us as beings with self-consciousness and self-reference.[17] The lion pursuing us after smelling our blood presumably does not experience us as self-conscious or as *Da-Sein*, whereas some forms of (human) sadism might well be tied to such an appresentation. A being without self-consciousness, an "externus consciousness," can be conscious in the sense of being totally taken up with or aware of the objects in his or her field of perception and thereby be, at the same time, utterly without any pre-reflexive self-awareness. Whether this can characterize humans is a debated issue. Some thinkers have wanted to distinguish neatly animal from human consciousness on this basis.

In referring to beings with such externus consciousness we would not need the quasi-indicator or quasi-indexical of "he himself" or "she herself" by which we impute to Others (in the third-person) self-awareness and a kind of self-reference, as in "The editor of *Noûs* thinks that he himself is a millionaire." In the case of "The editor of *Noûs* thinks that he is a millionaire" the speaker is not necessarily ascribing to the editor of *Noûs* the belief that he, the editor of *Noûs*, is aware that he (the editor of *Noûs*) is a millionaire and that the editor and millionaire are the same person.

One justification for killing or experimenting on some animals is that they are not being violated with cruelty because they are essentially "externus" or non-self-conscious forms of consciousness. Pain involves the self being affected without the self referring to itself. Can there be a self as a center of pain independent of the power for some sense of self-reference and self-consciousness? Is this not a place where both empirical-scientific observation and philosophical theory must work together or is there a purely analytical-essential issue here?

In any case it seems likely that there are animal forms of consciousness in which it would not be possible to use the quasi-indicator, such that we could say, "Ellie the earthworm believes that she herself is cause of this soil enrichment." This is perhaps because it is not clear that we can ascribe proper belief-attitudes to most kinds of animals. I will not pursue here the possibility that belief-intentions may have an essential connection with self-consciousness and self-reference.

Nevertheless, as with all members of the biotic community and even the biotic community itself taken as a whole or an ecosystem, we may think of analogous (Aristotelian) *tele* or, as some prefer, "interests" which would be, for the most part, essentially unconscious. This, again, is analogous to the situation of the parent of the infant or of the mentally handicapped child. The parent is aware of and responsible for the interests of the child in a way the child is not aware of them.

In the case of the biotic community, the authentic use of "we" by human beings involves something of a paradox. The use of "we" is most appropriate when the human beings remove themselves from the position of being able to represent the other members. In this sense human beings are most authentic members when they mute the use of "we." Any approximation of an appropriate saying of "we" would, of course, be based on the appresentation of the other members as embodied in the individual human or collective agency. That is, there is the awareness that the good of each is bound up with the good of all and that humans willy-nilly act in such a way that the well-being of the other members of the biotic community is affected. But there is the stubborn difficulty of authentically representing Others with whom one cannot enter into a conversation and/or whose interests one cannot presume to know.

In so far as humans have used "we" inclusive of the biotic community, it has typically been in the inauthentic forms of the royal, willful mode or the editorial, wishful mode. Another reason for the muting of the use of "we" is the difficulty of determining to whom the biotic community says "we"; who is the "you" being addressed who is outside this community? There is an outside only in prayer to a "being" who is in some respects transcendent or when parts of this community are, for whatever reason, fragmented against itself—as in we who are holding off the lion.

The birth of the rediscovery of subsistence economics seems to be, in part, centered around this necessity for human beings to remove themselves from the position to presume to say "we" and thereby mean to intend the biotic community. In contrast to the modern megamachinal economy where the work and biotic conditions of culture and financial well-being are rendered anonymous and invisible, there is advocacy of the pursuit of a new kind of *oikonomia* or householding which does not render invisible the consequences of our everyday economic agency. The new subsistence economic theory is keenly aware that the devastation of the rest of the biotic community caused by thoughtless human agency is an inherent feature of the megamachinal economy—which is to say a feature, as well, of the capitalist economy.[18]

In a transformation of membership in the biotic community, human beings would most properly say "we" when they were less in a position to say "we." They would resist representing what can only be invisible or anonymously present to them. But this transformation is not a recommendation that humans not appresent the rest of the biotic community and enter into a state of unconsciousness. The essential publicity of the world as the same for us all involves the ineluctable appresentation of all the Others. Following such a recommendation would not only involve the suppression of the "ontological dignity" of human beings, and perhaps some other nonhuman persons, but it would also lead to a more wanton destruction of the biotic community.

Notes

1. Paul W. Taylor, "The Ethics of Respect for Nature," *Environmental Philosophy: From Animal Rights to Radical Ecology*, eds. Michael E. Zimmerman, J. Baird Callicott, George Sessions, Karen J. Warren, John Clark (Englewood Cliffs, NJ: Prentice Hall, 1993), pp. 75–82. Hereafter this volume will be referred to as EP. See also Taylor's *Respect for Nature: A Theory of Environmental Ethics* (Princeton, NJ: Princeton University Press, 1993).

2. Husserl's critiques of "psychologism" in the Prolegomena to the *Logische Untersuchungen* (Tübingen: Max Niemeyer Verlag, 1968) are the basis for my reflections here.

3. The following authors by no means say the same thing but they are united in seeing the human animal as not merely ecstatically taken up with its environment but rather eccentric to or capable of a kind of transcendence of this environment's here and now importunities. See, for example, Robert Sokolowski, *Presence and Absence: A Philosophical Investigation of Language and Being* (Bloomington: Indiana University Press, 1978, 1996), especially ch. 1; Iso Kern, *Die Idee und Methode der Philosophie* (Berlin: de Gruyter, 1975); Max Scheler, *Man's Place in Nature* (New York: Noonday Press, 1978), ch. 2; Helmut Plessner, *Die Stufen des Organischen und der Mensch* (Berlin: de Gruyter, 1965), ch. VII; C. I. Lewis, *Values and Imperatives* (Stanford: Stanford University Press, 1969); C. I. Lewis, *The Good and Nature of the Right* (New York: Columbia University Press, 1955).

4. See, for example, Yves Simon, *Metaphysics of Knowledge*, transl. Vukan Kuic and Richard J. Thompson (New York: Fordham University Press, 1990), ch. 1.

5. See James G. Hart, *The Person and the Common Life* (Dordrecht: Kluwer, 1992), ch. 3.

6. See Arne Naess, *Ecology, Community, and Life-Style* (Cambridge, England: Cambridge University Press, 1990), especially ch. 7.

7. Holmes Rolston III, "Challenges in Environmental Ethics," EP, p. 141. See also Rolston *Ecology, Economics, Ethics: The Broken Circle* (New

Haven, London: Yale University Press, 1991). For the theme of entelechy in Husserl, see my "Entelechy in Transcendental Phenomenology: A Sketch of the Foundations of Husserlian Metaphysics," *American Catholic Philosophical Quarterly*, LXVI:2 (1992), pp. 189–212. The most elaborate ontological treatment of the topic in the phenomenological tradition is to be found in Hedwig Conrad-Martius, *Der Selbstaufbau der Natur: Entelechien und Energien* (Munich: Koesel, 1961). For a recent more popular but competent resurrection of the theme, see Rupert Sheldrake, *The Presence of the Past: Morphic Resonance and the Habits of Nature* (New York: Vintage, 1988).

8. Rolston, "Challenges in Environmental Ethics," p. 141.

9. Ibid., pp. 151–153.

10. Ibid., p. 144.

11. Ibid., p. 156.

12. In my wrestle with the "'is'/'ought'" in Husserl's social ethics in ch. IV of my *The Person and the Common Life*, I was blissfully oblivious of many of the issues which Hector-Neri Castañeda discusses in *Thinking and Doing* (Dordrecht: Reidel, 1975).

13. Cf. Mark Sagoff, "Animal Liberation and Environmental Ethics: Bad Marriage, Quick Divorce," EP, p. 84.

14. By this I wish to include Rolston, whom I regard as one of the richest voices in the field. See, for example, Rolston, "Challenges in Environmental Ethics."

15. For more detail in regard to "we" (but not the biotic community) in what follows, cf. my *The Person and the Common Life*, ch. 3, 5, and 6; also "I, We, and God," *Husserl-Ausgabe und Husserl Forschung*, ed. Samuel IJsseling (Dordrecht: Kluwer, 1990), pp. 125–149; and "'We,' Representation, and War Resistance," *Phenomenology, Interpretation, and Community*, eds. Lenore Langsdorf and Stephen H. Watson, with Marya Bower (Albany: State University Press of New York, 1996), pp. 126–144.

16. This is a pervasive theme in Husserl but most recently and ably defended by Hector-Neri Castañeda in numerous writings. For a brief statement see his "On the Phenomeno-Logic of the I," *Proceedings of the XIVth International Congress of Philosophy*, 3 (1968), pp. 260–266.

17. For this theme and what immediately follows I am dependent on some of Hector-Neri Castañeda's basic themes. See, for example, his *Thinking, Language, and Experience* (Minneapolis: University of Minnesota Press, 1989).

18. For recent literature, see Rudolf Bahro, *Avoiding Social and Ecological Disaster* (Bath, England: Gateway, 1994); *Woman: The Last Colony*, eds. Maria Mies, Veronika Bennholdt-Thomsen, Claudia von Werlhof

(London: Zed, 1988); Maria Mies and Vandana Shiva, *Ecofeminism* (London: Zed, 1993). See especially all the recent writings of Claudia von Werlhof (Innsbruck); for example, *Was haben die Huenher mit dem Dollar zu tun? Frauen und Oekonomie* (Munich: Frauenoffensive, 1991); "Im Grunde gibt es vor lauter Oekonomie keine Kultur mehr," *Der kalte Blick der Oekonomie*, eds. Arno Bamme, Wilhelm Berger, Caroline Gerschlager, Luise Guitzer (Vienna: Profil Verlag, 1993). For some of the foundations of this recent literature besides Marx's critique of capitalism, not necessarily his positive program, see Marshall Sahlins, *Stone Age Economics* (New York: Aldine de Gruyter, 1972); Ivan Illich, *Tools for Conviviality* (New York: Haper & Row, 1973); and Karl Polanyi, *The Great Transformation* (Boston: Beacon, 1944).

NINE

Life Beyond the Organism: Animal Being in Heidegger's Freiburg Lectures, 1929–30

William McNeill

"No doubt," Martin Heidegger wrote in 1939, "a good deal of time has yet to pass before we learn to see that the idea of 'organism' and of the 'organic' is a purely modern, mechanistic-technological concept."[1] According to this concept, living beings in general are interpreted as self-making artifacts—that is, as beings that emerge into their presence at hand in accordance with the rule of a preexisting form or *eidos*.

In its modern, technological configuration, the idea and *eidos* of each and every being is understood as a representation produced by the activity of the self-representing human subject, a subject that, through its own activity, produces, orders, and sets in place before itself and for itself all entities in their being (in their possible presence at hand) including itself. In this technological self-assertion of absolute subjectivity, the human subject is not only one organism among others, it is the organism of all organisms. Yet although the idea of "organism" as a self-making artifact becomes a central concept only in modernity, via the transformation of subjectivity undertaken philosophically by Descartes, the historical roots of this conception of life go back much further, namely, to the beginnings of science in Greek philosophy—beginnings on which Heidegger never ceased to meditate. In the present chapter, I propose to examine at some length Heidegger's most detailed and explicit analyses of living beings—analyses presented in a lecture course at the University of Freiburg during 1929–30 and which problematize the modern conception of living beings as organisms.

My purpose in this chapter will be threefold. First, I shall try to give a detailed overview of the most central analyses, with particular attention to Heidegger's attempt to distinguish animal life from human life. Second, I shall try to situate these analyses within the context of Heidegger's critical retrieval and transformation of the philosophical (Platonic and Aristotelian) foundations of our scientific and technological conception of the world. Third, in so doing I hope not only to illuminate the historical and critical force of these analyses, but to show why Heidegger's claims concerning the animal should not be regarded as another essentialist or humanist "theory" of the nature of animal life. This work will, I hope, contribute not only to existing debate surrounding this particular lecture course of Heidegger's,[2] but also to wider philosophical debates, especially in recent, post-Heideggerian French thought, concerning our conceptions of life in relation to ecological responsibility.[3]

1. Introduction: The Soul, Unity of the Body

A living being is generally understood as an organism that has various organs. Yet what exactly is an "organism"? What is the relation between the unity of the organism, classically defined as the "soul," and the individual sense organs: eyes, ears, etc.?

The question of the relation between the unity of a living being and its various sense organs was raised in a decisive form by Socrates in Plato's dialogue *Theaetetus*, not with respect to living beings in general, but specifically with respect to the human being. The issue arises in the context of a dialogue concerning the essence of human knowledge. The initial answer proposed is that knowing is *aisthesis*, sense perception, an apprehending via the senses. Yet what is it that does the perceiving in sense perception? Do we, Socrates asks, see with our eyes and hear with our ears? Or does the perception or apprehending of something necessarily involve something more than our specific sense organs? What does it mean to say that we see "with" our eyes? Is it the eyes as sense organs that do the seeing? Who or what is it that is seeing? Who or what is the "we" who see? Certainly, our specific sense organs are necessarily involved in all sense perception: we cannot see a sensible object without our eyes. Yet does this mean that it is the eyes as sense organs that actually do the seeing? Suppose that this were the case, says Socrates. Suppose that our eyes were actually doing the seeing, that our ears were hearing sounds, our nose were smelling, our tongue were tasting. This state of affairs, as Socrates puts it, would be uncanny. For each particular sense organ perceives its *own* particular sense object: the ear hears sounds, the eye sees color, and even our sense of touch is different at different points of the body. The various capacities for sense perception are dispersed throughout different locations on the body. There would thus be vision at one point of the body, hearing at another, and so on. Such a state of affairs would be truly uncanny, since there would be no one there who could both see *and* hear *and* smell simultaneously. There would be no *one* there, no unity or unifying activity in which the various senses could belong together and *be* at one and the same time. Thus, Socrates argues, in order for there to be *someone* who sees, hears, smells, and so on, these senses must "reach toward something like *one* idea [*eis mian tina idean*], whether we call it soul [*psuche*] or something else." (184 d1f)

Socrates' argument makes it clear that, in human apprehending at least, the sense organs (in Greek, *organon*) per se are not that which actively do the perceiving; rather, they are only that *through which* perception occurs. The sense organs are merely channels or "instruments" of perception, as the Greek *organon* (tool, implement) implies. The activity of perceiving as such is accomplished by the soul, by the apprehending or "seeing" (*noein*) of something more than the particulars disclosed by the various senses, namely, the unity of their belonging together in *one idea*, in one "vision." We cannot here examine the astonishing detail with which Heidegger in his 1931–32 course on Plato's *Republic* and *Theaetetus* analyzes the Socratic argument, but it is worth noting his emphasis that the Greek *idea* here (and the *noein* and *dianoein* it implies) does not yet refer to a *nonsensible* form opposed to the realm of *aisthesis*. *Idea* means, rather, "something seen in its being seen" (*das Gesichtete in seinem Gesichtetsein*), the *being seen* of a unity that has been sighted.[4] The apprehending (*noein*) of this unity throughout (*dia*) all differentiation of the senses and their objects is not simply an apprehending that occurs *by way of* the sense organs conceived as "instruments," but an apprehending that *stretches throughout* the various channels of sense perception, relates them to one another, and holds them together in their unity. It is on the basis of such a unity that any dispersion of sense perception is possible, a perceiving of "this *and not* that." Our sensuous, bodily dispersion is a dispersion *in* gathering and a gathering or unifying *in* dispersion. As gathering and unifying in advance of any sensory apprehending of particulars, the soul (which is here not yet isolated as an entity, but conceived and seen as an "activity," a being-seen) is, as Heidegger puts it, nothing other than that stretching (*Erstreckung*) that stretches throughout the various sense organs, enabling a gathered relating to sense-objects. It is the presence of soul as this relational stretching (the striving of Plato's *eros*) that first enables something corporeal to become organ-like, to be a body. "Only thus can something corporeal [*ein Körper*] become a body [*Leib*]."[5]

This Platonic view of the unitary being of a living body in relation to its sense organs carries a certain truth and persuasiveness with respect to the human body and its manner of existing. But does it also have certain limitations? Furthermore, can this view legitimately be extended to apply to all living beings, human and nonhuman? May plants and animals also be said to "have" a soul in this manner? We know that Aristotle will subsequently understand the soul as the form (*eidos*) of a natural body that is able to live; as such, the soul is said to be the primary actuality or "entelechy" (*entelecheia*) of any body that has organs, whether plant, animal, or human. (*De Anima*, 412 a20ff) Although Aristotle provides an extremely careful phenomenological analysis of the differences between various genera and species of living being, and although he denies that animals or plants in general have *nous* (the capacity of *noein*), his analyses nevertheless open the way for understanding each and every living being as a kind of "organism."

2. The Organism and its Organs

In his Freiburg lecture course from winter semester 1929–30, *The Fundamental Concepts of Metaphysics: World, Finitude, Solitude*,[6] Heidegger attempts to indicate what is problematic about the

Platonic-Aristotelian approach to understanding living beings, and especially animals, in terms of a fundamental form and principle called the soul. More precisely, he problematizes not so much the Platonic or Aristotelian conceptions per se, but their modern interpretation that makes itself known in contemporary scientific and technical conceptions of living beings as "organisms." According to such conceptions, an animal is basically an organism that has various organs. Each of the organs performs various functions that serve the underlying end of maintaining the organism itself as a whole. What the organism itself is and is capable of appears to be determined by the organs that it has. For example, it is evident that only those living organisms that have eyes can see. Having eyes is clearly a precondition of seeing; it makes vision possible.

But what does it mean to "have" eyes? And is seeing simply a result of having eyes? In the 1929–30 course, Heidegger begins his elucidation of the essence of the organism by trying to extricate our understanding of the organism and its organs from any instrumental conception. Yet the very word *organ*, stemming from the Greek *organon* ("working instrument," or *Werkzeug*, as Heidegger translates it), and related to *ergon* ("work," in German, *Werk*), itself suggests that an instrumental conception of living beings has been in play since the Greeks.[7] An "instrumental" interpretation may be defined as one that views the function of the organs in terms of an extrinsic end, purpose, or *telos*, and by extension regards the relation between the accomplishments of the organism (for example, seeing) and its organs (having eyes) as being "organized" in terms of cause and effect or means/end relations (we see because we have eyes; the eyes are a means to seeing).

Yet to what extent is an organ not an instrument? Both the organ and the instrument accomplish something; both are characterized by an end or purpose, by being "for something" or "in order to do something." A pen is for writing; the eye is for seeing. Yet may we conclude from this that both are pieces of equipment or instruments? *Is seeing produced by the eye?*, Heidegger asks. Does the eye have a *telos*, an end or purpose, *in the same way* that an implement does? Not at all. Seeing is not produced by the eye as the end of the activity of seeing in the manner that the use of a pen produces a piece of writing. For in the case of writing the use of an instrument produces an end product that is other than the productive activity

itself. The terms of Heidegger's analysis here are clearly Aristotelian, appealing to Aristotle's distinction between *praxis* and *poiesis*.
Writing is a form of *poiesis*, a *techne* where the end product lies
beyond (*para*) the activity of producing. In seeing, by contrast, there
is, according to Aristotle, no remainder beyond the activity itself at
the moment it is taking place. Thus vision, both perceptual and spec-
ulative (*horasis, theoria*), is a paradigm for *praxis* in the highest,
ontological sense. For here, the end or *telos* of the process is included
in the activity itself: at the same time we both see and have seen.
And life (*zen*), the living of living beings, is also a *praxis* in precisely
this sense of being an end in itself: at the same time, notes Aristotle,
we are at once living and have lived.[8] (*Metaphysics*, 1048 b18ff)
Whether this "simultaneity" of being held at the same time (*hama*)
in the presence of living and having lived, of being and having been,
is indeed attributable to animal life is something we shall have to
consider below.

The distinction between the organ and the instrument in terms
of the ontological status of their activity in each case is therefore
indicative of a fundamental distinction that must be made with
regard to the manner of being belonging to these beings themselves.
For whereas an instrument or piece of equipment is an independent
entity, something independently present at hand or ready to hand
and available for different people to use, the organ such as the eye is
in each case incorporated into a unique and singular living being:

> The pen is an *independent* entity, something ready to hand for *sev-
> eral different* people. By contrast, the eye, the organ, is, for those
> who need and use it, *never* present *in this way*. Rather every living
> being can in each case see only with *its* eyes. These eyes, and all the
> organs, are not independently present at hand like an item of use, a
> piece of equipment, but are incorporated into that entity which
> makes use of them. (320–21)

Thus, Heidegger proceeds to distinguish the organ, as having a
capacity (*Fähigkeit*) for something, from the instrument or piece of
equipment as having a *readiness* (*Fertigkeit*) for something. Readiness, he emphasizes, is here meant in a double sense: the piece of
equipment is ready both as completed or finished, and in the sense of
being ready or usable *for* something. Heidegger is here pointing to
an ambiguity in the meaning of "end"—which can mean either completion or purpose. (This corresponds to the ambiguity of the Greek

meaning of *telos*). Both the organ and the piece of equipment can serve some further end; and their essence is determined by this end in each instance. As we have just indicated, the nature of the end or "purpose" is fundamentally different in each case. Nonetheless, both the organ and the instrument might be said to serve some end, to be "ready for" something in the most general sense. But the instrument lies ready for doing something in lying independently before us; moreover, it is itself a *product* of a previous *techne*, whereas the living organ of the body is neither a product of human *techne* nor is it an independent, self-subsistent thing. It is therefore highly questionable whether we may consider the organ as something independent, since the eye taken by itself does not have the capacity to see, just as a piece of equipment taken by itself is not capable of anything at all, but requires the human hand to actualize its potentiality. The question to be raised is:

> Can the animal see because it has eyes, or does it have eyes because it can see? Why does the animal have eyes? Why can it have such things? Only because it can see. Possessing eyes and being able to see are not the same thing. (319)

It is *being able to see*, the potentiality for seeing, Heidegger points out, that first makes the possession of eyes possible and necessary. "An eye taken by itself is no eye at all." (323) The eye is not an instrument that exists on its own, only to be subsequently incorporated into an organism. Instead, organs, and their essence as organs, that is, as having capacities, always belong to the organism and develop out of the organism. We must therefore say not that organs have capacities, but that capacity belongs to and proceeds from the respective organism as a whole. The presence of a particular capacity as such thus precedes the organ corresponding to it: the organ develops out of the capacity. Heidegger illustrates this by reference to protoplasmic amoebae and infusoria, whose organs continually form themselves as and when required, and then disappear. Yet may we not conclude from the fact that specific organs develop out of the organism that the organism itself *produces* its own organs, indeed produces, reproduces, and renews itself within certain limits? Such a conclusion seems difficult to deny; moreover, it allows us to perceive a major difference between an organism and a machine. A machine has to be constructed by human beings and also regulated by them, whereas an organism is able to regulate itself.

Nevertheless, there is something about this conclusion that Heidegger wishes to resist. His resistance concerns the further conclusion that is normally drawn from these observations, namely the conclusion that, on account of its capacity for self-production, self-renewal, and self-regulation, the organism must have within it a specific active force or vital agent, an "entelechy." This conclusion, Heidegger insists, closes off the problem of the essence of life, for it implies some kind of efficient cause that originates and controls the movement and development of the organism, producing its organs (Heidegger speaks of a *Wirkungsmoment*). (326) It is questionable, indeed, whether we may speak of a *producing* of organs on the part of the organism at all. Organs are not produced in the way that an item of equipment is made ready. Heidegger underlines the independent character of the produced thing as opposed to a living, emergent, or disappearing organ by pointing out their different relatedness to *time*. In the case of, say, a hammer, it is in a certain way a matter of indifference how long the hammer is actually present or whenever it is destroyed. In the case of an organism such as a protoplasmic organism, the time at which the organs appear is, by contrast, critical. In the protoplasmic creature, each organ appears as and when it is needed. The organs are bound to the *duration and time of life*, the time of the living organism itself, and not in the first instance to an objectively ascertainable time (the time of something present at hand). The organs are bound to the lifetime and life process of the organism, to its capacity for living.

Heidegger examines various cases of protoplasmic organisms because they are best suited philosophically to the task of understanding the essence of the organ and its relation to the organism. Such life-forms appear to have no organs; at most their organs are "momentary organs." Although Heidegger does not develop the question of the *time* of the living being here, this critical temporal nature of the organs which emerges clearly in the case of protoplasmic cells helps to ward off an illusion that "repeatedly misleads" existing approaches to understanding the essential nature of organs. For in the case of those so-called higher animals which have an "enduring animal form," the illusion arises that the organs are something present at hand, something that remain constant, and that can be regarded independently and understood by analogy with instruments. Yet the temporal distinctions that become apparent when considering protoplasmic animals make it evident that the specific manner of being pertaining to living entities is fundamentally different from the being of the present at hand or ready to hand piece of equipment. "Organs, even though they appear to endure and to be present at hand, are nevertheless given only in *that manner of being* which we call *living* [*Leben*]." (329)

On the basis of these considerations, Heidegger argues that the "purposive" or teleological character of equipment and organ is fundamentally different in each case. The eye does not serve vision in the way that the pen serves to write. Whereas that which has been made ready serves or is "serviceable" (*dienlich*) for some (extrinsic) end, the organ as capacity must be understood as "subservient" (*diensthaft*) to the *potentiality* of the specific organism.

This distinction between the being of equipment, or instrumentality, and the being of the organ enables Heidegger to characterize more precisely the nature of capacity pertaining to the potentiality of the organ as opposed to the readiness of equipment. To say that something is ready-made (*fertig*) means not only that (1) it is completed; and (2) it is ready to serve for something; but means also (3) that "in its being it is at an end"—it cannot proceed any further. The piece of equipment *in itself* is unable to do anything; the pen, for example, in itself cannot write, just as the hammer in itself cannot hammer. Writing or hammering requires that an additional action is brought to the pen or the hammer from the outside, from beyond them: the possibility of their serving some end must, as Heidegger expresses it, first be "torn from the piece of equipment." In sum, "being a hammer is *not a pushing toward* hammering, the ready-made hammer lies outside a possible hammering." (330–31) This lying outside or beyond is to be contrasted with the way in which an organ such as the eye *belongs to* the capacity to see, because the capacity has the intrinsic character of subservience. Capacity, as Heidegger now formulates it, "*transposes itself into its own wherefore, and does so in advance with respect to itself.*" (331) This pushing toward and transposing itself into its own end in advance indeed characterizes what is "properly peculiar" to capacity; the hammer in its being, by contrast, "knows nothing of the sort."

The self-transpositional character of the capacity of a living organ marks its very being as living, as a kind of bodying-forth. Whereas using a piece of equipment for a particular end subordinates the equipment to a prescription that has in advance prescribed its possible usage (this being taken from the idea (*idea, eidos*) or "plan" in view of which the equipment was first produced), the living capacity itself requires no such external prescription. It is intrinsically self-regulating; and this self-regulation of its pushing toward its own end or "wherefore" characterizes capacity as *driven*. Capacity accomplishes itself as drive, as a driving itself forward or being driven forward that regulates in advance the possible range of accomplishment of the specific organ. Moreover, in its self-driving or driven character, each capacity traverses a particular dimension: its dynamic occurs as *traversal*. Yet the self-regulating traversal of a dimension is not to be taken in the spatial sense; the drives that are triggered in and as the actualization of various capacities are not merely extrinsic "occasionings" of the spatial movements of the living body. Rather, the dimensionality in question is that traversed by the capacities of the organs as living; the dimensional traversal is the very being of the living body, the pulse of living tissue. This traversal, as the movement of driven capacities, drives and extends in advance right through the unfolding of a capacity. The movement of living drives, Heidegger adds, can therefore never be understood along the lines of a mechanical or mathematical model, except by neglecting what is specific to the organs and organism *as living*.

These reflections allow us to address once more the question raised earlier: can the animal see because it has eyes, or does it have eyes because it can see? What the animal's eye can accomplish in each case, and the structure of the eye as organ, must be understood in terms of the capacity for seeing. The capacity for seeing, however, cannot adequately be determined in terms of the eye and its anatomical structure. This does not mean, of course, that empirical observation of the organ is irrelevant or could simply be disregarded. The anatomical structure of the bee's eye, for example, can help us to understand how the bee "sees" only if we consider it on the basis of the *specific* manner of being of the bee and its capacities. Heidegger cites a striking experiment in which the retinal image appearing in the eye of a glowworm was photographed. The photograph allows us to identify relatively clearly various features of a window within the glowworm's field of vision. The insect's eye, Heidegger comments, is capable of forming an image or "view" of the window. But does this tell us what the glowworm *sees*? "Not at all. *From what the organ accomplishes we cannot at all determine the capacity for seeing, nor the way in which whatever is accomplished by the organ is taken into the service of the potentiality for seeing.*" (336) Indeed, we cannot even begin to problematize the relationship between this insect's eye as organ and its capacity for seeing until we have considered the glowworm's *environment*, and the way in which the animal in general can have an environment. For the insect's eye is, as it were, "inserted" as something nonindependent between its environment and the seeing animal, where "inserted" means existing in the manner of the drive-like traversal pertaining to capacity.

Yet not only the environment must be taken into account, but also the animal or *organism as a whole* that "has" capacities. What constitutes, or what is the essence of, an organism as such? The question of the essence of the organism, which Heidegger approaches most cautiously, may be considered from two perspectives: (1) in terms of the nature of capacity; and (2) in terms of the relation between organs and the environment. Heidegger does not tease out these two threads so cleanly in his analysis; we do so here in order to show the intrinsic complexity of the analysis and the multiplicity of perspectives in play.

(1) The subservience that characterizes the nature of capacity as such has made it clear that each specific organ must be understood in terms of the way it is incorporated into and belongs to the *specific* organism under consideration. In analyzing the nature of an organ—which, as it were, constitutes the "between" or the "interface" between the organism as a living being and its environment—the analysis has thus had tacit recourse to a certain understanding of what it means to be an organism in general. The analysis of the nature of capacity pointed back to an understanding of the capacity for something in terms of a drive-like traversal in which the capacity transposes itself into its own end or "wherefore," that is, *into its own being.* For in being actualized, the capacity (for example, the capacity to see) does not lose itself or exhaust itself as capacity, but precisely retains itself as such a capacity, and does so in and throughout its driving traversal (seeing). This self-like character, however, does not belong to the specific organ as such, but to the capacity that the organ itself subserves and into which it is drawn. The specific capacities belong to and are regulated by the organism itself as a whole: it

is the organism as a whole that appears to be constituted by this *self-like* nature. The organism is the site or locus of the various capacities which, in turn, unfold from out of and subserve the organism as a whole. We have already encountered this self-like character of the organism, Heidegger reminds us, in noting that what is peculiar to the organism as opposed to a machine is that the organism (within certain limits) is *self*-producing, *self*-regulating, *self*-renewing. It is, as we say, *self-preserving*.

(2) This self-like, self-preserving character of the organism may also be considered in relation to the environment. Earlier, while discussing the features of certain protoplasmic creatures, Heidegger had noted that not only do the "momentary organs" that appear remain bound to the living process of the animal (unlike produced equipment), but that these organs never pass over into another body or substance. In the case of pseudopodia, for example, these protoplasmic creatures produce apparent limbs by which to propel themselves. "Yet when one of these apparent limbs of the animal comes into contact with that of another consisting of the same substance, it never flows over into the other or combines with the cellular content of the other. This means that *the organ is retained within the capacity* of touch and movement and indeed can only be superseded or replaced through this capacity." (329) The organs of a particular organism, even where they are highly fluid and changing (without the relative permanence of the human or "higher" organisms), never pass over into or lose themselves in the substance of another organism. In other words, the organs belong to an organism which, even at the fluid level of a protoplasm, has the character of self-retention and self-differentiation from other substances, including substances that are generically the same.

The question now is how this self-like character of the organism is to be conceived. The self-regulating and self-retaining nature of the organism has led, Heidegger argues, to a precipitous explanation of the selfhood of the animal "by way of analogy with our own selves," (332) so that we speak of an animal "soul," a vital force, an entelechy, or even ascribe consciousness to animal life. We should not deny a certain self-like character pertaining to the organism, for it lies in the very essence of capacity as such. In its driving traversal, a capacity does not depart from itself, but retains itself in and as the very movement into its wherefore. And yet it does so *"without* any so-called *self-consciousness* or even *reflection*, without any relating back to itself." (340) Every living organism exists in the manner of being "proper to itself," of being "properly peculiar" (*sich-zu-eigen, eigentümlich*), in other words, of belonging to itself. Yet not every living being belongs to itself in the manner of a human being or "person," that is, in the manner of *selfhood*. Heidegger thus now proposes to reserve the terms *self* and *selfhood*, taken in the strict sense, to characterize the way in which human beings belong to themselves, in contrast to the "proper being" (*Eigentum*) peculiar to the animal. With regard to the translation of these difficult terms, it should be noted that *Eigentum* normally means an individual's "property," what he or she owns, and *eigentümlich* would ordinarily be rendered as "peculiar." In the present context, both words thus carry the sense of something withheld from others, withdrawn or even refused, even something secretive. As we shall see, a certain refusal will shortly be identified by Heidegger as belonging to the being of the animal.

The organism as a unity of the living body that is constantly articulating itself into various capacities and yet retaining itself as a unity amid this multiplication and apparent dispersion of capacities unfolds and sustains its very being (living) as this unity. An organism does not simply "have" capacities as extrinsic properties, but thrives amid this articulating of itself into capacities. It lives as *capability* and *potentiality*. Its living is the very ability to articulate potentiality into a self-traversing movement into living capacities, a movement of traversal that is also a self-retention, a being "organized." Capability characterizes the essence of life. "Only that which is capable and remains capable, lives." (343) An organism, therefore, Heidegger insists, is not to be thought of as a present at hand entity that "has" various properties, capacities, and organs. "The term 'organism' is therefore no longer a name for this or that entity at all, but rather designates *a particular and fundamental way of being*." (342)

Thus far, Heidegger's analyses have served to put in question the instrumental view of the relation between organs and their activities. By emphasizing the unique way in which the organ is embedded in the living activity of the organism as a whole, Heidegger shows that the relation between an organ and its accomplishment is not an extrinsic means-ends relation as reductively conceived by mechanistic models of life. The organs are not simply instruments of the living body. Yet although this technical or instrumental teleology of the being of living organs, as the being of the organism itself, is readily refuted, there remains the possibility of a teleology of living being that is not so much technical (modelled around so-called "efficient causality") as practical (oriented toward "final causality"). According to this teleology, the being of the living entity or organism constitutes an end in itself. The relation between the organism, its organs, and their accomplishment is indeed not one of an *extrinsic* instrumentality conceived along productionist lines, but instead constitutes an *internal* teleology whereby the organs and their activities serve the higher, organizing end of the being (living) of the organism itself.[9] This end is both *origin* and *telos* of every moment of living activity; it is origin and telos of itself, of its own being and subsisting qua living.

This schema of a "practical," internal teleology is indeed that proposed by Aristotle in his classical treatise on the essence of life, *De Anima*. Although he initially appeals to "technical" analogies to approach the issue of life, Aristotle is careful to emphasize that these are merely analogies which are not appropriate to characterizing the nature of the living. It is the concept of *entelecheia*, appropriate to the realm of *praxis*, that Aristotle chooses in order to characterize the living being as an end in itself (the *psuche*). According to Aristotle, the soul is the primary entelechy of the living body, and such will be any body that has organs. As having (being) its own end in advance (namely, in advance of any particular moment of actualization), which is the sense of *entelecheia*, the living being is also precisely "in itself" (*en heauto*) *arche* of its own movement and rest. (*De Anima*, 412 b17f) Thus, Aristotle conceives of life in the most general sense, encompassing both animal and human, as *praxis*, as being an end in itself. (For Aristotle, the decisive distinction between animal and human is, of course, that humans can relate to that being-an-end as such, via *logos*, and thus be ethical and political beings.) Leaving aside for the moment the question of whether this characterization of *praxis* is appropriate even to understanding the essence of human existence, the next question that needs to be raised in the present context is whether the conception of internal teleology is indeed appropriate or adequate to living beings in general. Or is perhaps something about the otherness of other living beings obscured in adopting a schema (itself highly questionable) from the realm of human affairs in order to characterize all living beings?

In Heidegger's text, the possibility of this internal teleology has thus far been maintained precisely in the insistence that the organs and their capacities in each case *subserve* the being of the organism as a whole. But to what extent can an "organism" be characterized as being a self-contained, self-regulating whole? Is an organism origin and end of its own proper being, of its being gathered into "itself" in such a way as to have and dispose over the possibility of self-movement and rest? The viability and phenomenological appropriateness of this schema depend on the organism "itself" being accessible in its self-like character, or in its own "proper" being. And if the "organism," as a *living* being, is not adequately conceivable as something purely "present at hand" (a schema which, Heidegger suggests, is borrowed from the realm of *techne*, equating being complete (being-at-an-end) with the completedness of the produced "work" or product); if its own proper being is *not fully manifest* as such, how can we gain access to the living of this other being as such? Does the Aristotelian notion of the soul as *eidos* still import a technical or productionist approach into our understanding of other living beings, an approach that tends to obscure the character of their own proper being?

3. The Animal as Other

In showing the shortcomings of a technical-instrumental interpretation of the organs of an organism, the ontological inappropriacy of this schema came to light fairly readily. It soon became apparent that the application of an instrumental teleology was unsuitable, because it is taken from a realm of beings that are obviously not living (or at least not normally regarded as such). The being of equipment or tools (presence-at-hand and readiness-to-hand) is evidently not the same as the being of living beings. Of course, the predominance of a productionist-instrumental understanding of being in Western scientific and philosophical thinking has not prevented this schema from being applied to living beings also. By contrast with this first schema, the second, that of an internal-practical teleology, appears initially much less problematic with regard to its ontological appropriacy, for we recognize immediately that this schema is indeed more properly attuned to understanding the being of an entity as living. An indication of this is also the fact that whereas in our initial discussion of the organism and its organs, concerned with refuting equipmental teleology, the interpretations of the organism and its organs could in principle apply to *any* living being, raising the question of the appropriacy of an internal teleology of life immediately involves us in appealing to a possible distinction between *different kinds* of living being. Our concern now is not whether this schema is suitable for characterizing living beings in general, but whether it is phenomenologically and ontologically appropriate to those living beings which we regard as other than human (and, in this context, particularly those which seem most human-like; namely, animals). For we recognize that human existence can in some sense anticipate its own being and thus be an origin and end of its own actions, of itself as *praxis*.

In analyzing the relationship between organs, their accomplishments, and the organism, Heidegger did not simply overlook or ignore the possibility and even necessity of distinguishing between the living being of the human and that of other beings. Rather, this issue was constantly kept in the background, occasionally surfacing by way of a critical caution or reminder of the preliminary and tentative status of these analyses. As a question, the human/animal distinction thus serves as a critical limit to the preliminary analyses of the organism and its organs. For example, after recounting the glowworm experiment and recalling the need to consider the creature's relationship to its environment before drawing any conclusions as to what it sees, Heidegger cautions:

> The difficulty is not merely that of determining *what* it is that the insect sees, but also that of determining *how* it sees. For we should not compare our own seeing with that of the animal without further ado, since the *seeing and the potentiality to see of the animal* is a *capacity*, whereas *our potentiality to see* ultimately has a *character of possibility quite other* and possesses a *way of being that is quite other*. (337)

Of course, claiming that our way of being is "quite other" than that of the animal seems to raise various objections. How then can we know anything about the being of the animal without falling into a naïve anthropomorphism? Will not our interpretation of the animal necessarily be anthropocentric? How do we know what it is like to be an animal? If the animal is truly other, will not any attempt on our part to define its being necessarily reduce and erase its otherness? The question of access to the animal and to living beings that are nonhuman thus proves incircumventable; moreover, the prospect of our knowing what it is like to be an animal seems doomed from the outset. Yet perhaps such objections, which raise themselves repeatedly in contemporary debate, are themselves historically conditioned by the epoch of subjectivity. What is striking about such objections is that they presuppose that our perspective is at once subjective and purely human. They presuppose as unquestioned that human beings, through the subjectivity of their thinking, are undeniably at the *center* of the world, and that the "world," here conceived as the sum-total of beings (objects) in their being, is merely a result and "function" of human representation. The said objections presuppose both that we know what the human being is and that this conception of the world as our "representation" is unquestionable. Not only are these presuppositions historically determined, they are also phenomenologically and ontologically reductive with respect to the essence of life in general, whether human, animal, or other. In the remainder of this chapter, we shall try to indicate how Heidegger's account of animal life in the 1929–30 course undermines such subjectivity by shifting our perspective away from any supposed "interiority" of life and toward a transformed conception of world.

If the being of animals and that of humans were absolutely other, such otherness would of course not even be conceivable. The otherness of the animal remains, as Hegel would say, an otherness "for us." (How this "we" is to be determined can remain an open question for now; Heidegger's understanding of the being of the human being is not that proposed by Hegel.) It is an otherness that is manifest within the element of the Same, the element of *being*, an element which in the 1929–30 course is thought under the title "*world*." (Later, this will be thought by Heidegger as the finite event or *Ereignis* of difference in Sameness, an event in which the otherness of other beings is caught sight of in the moment or *Augenblick* of world).[10] Thus, in claiming that, for animals and humans respectively, "Seeing and seeing are not the same thing," (320) Heidegger is not claiming that there are *no* grounds whatsoever for comparison. It is a question, rather, of drawing critical distinctions that are first enabled by a certain underlying sameness, a sameness that is not to be conceived ontically (in terms of the underlying similarity of two entities) but ontologically (in terms of ways of being and in relation to world). In the case of seeing, for example, the seeing of animals and that of humans manifest a sameness in that both are evidently *ways of apprehending something* (using the word "apprehending" very loosely here), and as such, ways of being and of being in relation to other entities in the world. This does not preclude the possibility and even necessity of making distinctions with respect to the *way* in which something is apprehended in each case. (Heidegger will even claim that the animal does not "apprehend" anything, in a more strictly defined sense.)

In order to help clarify the grounds on which a comparison between the different ways of being of animal and human is possible, let us turn to the framework of the proposed "comparative examination." Heidegger's initial discussion of this issue, which occurs before the preliminary analysis of the organism and its organs, already brings to bear certain insights that will be decisive for addressing the question of access to beings other than ourselves.

The stone is *worldless* (*weltlos*); the animal is *poor in world* (*weltarm*); humans are *world-forming* (*weltbildend*): three "theses" which Heidegger proposes in order to frame his inquiry into world. (263) The three theses recall the possibility and perhaps even the necessity of distinguishing among humans, animals, and inanimate objects as fundamentally different kinds of entities. However obscure their grounds, these distinctions initially appear self-evident for us. Yet in terms of what criteria do we make such distinctions? Heidegger first considers the relation between the second and third theses: the animal is poor in world; man is world-forming. If by *world* we mean something like the accessibility of other beings, then what the theses are proposing seems straightforward. Human beings have greater access to other entities, their world is richer, it encompasses a greater range of accessibility; the animal has less access, it is "poor" in world compared to the richness of the human world. Yet may we simply understand poverty here as being intrinsically of lesser significance with respect to richness? Is the human a higher being than the animal? The reverse might well be true, notes Heidegger. Especially if we stop to compare the discriminatory capacity of a falcon's eye with that of a human being, or ponder the fact that "the human being can sink lower than any animal. . . . No animal can become so depraved as a human being." (286) Yet the fact that human existence bears ethical responsibility, and could in this sense be said to be "higher," need not be taken to imply that the human world is intrinsically more perfect or complete, or of intrinsically greater significance, but indicates only its radical otherness. All of which initially suggests only that "the criterion according to which we talk of height and depth in this connection is obscure." (286)

The thesis of poverty in world as characterizing the animal indeed suggests, according to Heidegger, that animals are in some way deprived of world; but such deprivation must not be taken as equivalent to having *no* world. This becomes clear via a comparison with the first thesis that depicts the stone as worldless. At the same time, the comparison helps us to understand positively the phenomenon of world as the accessibility of beings as such. We may say that the stone is worldless, that it has no world: this means that in principle it has no access to those beings in whose midst it is located. The stone may be in contact with the ground, but does not touch it in the way that the lizard sitting on the stone touches the stone. Above all, Heidegger emphasizes, neither of these ways of "touching" is the same as "*that* touching which we experience when we rest our hand upon the head of another human being." (290) The earth upon which the stone rests is not given *for* the stone; the stone has no access to anything *other* that surrounds it. The stone has no access to other beings. It gives no sign that other beings are present for it in any way.

In the case of the animal, the situation is more complicated. Whereas the surface upon which the stone rests is not accessible to the stone at all, the rock on which the lizard sits is indeed given in a certain way for the lizard—but, Heidegger hypothesizes, it is not given to the lizard "*as* a rock." This does not mean that it is given as something other than itself, but means: "not accessible *as a being* [*als Seiendes*]." (291–92) The thesis that the animal is poor in world, then, cannot mean that it is altogether without access to other beings. "Its *way of being*, which we call '*living*,' is not *without access* to what is around it. . . ." (292) On the one hand, the animal is not utterly deprived of world, if *world* means the *accessibility of beings*. To this extent we must say that the animal in some sense "has" world. On the other hand, if poverty in world indicates a deprivation, and deprivation means "not having," then it seems that the animal does not have world. Yet is the conception of world being used in the same sense when we say that the animal has, and yet does not have, "world"? It seems not. When we say that the animal *has world* then we mean world as the accessibility of beings, as some kind of openness for encountering other beings in general. This sense of world would therefore encompass both humans and animals as living beings. When we say that the animal *does not have* world, we mean that it does not have access to other beings *in the way that humans do*. Yet this makes highly problematic the question as to whether or not the thesis that the animal is poor in world can be a coherent thesis at all.

These reflections on accessibility serve initially to indicate the *fundamentally different ways of being* that pertain to the human being, the animal, and the stone. They have, Heidegger tells us, the sole purpose of eliminating the naïve approach which might think we were concerned with three beings "all present at hand in exactly the same way." (296) Human beings, animals, and stones are indeed all beings that appear and are present at hand *within* the world. Yet their respective *ways of being*, which in each case include a certain presence-at-hand (or possible presence-at-hand, at least for us), are not at all identical (*gleich*). These comparative (*vergleichende*) considerations help to highlight both proximity and difference with respect to the different ways of being in each case. On the one hand, the being of the animal, insofar as it is characterized by having access to other beings, is not entirely other than that of humans. Access to other beings, as Aristotle already saw, is a fundamental characteristic of both humans and animals. On the other hand, in this respect neither the human nor the animal have the same kind of being as the stone, which has no access to other beings. Likewise, the sense in which the animal does *not* have world cannot be understood in the same way as the sheer deprivation or not-having pertaining to the stone. From what perspective do we make such comparisons?

The question of our perspective upon each of the beings referred to in the three theses is primarily concerned not with the danger of anthropocentrism (which, Heidegger suggests, could perhaps be compensated for retrospectively), but with a question of principle regarding transposability—that is, regarding our ability as questioners to transpose ourselves *into* each of the beings to be investigated.

Heidegger approaches the issue by way of three correlative questions: Can we transpose ourselves into an animal, into a stone, or into another human being? Insofar as we ourselves are human beings, and exist in our own particular manner of being, the question is whether we are able to transpose ourselves into an entity that is other. Yet the very talk of "transposition," Heidegger stresses, is misleading. For transposing ourselves can neither mean factically entering the supposed "interior" of the other entity (thus taking on its very being), nor substituting ourselves for the other entity. Instead the point is, Heidegger notes, that transposing ourselves, as a way of understanding the Other, must precisely *let* the Other *be other*. With respect to the fundamental problematic it seeks to address, transposition is better understood as a "going along with" (*Mitgehen mit*) the Other in its way of being. The "decisive *positive* moment" of self-transposition does not consist in our relinquishing or abandoning ourselves, but "in we ourselves being precisely ourselves, and only in this way first bringing about the possibility of ourselves being able to go along with the other being while remaining *other* with respect to it." (297) The very term "transposition" is misleading because it suggests that the beings in question are in the first instance isolated spheres, each with their own interiority, between which a relation of access and mutual interaction would subsequently have to be established. Among other things, such a model—essentially a variant of the subject/object schema so central to modern representation— leaves unthought the possibility that a relation to the Other (however the Other is determined) may *precede* and even be *co-constitutive* of the so-called self and the possibility of its relation to itself. Allowing this possibility does not deny that each of the entities in question is, in its own specific being, indeed determined by selfhood (here understood in a purely formal sense).

Yet how are we to understand transposition as a going-along-with the Other? Heidegger begins by discussing the *first* question: Can we transpose ourselves into an animal? What is really being asked here is: Can we go along with the way in which the animal sees and hears things? It is self-evident for us in asking this question that the animal indeed relates to other things such as its food, its prey, its young, and so on. When we ask this, Heidegger remarks, we are assuming without question that "in relation to the animal

something like a going-along-with, a *going along with it in its access
and in its dealings within its world* is possible *in general,* and does
not represent an intrinsically nonsensical undertaking." (299) The
only question is whether we can factically succeed in this going-
along-with the animal. We make this assumption, it seems, because
we can see that both animals and we ourselves indeed have access to
other beings, because we have access to animals and they have
access to us, and it ought therefore to be possible in principle (or so it
seems) for each to *share* such access, precisely in going-along-with,
in sharing and participating in, the being of the Other.

What of the *second* question: Can we transpose ourselves into a
stone? The answer quite clearly seems to be "no," in this instance not
because of any inability on our part, but because the stone itself has
no sphere of transposability—no possibility of another being access-
ing its specific manner of being, which seems to be that of pure
presence-at-hand. Note that Heidegger adds a qualifier: there are
nonetheless ways in which we are able to regard purely material or
"inanimate" things not as such, but rather to "animate" them, namely
via *myth* and *art.* What is at stake in deciding whether a kind of
transposability is possible here, says Heidegger, is "the distinction
between fundamentally different *kinds* of *truth.*" The current investigation, we are reminded, is to remain within the bounds of the possible truth belonging to "scientific and metaphysical knowledge." (300)

In the case of the *third* question—Can we transpose ourselves
into another human being?—the very question, Heidegger indicates,
is meaningless. Not because a going-along-with the other human
being is impossible, but because we as human beings are *already*
transposed into other human beings in the very manner of our existing. Insofar as the being of human beings is *Dasein* (as analyzed in
Heidegger's 1927 treatise *Being and Time*), and *Dasein* intrinsically
entails *being-with-others,* it is fundamentally unquestionable for us
that we can, for example, "share with one another" the same comportment toward the same things, and indeed do so without this
comportment being fragmented in the process. As a specific way of
being that we ourselves in each case are, *Dasein,* as Heidegger
explained in *Being and Time,* is neither an isolated sphere nor an
interiority, but is, as its manner of being, an always-already-being-
in-the-world with other beings of its own kind (and in the presence of
other non-*Dasein*-like entities). Of course, this possibility of commu-

nity, of being-with (*Mitsein*), does not preclude our having factical difficulties in going along with the other human being. It does not exclude difference, but must precisely allow for difference within (and indeed as first enabling) community. Being with (Others), as Heidegger puts it, "belongs to the essence of human existence, that is, to the existence of every unique individual in each case." (301) There is no human individual who would not always already have been exposed to being in a world, to a being-in-the-world that is also a being with other human beings. Heidegger does not spell it out here, but the "unquestionability" of the sharing (*teilen*) at issue is due to the fact that "our" world of being-with-one-another is a world that is first disclosed in and through discourse, which itself enables communicative disclosure to Others, a "communicating" (*Mitteilung*: literally, a "separating and sharing-with") of our own being. The significance of this will become apparent later.

Where do such reflections leave us? An initial comparative consideration of the second guiding thesis, "the animal is poor in world," suggested that the animal has and yet does not have world. If we now consider what this means in terms of transposability or going-along-with, then it seems that we as human beings are in some way and to some extent already transposed into the sphere of animal life, into the realm of access to other worldly entities that characterizes living beings in general. Yet does this necessarily mean that the animal *has a world*? A series of difficult, yet crucial questions arises here:

> However, if an original transposedness on the part of human beings is possible in relation to the animal, this surely implies that the animal also has its world. Or is this going too far? Is it precisely this "going too far" that we constantly misunderstand? And why do we do so? Transposedness into the animal can belong to the essence of human beings without this necessarily meaning that we transpose ourselves into an animal's world or that the animal in general has a world. And now our question becomes more incisive: In this transposedness into the animal, where is it that we are transposed to? What is it we are going along with, and what does this "with" [*Mit*] mean? What sort of going is involved here? Or, from the perspective of the animal, what is it about the animal that allows and invites human transposedness into it, even while refusing human beings the possibility of going along with the animal? From the side of the animal, what is it that *grants the possibility of transposition and necessarily refuses any going-along-with*? What is this *having and yet not having*? (308)

The animal at once admits the *possibility* of a certain trans-posedness of human beings into it, and yet necessarily *refuses* our going along with it. We cannot go along with the way in which the animal sees something in the way that we can go along with the manner in which another human being sees something. The animal has, or better *is*, a certain sphere of transposability, and yet does not appear to have what we call world (which for us is always that of an historical community). Yet the animal's not having world, its refusal of our going along with it, is possible, notes Heidegger, only where there is a potentiality for granting transposability and having world. Such refusal is not a sheer not-having (not having even the possibility, as with the stone). The term "poverty" (*Armut*) desig-nates precisely this "not having *in* [or *while*] being able to have [*das Nichthaben* im *Habenkönnen*]." Nevertheless, the refusal in ques-tion, Heidegger emphasizes, is not due to any inability intrinsic to the finitude of human knowing, but "is grounded in the essence of the animal." (309)

4. The Being of the Animal: Organism and Environment

The above considerations have helped to set into relief the way in which the being of animals manifests its own specific otherness to us, the way in which its own proper being announces itself within the human world. Heidegger's formulation of this otherness as a "not having in being able to have" indicates that this otherness of animal being is neither absolute otherness nor a dialectical determination that would represent the being of animals and that of humans as dif-ferent stages of one underlying order of being, of the Same conceived in the manner of the Hegelian Absolute. Indeed, Heidegger's formu-lation here seeks precisely to resist such a homogeneous ordering of living beings. For this reason, the "poverty in world" that names the *aporia* of animal being also resists any hierarchical ordering of the being of the animal compared to that of the human with regard to such criteria as completeness or perfection. Before considering this issue further, however, let us turn to Heidegger's concluding discus-sions of the being of the animal and of the organism.

Following his preliminary analysis of the organism and its organs, Heidegger develops a complex and nuanced interpretation of the "self-like" character of the animal organism, of the "peculiarity" of its proper being. We cannot here present the detailed analyses of animal being as "driven" and drive-like, analyses which the 1929–30 course unfolds in relation to certain results of experimental biology, but shall merely summarize the main conclusions. The organism's self-retaining is its remaining "with" itself (*bei sich selbst*), and this without any self-reflexivity. But in the case of animals, their remaining with themselves and keeping to themselves is also an "eliminative" moving away from those entities that manifest themselves to the animal. Heidegger characterizes this strange absorption (*Eingenomm-enheit*) of the animal in and into itself as *Benommenheit*, captivated behavior or "captivation." Captivation designates the being of the animal, "the inner possibility of animality itself," and yet it is quite different for each animal species. (349) Such captivation is still an openness, since the animal is, after all, open to encountering other things; it has access to other entities in general. But is this openness the same as our openness for other entities; is this access the same as our access? Heidegger cites some results from experimental biology in arguing for a decisive difference between the openness of the animal's being and that of the being of humans. The animal is certainly open for and can be affected by other things around it; it is open for an environment in general, but, Heidegger argues, it can never ascertain, grasp, or apprehend (*vernehmen*) these other things *as such*, as being what they are, and as being present in the way that they are. Its captivation is such that it cannot apprehend other entities *as beings* in their being present at hand. The animal has the possibility taken from it (*genommen, benommen*) of apprehending something *as* something. Yet its captivation is not "some kind of rigid fixation on the part of the animal, as if it were somehow spellbound." (361) Instead, captivation enables the kind of "leeway" specific to the animal's openness for its environment, its openness for encountering things within the limits of its driven behavior.

To say that the animal is unable to apprehend beings as beings (*Seiendes*) is to say that it is unable to apprehend them in their being (*Sein*), that is, in respect of the fact that they "are": that they are this or that; that they are present here now and not absent; and so on. Yet this in itself implies something further:

> This driven behavior does *not* relate itself—and as captivated behavior cannot relate itself—*to what is present at hand as such*. What is

present at hand as such means what is present at hand in its *being* present at hand, as a *being*. Beings are *not manifest* for the behavior of the animal in its captivation, they are not disclosed to it, and for that very reason are *not closed off from it* either. Captivation stands outside this possibility. As far as the animal is concerned, we cannot say that beings are closed off from it. Beings could only be closed off if there were some possibility of disclosure at all, however slight that might be. But the captivation of the animal places the animal essentially outside of the possibility that beings could be either disclosed to it or closed off from it. . . . (361)

Taken in itself, in what is most proper to it, the animal in its living moves outside of the play of disclosedness and concealment, beyond the possible alternative of being or not being. This means, more precisely formulated, that in the animal's behavior there is *"no letting be* of beings as such—none at all and in no way whatsoever, not even any not-letting-be." (368) Its openness is certainly an access to things outside it, yet it is also characterized as an inability to attend to *(sich einlassen auf)* things as such. Rather, in its specific openness, the animal is driven around within its manifold drives in such a way that it "finds itself suspended, as it were, between itself and its environment, even though neither one nor the other is experienced *as* a being." (361) The animal is enclosed within an encircling ring *(Umring)*, within which it is open for whatever can disinhibit its drives, for whatever can "affect" it or "trigger" its capacities. The animal "always intrinsically bears this disinhibiting ring along with it and does so as long as it is alive. More precisely, the animal's living is precisely the struggle [*Ringen*] to maintain this ring or sphere. . . ." (371) This self-encircling is a way of living that is a strange absorption in itself; but this does not mean that the animal is absorbed in some so-called interiority. (371) On the contrary, the animal lives and moves, it "behaves" *(benimmt sich)* precisely in a continual openness for whatever manifests itself to the animal in its environment. The being of the animal, as driven behavior that is responsive to the entities that show themselves to it, is not at all enclosure in a capsule or closed sphere. (377) And yet this manner of living appears to close itself off, or be closed off from, our way of being.

We shall consider the validity and wider context of these claims in the final section of this chapter. But first let us pause to consider, within a somewhat broader perspective, the implications of this characterization of the being of the animal with respect to our earlier question of the unity and self-like character of the organism—what Heidegger referred to as the peculiarity of its own proper being. Heidegger's analyses appear to be conducted at a certain limit of scientific and metaphysical inquiry; more precisely, they appear to take such inquiry regarding this theme to a certain limit. In so doing, they not only problematize the mechanistic and physicalist conceptions of life, which reduce life to mechanistic or purely material processes, but also complicate a certain naïveté in prevailing Darwinist and neovitalist approaches.

Our earlier consideration of the living being as an organism, while rejecting mechanistic conceptions of the organism and its organs as reductive and inappropriate, was nevertheless led to assert the necessity of a certain "self"-like unity of the organism. This appeared necessary simply on account of the organism's self-retention, its retaining itself as such despite all interaction with its environment. Of course, this character of self-maintaining is in a purely formal sense found in every entity that is *this one* entity and not another. Yet the self-like character of an organism is unlike that of a stone, insofar as the organism, in its way of being, is open for being affected by other entities around it, and indeed in such a way as to move itself in response to them, to "behave" accordingly. The pressing question is what kind (if any) of relation to "itself" the animal has in such behavior; what kind of "movement" this is (especially since it is not simply movement in space, but also a movement of living, of the living "process" as such—something Heidegger notes is crucial to understanding animal life, but which he does not pursue at length in this course (see 385–88)); and what it means to say that the animal moves "itself."

In general it can be said of scientific studies of animal or organismic life that they begin by regarding the animal as an *entity* and proceed from there to examine (via experiment, observation, and so on) its specific *way of being*. Depending on the presuppositions at work, this way of being may be regarded in advance in a mechanistic manner, that is, as "functioning" in terms of laws of extrinsic cause and effect; or it may be regarded in terms of an internal purposiveness and teleology, whereby the animal's way of being is intrinsically self-regulating, unfolding in accordance with an "entelechy" (vitalism). Both of these approaches are inherently metaphysical insofar as they proceed from an entity to discover its being, its concealed truth and ground. *What* the animal, as an entity, truly *is*, in the *manner of its being*, is to be uncovered by observing and inferring the hidden laws that govern and regulate its being. These laws in their unity and coherence are to be made visible in language, in the *logos* of scientific discourse, which thereby formulates the formerly concealed *eidos* of the entity in its own proper being, in the being of itself, its "being-a-self." In Aristotelian metaphysics, such an approach ultimately arrives at the permanent truth of the being of the entity; in modern metaphysics (science), such observation, in keeping with a transformed sense of *theoria*, is in advance subservient to the essence of technology: it discovers "truths" that serve only an ongoing production of "truth," of language, of being, and of beings (not least of "living," "genetic" "material"). What is problematic about both approaches is that they presuppose in advance and from the outset that entities *in themselves* have the character of *eidos* ("form") and of *logos*, that the *being* of entities (here, of living beings) has in the first instance and in general the character of a "*self*" (of self-subsistence and identity) that is reducible to and accessible as *logos*. With respect to determining the being of living beings as "organisms," both mechanism and vitalism from the outset presuppose as known what is in fact most enigmatic, the enigma of living beings as such.

How does Heidegger's approach in the 1929–30 course problematize such approaches to understanding the being of living beings? From the beginning, Heidegger's analysis takes the "organism" not as an already existing, fully determinate entity whose definitive being is presupposed to be accessible in the presence-at-hand of its *eidos* (whether conceived as outward, empirical form, or as concealed "entelechy"), but as the *way of being* of an entity which, existing in and as this way of being, is fundamentally *open* to an environment, yet in the case of the animal in such a way as not to be open to itself, that is, to its own way of being as such, in such openness. This fundamental openness of the organism as a way of being means not only that the animal should not be conceived as an isolatable entity that then "has" a way of being; but that the holistic and self-like character of an organism cannot be properly conceived as already circumscribed in advance in the manner of entelechy, of being in advance its own end. The self-like character of the animal as organism, rather, must be conceived as a finitude of being, but a finitude which—as we shall attempt to clarify in the next section—is not accessible to the animal as being such.

The extent to which Heidegger's analyses in the 1929–30 course, in engaging with contemporary theories of biology, at once extend and radicalize prevailing late nineteenth and early twentieth century conceptions of the organism is clarified in particular in section 61 of the course in the context of his remarks on the research of two leading biologists, Hans Driesch and Jakob Johann von Uexküll. In the research of Driesch, the mechanistic and instrumentalist conception of the relation between the organism and its organs is surpassed in favor of a holistic view of the organism. According to this view, "[w]holeness means that the organism is not an aggregate, composed of elements or parts, but that the growth and the construction of the organism is governed by this wholeness in each and every step." (380) Although this approach avoids the naïve mechanistic conception that tries to recompose the living organism out of elementary cells, themselves conceived in physico-chemical fashion, it leads Driesch to regard the organism in terms of purposiveness, as governed by a certain force or entelechy. But a decisive shortcoming in this vitalist or neovitalist approach (which, Heidegger remarks, is "just as dangerous as mechanism" with regard to biological problems) is that the organism is isolated in advance from its environment: ". . . the organism is certainly grasped as a whole here, yet grasped in such a way that the animal's relation to the environment has not been included in the fundamental structure of the organism. The totality of the organism coincides as it were with the external surface of the animal's body." (382) By contrast with the research of Driesch, the investigations of von Uexküll adopt a more "ecological" approach that emphasizes the animal's relation to its environment. Despite the wealth and importance of von Uexküll's empirical observations, however, the philosophical and theoretical interpretation of the organism's intimate relation to and interdependence upon its environment is, Heidegger suggests, barely adequate. Not only is it problematic to speak, as von Uexküll does, of an "environing world" (*Umwelt*) and an "inner world" (*Innenwelt*) of animals (since to do so meaningfully presupposes that the meaning of "world" has been adequately clarified); but the approach to understanding the organism's relation to its environment is continually led astray by the prevailing

Darwinistic interpretation of adaptation. "In Darwinism such investigations were based upon the fundamentally misconceived idea that the animal is present at hand, and then subsequently adapts itself to a world that is present at hand, that it then comports itself accordingly and that the fittest individual gets selected." (382) Nevertheless, von Uexküll's investigations indeed prepare the possibility of "a more radical interpretation of the organism, according to which the totality of the organism would not merely consist in the corporeal totality of the animal, but rather this corporeal totality could itself only be understood on the basis of that original totality which is circumscribed by what we called the *disinhibiting ring*." (383)

These remarks help to clarify the sense in which Heidegger's analyses problematize neovitalist conceptions of the organism, which ultimately appeal to an entelechy, but also problematize more fundamentally the ascription of an intrinsically self-like character and of a world to the animal precisely by the way in which the animal's open relation to its environment is taken up into the fundamental characterization of the animal's being. As a way of being, the animal is neither an entity that is simply present at hand "within" an environment or surrounding world which is also present at hand, and to which it *then* relates (375), nor is its being an already present end in itself. Rather, as organism the animal is a fundamentally open way of being in relation to its environment, a manner of being open to the approach of other entities—a peculiar way of being that does not hold itself back as such in the face of such an approach (cf. the bee experiment described at 350–62), but is absorbed and captivated in the manner of assimilative and eliminative behavior.

We can see already from these reflections that Heidegger's analyses problematize from the outset any attempt to understand the being of the organism or of the animal on the basis of a presupposed *eidos*. Not only is it reductive to regard the organism from the outset as an entity circumscribed by its already existing, present at hand form or figure, the "morphological unity" of its corporeal body; it is no less reductive to presuppose that an organism, in its way of being, simply "has" or is an already existing "organization," fundamentally present at hand and accessible in principle to an eidetic *logos*, that is, to a theoretical discourse that would simply describe what is already given and present at hand. Whether and to what extent Heidegger's own discourse, in claiming to describe the being of the animal, is also problematized through these very analyses is something we shall have to consider in our concluding remarks.

Given this characterization of animal being as open for those things that disinhibit its drives yet unable to attend to them as such, Heidegger identifies what now appears to have been misleading in the initial thesis that the animal is poor in world. When it was said that the animal both has and does not have world, the concept of *world* was being used in an equivocal and "underdetermined" sense. In saying that the animal has world, we meant that it has access to other things around it, unlike the stone. In saying that the animal does not have world, we meant that the animal refuses our going along with it in the way that we can go along with other human beings, in the sense of sharing a common comportment toward the same things, toward things to which we have a common access. Heidegger's claim concerning captivation, however, now suggests that the animal does have access to things that actually are, but that only we are able to experience these things and attend to them *as beings*:

> On the basis of our interpretation of animal *captivation*, however, we can now see *where the misinterpretation lies*. The animal certainly has access to . . . something that actually is. But this is something that *only we* are capable of experiencing and having manifest *as beings*. When we claimed by way of introduction that amongst other things world means the accessibility of beings, this characterization of the concept of world is easily misunderstood because the character of world remains underdetermined here. We must say that world does not mean the accessibility of beings, but rather implies *amongst other things* the accessibility of beings *as such*. (390–91)

If this insight is correct, then it seems we must conclude that the animal in fact *has no world*. This cannot of course mean that its being coincides with the worldlessness of the stone. The animal indeed has something that the stone does not have; its being open in captivation is "something the animal *essentially has*." (391) We can therefore now provide a more appropriate formulation of the enigmatic "having and not having" of the animal: the animal displays a not-having of world in having an openness for whatever disinhibits its drives. (392)

Does the clarification that *world* means not simply the accessibility of beings but (*inter alia*) the accessibility of beings *as such* enable us to clarify the proper being and proper peculiarity of the animal? We can now see—or so it seems—that the thesis that the animal is poor in world goes too far. For it is only from *our* perspective that the animal can be said to be poor in world. If by *world* we mean the human world, then we cannot say that the being of the animal *in itself* is constituted by poverty in world. The thesis does not represent an interpretation of the specific essence proper to animality, but "only" a "comparative" illustration. (393) It seems, therefore, says Heidegger, as though we must discard our thesis altogether, since it gives rise to the mistaken opinion that "the being of the animal in and of itself" is deprivation and poverty. (394)

Nevertheless, Heidegger does not hasten to this conclusion, but insists on the need for a critical caution. Is not this suspicion of a misinterpretation again based upon a metaphysics of subjectivity, itself derived from the medieval interpretation of the being of beings as substance, an interpretation prepared in part by Greek philosophy? Does it not presuppose that the animal could in principle be accessible as it is *in itself*, isolatable from its intrinsic relations to other entities and thus determinable in its being—precisely a presupposition that Heidegger's analyses have been at pains to refute? And have we not once again presupposed a naïve anthropocentrism when we say "it is only from *our* perspective . . . ," only from the perspective of "our," "human" world? In what sense do we "have" this perspective, in what sense do we *have a world*, given that "we" are not simply entities that crop up among others, but are more fundamentally characterized by an access to other beings as such? What does it mean that we "stand" in an openness to other beings as such, that we apprehend other entities in their being? Who are the "we" who, according to the third thesis, are said not merely to have a world or (as in *Being and Time*) to be "in" a world, but to be "world-forming"? Is "world" adequately determined as an openness to or accessibility of beings as such?

Given that we still know very little of the essence of world, remarks Heidegger, we have no right at this stage to alter the thesis that the animal is poor in world, or simply to reduce it to the statement that the animal has no world, which might lead us to regard this not-having as "a mere not-having, rather than a deprivation." (395) Instead, we must leave open the possibility that the animal's not having world must indeed be understood as a deprivation. The present stage of the analysis invites a renewed meditation on what is meant by world.

5. The Phenomenon of World

Thus far, Heidegger's analyses have sought to understand the organism in terms of its living, and not as a mere entity: "the organism" is not meant to refer simply to a present at hand entity; and the specific being of the animal organism (the animal as a way of being, as "captivation") is not to be understood as presence-at-hand. Indeed, nature in general is inadequately conceived as "the wall which it becomes when turned into an object of scientific-theoretical observation." (403) It is characteristic of theoretical and scientific inquiry that it levels out distinctions in ways of being pertaining to different kinds of entities, investigating all entities only insofar as they can be thematized and objectified in their presence at hand. That different kinds of entities do have fundamentally different ways of being is, by contrast, precisely what we presuppose in our worldly actions and comportment toward other beings: we do not relate to another human being in the way that we might relate to an animal or to a stone. Moreover, in beginning with entities that are *isolated* and objectifiable in their presence at hand, the modern scientific worldview constructs retrospectively a "world" which (schematizing somewhat rapidly and without taking full account of the transformation of science into technology) consists of the subsequent linking and coordinating of these isolated elements in mathematically conceived space and time. In such a "world" there is no space or time for the irreducibly finite action of the individual whose originary world is historically and ethically determined; the finitude of space and time is excluded in this theoretico-technical construct. In short, what is always and necessarily excluded in the scientific worldview are the worlds from which science itself originates (worlds which are intrinsically differential and which do not first need to be constructed): the finite action and activity of the scientist never enters the scientific "picture" as such; as a finitely acting being, the living individual is a matter of indifference to the force of scientific truth.

We have seen that in characterizing the being of the animal as captivated behavior or *Benommenheit*, Heidegger not only denies that animal being should be reduced to that of a present at hand entity, but he also insists that the animal's multiple relations to its own environment are co-constitutive of, and must be incorporated into, any theory of the being of the animal. Given that the "organism" is a fundamentally *open* way of being, it is evidently problematic even to claim that we could conclusively define, that is, delimit in a definitional *logos* that would circumscribe its being, *what* "the animal" in its essence "*is*." Even Heidegger's characterization of the *way of being* of the animal as *Benommenheit* neither claims to be a conclusive theory of animality that would be valid for all time, nor does it present a blanket theory of animal being that could simply be "applied" indifferently to all animals. Nor, finally, does it present a definition that would simply allow us to oppose animals on the one side to human beings on the other.

The first point, which follows simply because the being of language is itself intrinsically historical, that is, finitely temporal, is made by Heidegger himself with respect to a very specific history. Following his summary of what is meant by *Benommenheit*, Heidegger remarks:

> Certainly we do not mean to imply that this represents the definitive clarification of the *essence of animality* beyond which there is no need to ask any further for all time. Yet it does represent a *concrete characterization of that fundamental conception in relation to the essence of life* within which every consideration of the essence of life moves. It was one which was long neglected precisely in the nineteenth century . . . because it was suppressed by the prevailing mechanistic and physicalist approach to nature. (378)

This remark relates to an earlier comment which we recalled above; namely that the present inquiry is "for the moment" to remain within the bounds of scientific and metaphysical truth—kinds of truth which, he adds, "have together long since determined the way in which we conceive of truth in our everyday reflection and judgment." (300) In the 1929–30 course, Heidegger not only engages with contemporary scientific theory of animal life, but seeks to ground such theory philosophically: on the one hand, showing some of the fundamental presuppositions of such theory (ontological presuppositions concerning the very concept of biological life, and which are not accessible to the science of biology as such but only to philosophizing); and on the other hand, grounding such presuppositions in a more fundamental experience of "world." In so doing, however, the 1929–30 course not only retrieves in a critical and transformative manner a fundamentally Aristotelian, ontotheological framework; it also problematizes the foundational primacy attributed to theoretical contemplation as our originary mode of access to the world.

Regarding the second point, the characterization of animal being as captivated behavior would represent a metaphysical theory of "the animal" in general only if all animals, in this manner of being, were present at hand in the same way. But the thesis concerning animal being as "poverty in world" and as captivated behavior is meant precisely to deny this reductionism (although this does not mean, of course, that a certain kind of presence at hand does not also pertain to the animal in each case): in characterizing the being of the animal as *Benommenheit*, Heidegger is insistent that "animals for their part are *not something present at hand for us* in their being. . . ." (402) That is, they are not present at hand for us *in the way that scientific theory conceives them to be* from the outset. And this also means that Heidegger's thesis on animal being is itself not reducible to a "theory" of animality. Rather, it provides us with a way of seeing and approaching animal being that draws attention to what is suppressed and excluded by any scientific theory (not just those theories of the late nineteenth century).

The way in which Heidegger's thesis transgresses the "dimension of truth pertaining to scientific and metaphysical knowledge" becomes fully visible only toward the end of his reflections on animal being, as the phenomenon of world is brought increasingly into view. Resisting any notion that the thesis of animal being as captivation could simply be applied indifferently as a blanket theory, Heidegger stresses the need for attentiveness to the quite specific differences between various animal species. The encircling ring that constitutes the animal's captivation varies from animal to animal. Every animal and animal species is encircled by its own encircling ring, which in each case determines the openness of the animal for whatever things within its environment can disinhibit its specific drives. Yet not only is the encircling ring of the woodpecker different from that of the squirrel, which differs in turn from that of the woodworm; these encircling rings are themselves not present at hand spheres "laid down alongside or in between one another." Instead, they *intermesh* with one another:

The woodworm, for example, which bores into the bark of the oak tree is encircled by *its own* specific ring. But the woodworm itself, and that means together with this encircling ring of its own, finds itself in turn within the ring encircling the woodpecker as it looks for the worm. And this woodpecker finds itself in all this within the ring encircling the squirrel which startles it as it works. Now this whole context of openness within the rings of captivation encircling the animal realm is not merely characterized by an enormous wealth of contents and relations which we can hardly imagine, but in all of this it is still fundamentally different from the manifest-ness of beings as encountered in the world-forming *Dasein* of the human being. (401)

The encircling rings of living animals intermesh with one another and are "transposed" into one another in a way that differs fundamentally from all mere presence-at-hand. The being of living beings, moreover, is such that in it there becomes manifest *"an intrin-sically dominant character of living beings amongst beings in general,* an intrinsic elevation *[Erhabenheit]* of nature over itself, a sublimity that is lived in life itself."* (403) Yet none of this intersecting of the encircling rings that constitutes the being of living beings is simply present at hand for human beings. Instead, human existence or *Dasein*, Heidegger emphasizes, is *itself* transposed in a peculiar way into the encircling nexus of living beings. Yet does this mean that we humans perhaps find ourselves circumscribed by our own specific encircling ring that grants us our peculiarly human perspective upon things, just as other living beings have theirs—"as if we were now on the same level as the animals, both them and us standing over against a wall of beings with the same shared content, as though the animals amongst themselves and we amongst them simply saw the same wall of beings in different ways, as though we were simply dealing with manifold aspects of the same"? (403) It is precisely this kind of theoretico-analogical relativism (which is also the essence of scientific objectivity, that is, of the metaphysics of representational subjectivity) that Heidegger's analysis seeks to resist:

No, the encircling rings amongst themselves are not remotely com-parable, and the totality of the manifest enmeshing of encircling rings in each case is not simply part of those beings that are other-wise manifest for us, but rather holds us captive *[hält uns . . . gefangen]* in a quite specific way. That is why we say that humans exist in a peculiar way *in the midst [inmitten]* of beings. In the midst of beings means: Living nature holds us ourselves captive as human beings in a quite specific way, not on the basis of any particular influence or impression that nature exerts or makes upon us, but rather from out of our essence, whether we experience that essence in an originary relationship or not. (403–04)

The claim that the ways in which entities are given and show themselves are fundamentally different among living beings, whether animal or human, cautions us against the prejudice that there is simply one world, composed of a sum-total of present at hand entities, to which different beings would have different access depending on their individual perspective. The honey that appears to a bee as its food may not appear to a cat at all—not even as something toward which it could be indifferent (for this would presuppose the cat being able to adopt a stance toward the honey, as well as the honey being given for the cat *as being honey*). But this does not at all mean that the way in which something appears is primarily dependent upon a "subject" or upon the particular living being in question—not even in the case of the human being. Furthermore, as Heidegger here indicates, human beings are not above or beyond nature in the sense of being different, as beings, from living nature (the fundamental or originary difference between human and animal is not an ontic difference). The point is that living nature (as *phusis*) in us, which indeed "holds us captive in a quite specific way," exists in a way of being that is other than that of other kinds of living beings. It is ontologically other, other by virtue of its being "ontological," or better, historical. In Heidegger's understanding of "essence" (*Wesen*), the claim that the animal is other in essence than the human does not refer to essential essence in the sense of "whatness" or substance (*essentia, ousia*) characteristic of metaphysics, but to the respective ways of being of human and animal, the kind of presence each displays.

In order to substantiate and clarify these claims we must examine more closely the concept of world and its relation to selfhood, keeping in view Heidegger's earlier claims about animal being as captivation. Here we shall also go beyond what is explicitly said in the text of the 1929–30 course.

In examining the claim that "the animal is poor in world," Heidegger indicated provisionally that this thesis is sustainable only if by "world" we mean not simply the accessibility of beings, but ("amongst other things") the accessibility of beings *as such*, as beings.

Yet this determination too is not sufficient to comprehend fully the phenomenon of world. What is meant by "world"? For us, entities are not only given and accessible to us as manifest beings, as being in each case this or that; they are also simultaneously given *as a whole*, in a certain togetherness and unity. They belong together in such a way that no entity is ever given in isolation; and yet each and every entity is manifest in its particularity, as being the entity that it is. But this "whole," which we understand as our *world*, is not at all reducible to the sum-total of manifest beings, nor to a totality of beings that exist in themselves. Rather, this "whole" must already be given *in advance* in order for it to be possible for us to have access to any entity *as being this particular entity*. The possibility of beings first being given and appearing as such, in their specific being, is first enabled by this prior forming of a whole. For to have access to any particular entity as being this entity is *already* to see it *in an originary relation to* other beings, as being *this* entity *and not another*. ("Originary" here means, among other things, prior to ascertainment by a theoretical *logos*.) A differential unity, a belonging together in mutual difference, always already precedes any appearing of identity. In the 1929–30 course, Heidegger relates the prevailing of this differential unity to Aristotle in identifying it with the simultaneous *synthesis* and *diairesis* that first enables the specific openness in which apophantic discourse (the *logos apophantikos*) is grounded. Apophantic discourse is discourse which makes the specific claim solely to point out and manifest that which already is in its presence at hand. (Such is precisely the theoretical discourse of science.) The happening of this differential belonging-together, that is, of the openness of beings as a whole at each moment, is equally an event of freedom: it first enables our being-free for other beings as other. As the prior formation of world, this event first enables not only the *logos apophantikos* as such, but every *logos*. For every discourse speaks, knowingly or not, from out of and into this prior forming of a whole.

We do not have the occasion here to pursue at greater length this rootedness of *logos* in the happening of world. But granted that *world*, at least for human beings, entails not only the accessibility of beings as such but the accessibility or manifestness of beings as such and *as a whole* (in the specific sense indicated) (412)—granted also that there is a prior forming of world (prior, that is, to the manifestness of particular beings as such)—the pressing question remains of *how* this "forming" of world occurs. Is it the human being that in each case forms the world, as Heidegger's third thesis, "Man is world-forming," might seem to claim? If so, are we not after all trapped in a kind of anthropocentric perspectivism in which human beings, whether as individual or collective subjects, somehow form and thus "have" their human world, from which they could know nothing of the "world" or "worlds" of animals? Is not the world, in which we already find ourselves, "our world" after all, as we put it above?

That the world is not at all simply "our" world, that it is neither the property of, nor something first formed by the activity of, human beings, is indicated by the fact that the only human beings that exist are individual beings that have already become manifest as such, within and in the midst of a world of Others, a world that already exists in preceding them. Only within an already prevailing world can individual beings first become manifest as such, not only to Others, but to themselves as individual beings. The being of an individual human being is first enabled by this precedence of a world (which is to say, by the precedence of history). Thus, Heidegger writes, "it is not the case that the human being first exists and then also one day decides amongst other things to form a world. Rather world-formation is something that occurs, and only on this ground can a human being exist in the first place." (414) As Heidegger also indicates here, "world" is not simply a phenomenon that already exists, but an *event* that occurs and continues to occur: it forms itself, it is intrinsically poietic, transformative. But this event does not happen without or somewhere beyond human beings either: it occurs in and through human beings who partake in the happening of this event although they do not originate it as "subjects." Thus, Heidegger explains, it is not the individual human being who is world-forming, but the human being in his essential humanity, in his (futural and historical) being (*Sein*), in his openness to and for a possible world, in the happening of disclosedness in and through him: "the *Da-sein* in the human being is world-forming." (414)

In what way do we in each case first come to ourselves and first become manifest to ourselves as such, as an individualized, existing self, through this event of world-formation that occurs through the *Da-sein* in us, that is, through the historical disclosure of worldly freedom? Not through any self-reflection or theoretical speculation, but more originarily through the phenomenon of attunement (*Stimmung*). The happening of attunement holds and maintains us in the thrownness of our concrete, bodily existing: in its originary unity with world-formation, it manifests us in our already having been, in our having been thrown in each case into the finite happening of a particular, situated, historical world. Such happening of attunement is the way in which we originarily approach and find ourselves as precisely *ourselves* in each instance, and not Others. It is the event of our emergence into the manifestness of a finite world, a happening of the manifestness of a whole into which we are held in advance, and thereby held open to Others and to ourselves. As such, attunement is the specific way in which living nature "holds us captive" in the midst of beings as a whole.

> *Dasein* places us ourselves before beings as a whole. In attunement, one *is* in this way or that—and this therefore entails that attunement precisely makes manifest *beings as a whole* and makes us manifest to ourselves as we find ourselves situated in the midst of beings as a whole. Attunement and being attuned is by no means a taking cognizance of psychological states, but is rather a way of *being borne out* [*Hinausgetragenwerden*] into a manifestness of beings as a whole that is in each case specific, and that means: into the manifestness of *Dasein* as such, as it finds itself situated in the midst of this whole in each instance. (410)

The primacy of attunement in the disclosure of our being entails that living nature, in holding us captive, is never reducible to an object of theoretical contemplation. Instead, it is that to which we are always already bound in advance, that which binds us prior to all our activities and actions. Yet it binds us in the peculiar and enigmatic manner that the binding character of those beings that surround us and press upon us *first approaches* us from out of the openness of a finite, historical world. (By contrast the German for "poverty" in the animal's alleged "poverty in world," namely, *Armut*, implies the lack of a certain attunement, of a certain mood, even of a certain courage or gathering of oneself, of a certain "cheer" or "spirit"—all of which are suggested by the German *Mut*.[11]) The manifestness of beings as a whole in each case approaches us as a manifestness that *precedes us in already having been*, such that the disclosure and openness of living nature for us is always already historical. If the happening of world is itself an emergence, a coming into being, and indeed one that first enables our own historical emergence as a self in each case, this futural character of world-formation is nevertheless always bound in advance to manifestation in and through particular living beings whose existence is at once finite and historical.[12] The happening of world is thus "bound" in the twofold sense of being tied to and borne by a particular, factical situatedness in the midst of beings, and in that the possibilities it enables are in each case *restricted* in advance to possibilities that are projected and come toward us *from out of* a disclosedness of beings that have already been, that is, that are manifest in a worldly and historical manner. (Cf. 527–28) The event of world-formation frees beings as a whole to manifest themselves historically, and only thereby frees us to respond to and take up a stance toward beings as a whole amid this situated happening of worldly freedom. Freedom, as Heidegger would later emphasize, is not the property of human beings.

These considerations, which go somewhat beyond the explicit text of the 1929–30 course, make it apparent that a peculiar *poiesis* happens in and through human beings, a *poiesis* of which they are not the origin (Heidegger relates it to Aristotle's so-called *nous poietikos*). Nevertheless, this originary *poiesis* itself *enables* that peculiar manner of being an origin that is proper to human beings: the possibility of *action*, of coming into being as freely responding to that which has already been. Our everyday actions, as in each case a factical response to that which already is, presuppose an originary responsiveness and responsibility in and through which beings first manifest themselves and come to be, come to stand in the light of a particular historical world; in short, they presuppose what Heidegger would later call the event (*Ereignis*) in which language comes to pass. The being of world itself indeed presupposes, or rather *is*, this always already having been drawn into language as an event that precedes us, as the precedence that history itself is. The coming to be of a world is in each case first enabled by our being held open (prior to any self-disclosure or presence as such) for the happening of language. For language is that which has always already been in being always yet to come.

6. The Time of Life: Self and World

We cannot pursue these themes at length here, themes which, emerging from the 1929–30 course, clearly foreshadow the discussion of the strife between world and Earth in "The Origin of the Work of Art" (1936) and the more explicit writings on the *Ereignis* of world as the *Ereignis* of language in Heidegger's later work. In my concluding remarks, I would like, rather, to reconsider some of Heidegger's claims concerning animal being in the light of the preceding discussion of world, specifically in relation to the question of selfhood.

According to the characterization of animal being as captivated behavior, such captivation entails among other things an absorption (*Eingenommenheit*) of the animal into itself. (367) But this does not mean that the animal in its way of being, living, is preoccupied with itself or even has access to itself, that is, to its own way of being, as such. Quite on the contrary. The animal neither has nor exists as a self in the way in which we do. The animal's captivated behavior is absorption in the sense of a being absorbed into "the totality of interacting instinctual drives," a totality in which the unity of the animal's body as a living body is grounded. (376) As we have seen, this absorption does not, however, mean enclosedness or encapsulation in an interiority. It is precisely an *openness*—a way of living that is a remaining open for whatever is accessible. As a consequence of this very openness of the activity of living, the animal is always more than it already is: it exceeds every "already" in an incalculable manner that can never be theoretically discerned. Which is also to say that the animal in its living is in each case a specific kind of emergence and approach: as Heidegger puts it, the animal "approaches" or "comes toward" the Other in "opening itself" to the Other. (369) And yet, according to Heidegger, this Other is never manifest as a being (*Seiendes*), that is, in its being (*Sein*). Whatever disinhibits and triggers the animal's driven behavior in affecting its specific sensibility "withdraws itself as it were constantly and necessarily" from the specific openness of the animal's captivated behavior. (370) This self-withdrawal of that which appears and presents itself to the animal implies that the animal is in effect captivated by the ongoing flow of presentation of whatever presents itself, of that which it "deals with" in the manner of "elimination" (*Beseitigung*)— the German term here implying moving things aside, letting them pass to the side. This "elimination" precisely lets the animal maintain its ongoing activity as living, lets its own specific emergence move on, so to speak. But this moving on is a continual exposure to and dependence on whatever presents itself even as it withdraws, presents itself in its very withdrawal. This entails that the animal, "taken" as it is by the ongoing flow of presentation, borne along and carried along by it, is unable to take up a free stance outside the presence of whatever is present as its environment. Neither the specific being (presence) of the animal itself nor that of whatever appears and presents itself to the animal are able to attain any permanence in the midst of this temporal flow of presentation. Thus Heidegger writes that, for the animal,

> [t]hat which disinhibits . . . must constantly in accordance with its essence withdraw itself. It is *nothing enduring* that could *stand over against the animal as a possible object* [*kein Bleibendes, das dem Tier als ein möglicher Gegenstand gegenübersteht*]. . . . The self-withdrawal of that which disinhibits corresponds to the essential *inability to attend* to it which is involved in behavior. . . . (372)

Correlatively, the being of the animal itself lacks the specific enduring or remaining that enables an attentiveness to whatever is present as such, as being present:

> Since that which disinhibits behavior essentially withdraws and eludes it [*aus dem Wege geht*], so too the relation of behavior to that which occasions it is a *not attending to it*. No permanence as such is ever attained [*Es kommt nie zu einem Bleiben als solchem*], nor indeed any change as such. (370)

In order for a living being to be able to achieve an endurance beyond or in excess of the temporal flow of presentation, it (its living presence) would have to take up an independent stance in relation to something outside of and beyond not only that which is presenting itself, but beyond the present of whatever is presenting itself at each moment. Such a stance is, for us, a dwelling in the element of language. It is what we call being. In being brought to language, things too first attain a certain endurance and permanence of presence; they come to stand over against us (our own presencing) in various kinds of presence at hand. Only where there is language can that which presences come to stand in the relative and unitary constancy of its manifold presentations. Such permanence is not atemporal or eternal, but an enduring in the manner of the specific temporality of *historical* time.

What does this imply with respect to the activity of the animal in each case? The beginning of the animal's activities, such as moving, feeding, and so on, is never a free origination in the manner in which human beings can freely initiate and thus be an origin of their actions. This is because the animal does not exist in a free (world-forming) anticipation of being in general, whether its own being or that of Others; it does not come to stand within the freedom of and openness to a world, that is, to that whole that first enables something to be apprehended as *being* what it is, as being in such and such a way, or as being in relation to something else. The animal's activities and movements are always responsive to and triggered by whatever presents itself in the animal's immediate environment. Yet none of this entails that the animal is a purely passive being, merely at the mercy of whatever presents itself to the animal as it withdraws. The animal is still able to move and "act" in a manner that is not *wholly* or exclusively determined by its immediate environment. Although Heidegger, so far as I am aware, nowhere clarifies this sufficiently, the animal in fact has and must have a certain ability (again different for each specific animal according to the manner of its behavior and captivation) to relate to something *as* something, although not, indeed, *as being* something. It is indeed a precondition of the animal's being able to move that it has an ability to relate to something beyond the field of its own specific presence at any particular moment. Aristotle already understood this necessity for a living being to exist in a differential relationship to the momentary field of presence of its immediate environment if it is to be able to move. A cat responds to the presence of a mouse *as* its potential dinner, or *as* something to play with; it responds to the presence of a dog *as* a potential threat—*and not* as its food (but this "and not," which in the case of the animal occurs not through the free element of *logos*, but is bound to the momentary presence of the particular, is presumably not open to the animal *as such*). This entails that what is not immediately present (in the latter case, its food) is and can indeed also be present *in a certain way* for the animal (which is also a precondition of the fact that certain animals can be trained and acquire "learned behavior"[13]). (Aristotle called this faculty *phantasia*.) But in what way can that which is not immediately present still be present? For the animal, the presence of that which is not immediately given in its environment is a presence by association: it is triggered precisely by that which is present at a given moment. The animal is exposed to the presence of what presents itself in the immediate moment in the sense of being captivated by it and having to behave accordingly in response. This response would of course be very specific, dependent on the way in which the animal's previous exposure to various entities has been "incorporated" into its driven behavior, and on what transpires in the free play of presence and absence to which the animal is exposed on each occasion; animal response does not follow the rule of cause and effect. But this precisely means, as we can now see more clearly, that it would indeed be going too far to say that the animal either has or does not have world: its living entails the forming of a certain whole, of a wholeness of its relations that is the openness of an encircling ring—and yet this living does not irrupt or break out into the taking up of a *free stance* in the midst of this whole, a stance that would free it for its own presence.

The implications of these reflections become clearer if we consider the question of whether the animal has a relation to *itself* or not. The above considerations imply that the animal indeed has something like a *sense* of self. The animal senses itself, that is, its embodiment, in emerging out of itself and in moving, but only in response to whatever is immediately given to it within what Heidegger calls the encircling ring of its specific openness for being affected. Such a sense of self, though, is quite other than the human sense of selfhood. In its absorption into its own living, into its own openness for . . . other entities, the animal is never "with itself [*bei sich selbst*] in the proper sense" (374), the German preposition *bei* here implying "in the presence of. . . ." Rather, Heidegger writes,

> The specific selfhood [*Selbstsein*] of the animal (taking "self" here in a purely formal sense) is its being proper to itself, being its own [*Sich-zu-eigen-Sein, Eigentum*] in the manner of its driven activity. The animal is always driven in a certain way in this activity. This is why its being taken [in the sense of given over to, or "preoccupied" with whatever it is absorbed in: *Hingenommensein*] is never a letting itself attend to beings, *not even to itself as such*. But this driven activity does not occur within a self-enclosed capsule; on the contrary, on the grounds of the way in which the instinctual drives themselves are preoccupied [*aufgrund der Hingenommenheit der Triebe*] it is always related to something else. (376–77, emphasis added)

The claimed inability of the animal to attend to itself as such (that is, as being itself) is not disproven by the fact that birds preen themselves or that cats clean their fur. The claim is that the animal is unable to let itself (its own being) be, because it is unable to let be in general. Letting be (*Seinlassen*) in the sense of attending to . . . is not at all to be understood as a passive disregard, but as a taking into care in the manner of entering into the historical happening of a world. The animal's absorption into itself means that the animal cannot exist in the manner of being-a-self (or of self-consciousness), even though it "has" (or rather, "is") its own proper way of being (living) which is intrinsically retained in this absorption. This means that the animal, as a way of being, is indeed "outside of itself," but not in such a way as to have a *free* relation to its own being, that is, to *stand* outside itself in its own being. For this reason, its being is not "ecstatic" in the strict sense of the word (as used in *Being and Time* to characterize the temporality of *Dasein*). Its being does not entail *stasis*, that is, having assumed a *stance* (*Haltung*) outside of its own being, a stance that nevertheless enables a free presence-to-self in the manner of human existing. Thus, Heidegger remarks, human activity is "comportment" (*Verhalten*) rather than behavior. (345–46) "But all comportment is possible only in being held in a certain restraint [*Verhaltenheit*], maintaining a stance [*Verhaltung*], and a stance [*Haltung*] is given only where a being has the character of a self or, as we also say, of a person." (397–98) Such presence is (among other things) a remaining "with" (*bei*), that is, in the presence of oneself in each case, which is to say, in the presence of one's own having-been, of oneself as Other—not as any arbitrary Other, but as the Other in and of oneself, the still indeterminate Other that in each case "holds us captive" in our historical thrownness in the midst of beings as a whole. It is a futural openness for one's own having been, an openness that is "held" (*gehalten*), as presence, in the manner of the *Augenblick*, the momentary "glance of the eye" that catches sight of beings as a whole in their worldly presence and that stands at the heart of both *Being and Time* and the 1929–30 course (and indeed all of Heidegger's work). "Oneself" here means, therefore: thought as and in terms of *Dasein*, as being-in-the-world, as the having-been of a *world* that includes the being one has and will have been in one's worldly appearing to Others. Assuming a free relation and stance toward one's own being presupposes a free yet binding relation toward the being of beings as a whole, toward the phenomenon of world that first lets beings appear and be as such in their singularity.

By contrast, the animal in its absorption displays a peculiar non-remaining with either its own (thrown) being or that of Others, that is, with being as that which has been (historical). The animal's "thrownness," its being captivated as a particular emergence in living nature, is ahistorical. The animal shows an openness to what is to come by means of a turning away from, a non-attending to, presence—in a nontarrying in the presence of Others. The being or *Dasein* of human beings, by contrast, is precisely this tarrying and dwelling in the presence of Others (including oneself as "Other"), *a presence that exists only as having-been.* This tarrying in being held in a presence and toward other beings as a whole can be understood as the happening of an always indeterminate future, as an originarily responsive letting-be (*Seinlassen*). In enabling beings to arrive (to while in presence), it entails a holding oneself in this presencing, an originary letting-happen (or letting-arrive) of *world* as completion (*Ergänzung*). This forming of a whole enables the togetherness in keeping to themselves while presencing of other beings: a belonging together as a coming to be (presence) together in having-been.

With regard to the time of life, we can thus say that whereas the animal, in its radical openness, is refused the possibility of any return to its own having-been as a having-been in the presence of Others—which, as we can now better appreciate, is precisely the *refusal* in which the animal shows itself to us in its specific otherness—and is thus excluded from an active participation in the temporality of the world as such, human beings are necessarily held in and drawn into this possibility. Their presence can only ever be a presence that has already been; their future presence will always be a presence that will have been: with respect to the presence of what is present, they exist in an essential absence. And this is the possibility and necessity of their actions, of their existing futurally and, from out of what has been, bringing forth in their actions what has never yet been—of their being an origin that remains indebted to an historical world as a world of Others. In the concluding remarks of the course, Heidegger characterizes the occurrence of this held presence, of the moment of human existing and acting, as the happening of an essential absence that is at once worldly, historical, and finite:

> In the occurrence of projection world is formed, that is, in projecting something erupts and irrupts toward possibilities, thereby irrupting into what is actual as such, so as to experience itself as having irrupted as an actual being in the midst of what can now be manifest as beings. It is a being of a properly primordial kind, which has irrupted to that way of being [Sein] which we call Da-sein and to that being [Seienden] which we say exists, that is, ex-sists, is an exiting from itself in the essence of its being, yet without abandoning itself.
>
> Man is that inability to remain and yet is unable to leave his place. In projecting, the Da-sein in him constantly throws him into possibilities and thereby keeps him subjected to what is actual. Thus thrown in this throw, man is a transition, transition as the fundamental essence of occurrence. Man is history, or better, history is man. Man is enraptured in this transition and therefore prevails as "absent." Absent in a fundamental sense—never simply at hand, but absent in the essence of his prevailing, in his essentially being away, removed into essential having been and future—prevailing in absence and never at hand, yet existent in his essential absence. . . . (531)

What does this absence intrinsic to the momentary presencing of human existence imply with respect to the divergence between human and animal ways of being? In recalling his earlier analyses of the fundamental attunement of boredom from the same course, an attunement that brings us before beings as a whole and thrusts us into the momentary necessity of having to act, Heidegger recalls how the Augenblick shows itself as the opening up of "the entire abyss [Abgrund] of Dasein in the midst of Dasein." (411) It is the abyss of our historical being, the abyss of the task of having to be historical even in the thrownness and finitude of our living singularity (for us, the inevitable "solitude" (Einsamkeit) and individuation (Vereinzelung) in our having to be with Others), the abyss of our manner of being held captive in the midst of living nature. This being held captive (gefangen) is, Heidegger insists, quite different from the animal's captivation (Benommenheit), for between these two manners of being "there lies an abyss that can be bridged by no mediation whatsoever." (409) The anti-Hegelian tone of this claim should not, however, mislead us into thinking that there is no belonging together of these diverse and different ways of being. More precisely, as becomes apparent by the end of the course, we should say that the abyss in question is the "between": it is the happening of that between which enables a finite, differential belonging together in distinction, the happening of an historical world.[14] In the concluding paragraphs, Heidegger identifies the happening of this "originarily *irruptive* 'between'" as the irrupting into the midst of beings of the ontological difference itself (the difference "between" being and beings), or better, of the *event* of originary difference that occurs as the formation of world and that first lets beings become manifest as such, in their being. (530–31) It is the event of that distinction which "ultimately . . . *makes possible all distinguishing and all distinctiveness* . . . ," all *krinein*. (517ff) Nevertheless, if our insight into this "abyss," the happening of worldly freedom itself, calls for "the complete divergence of the two theses [concerning the animal and the human being]" (409), this does not mean that the theses are unsustainable as such. The thesis of the animal's world-poverty as "not having in/while being able to have" world, in its divergence from the thesis that the human being is world-forming, precisely lets "the essence of world light up." (409) The entire analysis of animal being, we must recall (and Heidegger is emphatic about this), is subservient to this leading task.[15] Only if we isolate the analyses of animal being from their proper context, as tends to happen in contemporary debate, does the thesis that the animal is "poor in world" appear merely to reinscribe a fundamentally traditional, metaphysical "theory" distinguishing the animal from the human. (This does not of course mean—as the present chapter has tried to indicate—that the thesis does not retrieve traditional philosophical resources; the point is that in so doing, it also critically transforms and rethinks such resources.) By contrast, attentiveness to the way in which the thesis is situated in relation to the phenomenon of world shows why the being of the animal and that of human *Dasein* cannot simply be opposed to one another as present at hand realms being described by a purely theoretical discourse. The "abyssal" opening up of the happening of world, as the happening of historical freedom, is not that of a present at hand abyss or difference that exists between two already existing entities. It is the opening of the ongoing and never completable task of our ethical responsibility toward not only other humans, but all Others, living and otherwise. The momentary event of presencing that lets beings be is in this sense protoethical, the criterion of all criteria.[16]

Heidegger's attentiveness to the poietic, world-forming occurrence of this "momentary" event indicates that the *Augenblick* not only names the way in which we are held in having-been and future, and thus exist and come to presence only in and as the "essential absence" of a rapture or transport; it also marks the site of the opening up of a world that has always already called us into being, called upon us to irrupt into the freedom of a world and to assume a free stance toward the beings manifest within this happening of world. Having entered a world, we are always already absent in the sense of having-been, of dwelling in advance in the happening of a world whose presence calls us from beyond our time. Existing in the world, our "own" time is always already that of Others, both of the Others of other historical worlds and of other beings whose way of being is not historical, that is, does not carry the weight of our responsibility. In acting, in coming to be ourselves, we have always already exited from any time that could be exclusively our own in entering the time of Others as the time of a world. "Our" time will always have been that of Others in whose presence we dwell.

The *Augenblick* thus shows itself as the veritable abyss of world, an abyss that does not lie between different entities as beings present at hand, but that is the finite opening enabling and calling for our attentiveness to Others—to all Others—in the context of their worldly presence. It is the call to presence that calls upon us to act in response to Others who have themselves come to presence in an historical world. As open for Others who appear in such a world, we always already exist in a certain attending to Others, even where we no longer respect and honor them as such. Such respect was once called *theoria*.[17]

Notes

1. Martin Heidegger, "*Vom Wesen und Begriff der Πηθσισ: Aristoteles, Physik, B1,*" *Gesamtausgabe Bd. 9: Wegmarken* (Frankfurt: Klostermann, 1976), p. [325]; "On the Essence and Concept of Πηθσισ: Aristotle, *Physics*, B1," transl. Thomas Sheehan, *Pathmarks*, ed. William McNeill (Cambridge: Cambridge University Press, 1998).

2. See in particular Michel Haar, *Le chant de la terre* (Paris: Éditions de l'Herne, 1985); Jacques Derrida, *De l'esprit* (Paris: Galilée, 1987); and David Farrell Krell, *Daimon Life* (Bloomington: Indiana University Press, 1992).

3. For a helpful overview, see Verena Andermatt Conley, *Ecopolitics* (London: Routledge, 1997).

4. Martin Heidegger, *Gesamtausgabe Bd. 34: Vom Wesen der Wahrheit* (Frankfurt: Klostermann, 1988), p. 173.

5. Ibid., p. 177.

6. Martin Heidegger, *Gesamtausgabe Bd. 29/30: Die Grundbegriffe der Metaphysik: Welt—Endlichkeit—Einsamkeit* (Frankfurt: Klostermann, 1983); *The Fundamental Concepts of Metaphysics: World, Finitude, Solitude*, transl. William McNeill and Nicholas Walker (Bloomington: Indiana University Press, 1995). Page references that follow are to the German edition (cited at the top of the page in the translation). Translations have been modified where appropriate.

7. Whether this "simultaneity" of being held at the same time (*hama*) in the presence of living and having lived, of being and having been, is indeed attributable to animal life is something we shall have to consider. See section 6 of the present essay, on "The Time of Life."

8. *Gesamtausgabe Bd. 29/30*, p. 312

9. For a discussion and defense of such teleology with respect to animal being, see Martha Craven Nussbaum, "Aristotle on Teleological Explanation," *Aristotle's De Motu Animalium*, Essay 1 (Princeton: Princeton University Press, 1978), pp. 59–106.

10. Later, this will be thought by Heidegger as the finite event or *Ereignis* of difference in Sameness, an event in which the otherness of other beings is caught sight of in the moment or *Augenblick* of world. On the *Ereignis* of difference, see Martin Heidegger, *Identität und Differenz* (Pfullingen: Neske, 1957); *Identity and Difference*, transl. Joan Stambaugh (New York: Harper & Row, 1969). With regard to Hegel, see the essay *"Die Onto-theo-logische Verfassung der Metaphysik"* ("The Onto-theo-logical Constitution of Metaphysics") in the same volume.

11. See especially Heidegger's comments on pp. 287–88, and the translators' note on p. 182 of the English. On the question of "spirit" in relation to the 1929–30 course, see Derrida, *De l'esprit*.

12. It is therefore peculiarly mistaken to claim, as does Didier Franck in his commentary on the 1929–30 course, that "the ecstatic constitution of [*Dasein's*] existence cannot be reconciled with its incarnation." Attuned manifestation is as such always already ecstatic-existent; ecstasis is always ecstasis of a (singular and living) body. See Didier Franck, "Being and the Living," *Who Comes After the Subject?*, eds. Eduardo Cadava, Peter Connor, and Jean-Luc Nancy (New York: Routledge, 1991), p. 144.

13. Cf. *Gesamtausgabe Bd. 29/30*, Section 54.

14. In this sense Heidegger, in the "Letter on 'Humanism,'" will later speak of our "abyssal bodily kinship with the animal," which is precisely a kinship of worldly being in the midst of living nature. See Martin Heidegger, *"Brief über den 'Humanismus,'" Gesamtausgabe Bd. 9: Wegmarken*, p. [157]; "Letter on 'Humanism,'" transl. Frank A. Capuzzi and John Glenn Gray, *Pathmarks*, ed. William McNeill.

15. Cf. sections 39 to 42, in particular pp. 262–63.

16. Unlike Derrida, I would argue therefore that we indeed find in Heidegger's discourse on animality grounds for claiming that we do have a responsibility toward the living in general. Furthermore, I find in Heidegger's text no sense in which *Dasein* may be said to be "better" than a living thing. See Jacques Derrida (with Jean-Luc Nancy) "'Eating Well,' or the Calculation of the Subject: An Interview with Jacques Derrida," *Who Comes After the Subject?*, eds. Cadava et al., pp. 112–13.

17. I discuss the complex relations between *theoria* and the *Augenblick* in Heidegger's work in *The Glance of the Eye: Heidegger, Aristotle, and the Ends of Theory* (Albany: State University of New York Press, 1999).

TEN

Into the Truth with Animals

 *Carleton Dallery*

How shall we be with animals? Depends on the animal. And
on its congeners. And on its multiple relations within its ecosystem. Depends on us too—how various we are! Where shall we
start?

For many in today's acrimonious controversy over human practices toward animals, that answer is too relativistic. It is therefore
not of a sort that can generate placards, campaigns, and demonstra-
tions in municipal council meetings when the question of deer control comes up. And yet, it is the traditional answer. Humans have
always had discriminating relationships with animals, even within
one species, as the old science of breeding attests. Evidence for dis-
criminative perception goes back as far as the Paleolithic, which I
shall ponder momentarily.

But the answer is not helpful, as far as it goes. What is clear today
is that people all over the world—in different cultures, and in different social locations from remote villages to urban policy chambers—
are trying to re-configure our discriminations about animals on an
individual level and on the broadest ecological level. Not only are
species disappearing, but the behavior of many species is undergo-
ing change in astonishing ways, and the environments of a great

many species are being irretrievably altered by human intrusion—dams, deforestation, highways, sound barriers, flows of waste and damaging chemicals, and many other things. No formula will ever do justice to the variety of species, the variety of life-cycles, and the variety of interrelationships among species, including the human species. Consequently, a long and urgent task awaits us. It is surely part of a more inclusive task: the restoration of the excluded—people and others cut off from sustenance and fulfillment by human actions, systems, and negligence. The beneficiaries of the "logic" of exclusion, as some call it, will not let the task be easy.

Can we discover responsibility and reciprocity in relations among human beings and animals? Or is our responsibility merely a construct or hypothesis based upon either rights of animals or calculated utility-values in terms of human advantage? Both sorts of approach have strong support in current discussions. Rather than enter those disputes, what I shall try to do here is sketch out a case that responsibility and reciprocity—even though these are interpretive terms carrying complexes of associated meanings—have their roots in ontology, Being, the way things are, truth. According to many recent interrogators of "the human thing," including some philosophers, there is no one privileged mode of access to that ontological source or ground. In today's academic climate, it is worth emphasizing that language is not a privileged (or the only) mode of access. In fact, it might be time to raise the alarm that those who live and work *only* in language, in the coming-and-going of words, may risk departing truth to the extent that their talk excludes work and discipline within other sensory and kinetic modes in relation to concrete, resistant domains such as animals, the soil, and their own bodies. But it is not easy to sit down, shut up, and pay very careful attention to whatever else there is besides our selves, our identities, our fantasies. Or, better, to *stand up* and welcome silence. There is no external reward for doing so.

Let it be granted immediately that in human relations with animals, with animal populations, and with living nature as a whole, we can discover every sort of neglect, cruelty, exploitation, distortion, and silliness that we can find within the solely human realm. This should be obvious, and specific examples deserve close study. My question, though, is of a different order.

On the Paleolithic

The cave artists of the Paleolithic have not told us what they were up to. All we have are their works. We can wonder at them and we can wonder about them. Can we see in them a relationship of reciprocity, something deeper than object-assessing observation? Note first that not all contemporaneous species were memorialized on cave walls. We might say there was a "prestige group" of beasts. Some just did not make the cut. It is remarkable that the many works discovered have so much in common in terms of selection and style, even acknowledging their diversity. We may speculate that their creation involved much social process outside the cave chambers and were complemented by other modes of expression such as bodily performance and vocal expressions. Whether or not magical expectation was in play, no one really knows, though such an interpretation has had its supporters. There was something about those beasts that the cave artists brought into the fire-lit space with them, brought into their own bodily movements and their selection of means (different dyes, for example) for depicting animal forms-in-motion. The fact that so many of our contemporaries still marvel at these designs suggests that what the artists brought into the painting and brought to life is still there for us. The artists translated aspects of the form and movement of the animals into two-dimensional signs that surpass in impact any "realistic" image. According to recent interpreters, the images are not done as attempts to stereotype the species or to mark general use-values. The more finished ones have features that suggest individual variations.[1] Taken as a genre, the images show a style of perception that is kinetic and intimate. The main evidence of a sense of species difference (as we would call it—a radical difference, in any case) between beast and human is the astonishing paucity of human figures on the walls—most or all of which are stereotyped stick figures.

Intimacy and acuity of human perception of animals have a checkered history. Intimacy has often been lost to distance and objectification; acuity has often been lost to glorification, exaggeration, projective elaboration, and preoccupation with "essential" and symbolic characteristics. Much has been written on this history and its various manifestations in the arts and historical records, and much more remains to be elucidated. However, our present discussion has a different focus. My concern is to suggest that from the earliest evidence human beings have been able to express animal movement and individuality in a fashion that does not rely on human status, on mastery of the creature, on abstraction according to essence, on utility, or on relations of some sort of ownership. This ability, in some of its manifestations and possibly in all, cannot be separated from processes of choice-making, uses of means, discussions and development of skill over time, and presentation before communities—in other words, "performance." What this complex suggests is that the long history of expressing and working with animal movement and form is, at the same time, a history of self-discovery on the part of human beings—a history of asking not only what is this (animal, animal behavior), but also what am I, what are we, how are we? I do not mean that such questioning took the form of verbal inquiry—interrogations using the question mark. I mean that the presence of animals within and at the margin of human communities has evoked a huge variety of expressive renditions of the human-animal relationships, with many changes over time and in contact with new cultures. This heritage can be seen as exploration, variation, self-discovery, the affirmation and denial of boundaries, and the discovery of the transcending of boundaries.

In some cultures, animal species have been used to answer or stabilize questioning about human beings in relation to them, as examples of magical and symbolic practice show. Probably every reader has a preferred list of such beasts—lions, horses, ravens, owls, doves, coyotes, and how many others! We could say that animals—not only mythical ones but real ones—have been resident in the "text" of the human adventure. In a way, their role may be typically to remind us that there is life beyond the text, puzzles and behaviors we just don't get.

Then how did animals drift to the margin of the human world in industrial culture and at times in other cultures? How is it that whole philosophies and whole theologies have little or nothing to say about human-animal relationships, and that so many are almost obsessively concerned to establish the difference between human and animal nature? One answer begins by looking at other living beings allowed to drift to the margins, to remain unspoken about. Let the reader ponder only two categories of marginalized people, and it will become evident that the process of marginalization and exclusion has had a primary place in much philosophical and ideological thinking. Even when I use the phrase "human-animal," I risk slipping into an exclusionary logic simply because the confident assumption of human difference and status is so entrenched. Why the risk? Because I am working at the most general level, asking or answering a question without taking into account the diversity and shifts of concrete relationships across species-differences. A label of caveat could be pasted on texts such as this: warning, assumptions at work!

The logic of exclusion works by starting with an assumption of difference, often an assumption of uniqueness, and then proceeds to question about the content or nature or worth of that difference. An example from the field of international relations might elucidate this point. Here, the logic of exclusion starts by assuming the nation-state to be the basic and enduring unit in the field of relationships. The field or network is not primary; nor are other social, economic, and cultural players such as social movements. In the so-called Realist school of international relations the position and the tasks of the nation-state are of ultimate importance. Everything else is on the margin. In philosophy, the question of what is essentially human begins from a presupposition of difference, and can easily—but not necessarily—advance to a tacit or explicit exclusion. Hostility toward the "base," the "bestial," the "lower," and the "fleshly" within certain moral philosophies manifests an exclusionary logic. Philosophies and ideologies of civilization as contrasted or opposed to the "Others," the "natives," the "third world," the "periphery," depend on an exclusionary move. Collectors of "primitive" art—who distinguish the art from the multiple objects of craft and utility within a culture—practice an exclusionary logic.[2] More often than not, I believe, the makers of such objects cannot recognize that exclusion. Laboratory sciences that study individual animals in experimental settings, for all the positive gains in knowledge, nevertheless depend on a valuation of exclusionary methods: the animal in its habitat behaves differently; the animal in contact with human beings in different contexts behaves differently.

Rather than condemn the logic of exclusion as an evil mistake, I propose we examine its workings in terms of its complex history, its assumed—even if not admitted—gains, and its discernible costs or burdens. In fact there are so many varieties of exclusion in operation that it is misleading to speak of it, as I have done, as an "it." The metaphysical motto of exclusion, "Truth is one, error multiple," may have to be replaced by one that affirms "Truth is multiple." At the very least, it is so complex, so demanding on our ability to assume a variety of perspectives, that it sounds dreamlike today to say "Truth is one."

To return to the matter of human beings in relation with animals: what if, like the ethologists observing members of a single species, we examine cases of human beings in interaction with animals? Do we need to assume a defined "object" for our examination? Not at all. We are not constrained to divide our field of study into isolated "kinds." We can look at multiple relations, as indeed the field of ethology has been doing, most especially in studies of the high canopy of the rain forests. All we need do is drop assumptions of one-sided initiative or control by one kind of being and watch, listen, or just hang around attentively.[3] We probably also need to drop or attenuate assumptions about a unitary location of what we examine, such as "consciousness," or "the mind of Man," or "the text," or the unitary, boundaried object standing separate from all other objects. When researchers in the 1970s "hung around attentively" watching infant-caregiver interactions, they were surprised to discover that the infants influenced their caregivers (human beings and some other primate species). The least we achieve by attenuating assumptions about unitary location is that we become capable of surprise.

There are written works that give us examples of hanging around attentively, some of them in the first person. I shall discuss only three of them, first as examples of a certain attentiveness, and second as bearers of profound insight into humans-with-animals, the implications of which deserve exploration beyond what I can provide in this chapter. The three works are Diana Starr Cooper's portrayal of the Big Apple Circus, *Night after Night* (1994); Vicki Hearne's *Adam's Task: Calling Animals by Name* (1984); and Monty Roberts' *The Man Who Listens to Horses* (1997). In all three, we hear about human beings and animals in a ring—not an insignificant feature. In all three, the acuity and intimacy evident in the behavior of the human beings is paralleled in the behavior of the animals. And in all three, there are "third parties" to the performances in the rings—owners, students, audiences, colleagues.

Circus

At this point, I am aware that certain "defenders" of animals are sure to be hostile: animals confined in a ring? human beings more or less in charge? people looking on? "It's unnatural." "It's domination and subjection." Well, this is an important question. Just what does it mean for an animal presence to be "natural"? To consider inter-species performance within a ring "unnatural" is an ideological position, and a popular one; it is not a philosophical or scientific one.

Cooper's brilliant and multilevelled exposition is not only a delight, it is a thought-provoker. Woven into the evocative and cele-bratory prose are philosophical themes that invite reflection. For those who can read beyond the text, it is remarkable that her appre-ciation of circus includes an affirmation of the ancient roots of circus, its pre-modern nature, and a critique of certain aspects of modernity which the experience of circus makes manifest. In this regard, it is important to note that in classical fashion Cooper does not allow that everything with the public name of "circus" ought to be consid-ered within the tradition.

What is a circus?

According to Paul Binder, co-founder of the Big Apple Circus, "[c]ircus is the art form most closely involved with the relationship between animals and people." Cooper adds that "circus is the art form most directly concerned with exploring the conundrum and the fact of people *as* animals."[4] But wait: there is a social structure in the circus. Not only is there an audience, there is someone in charge—the ringmaster! Already, readers of a certain ideological cast will protest: Hierarchy, authority! For Cooper, circus is a kind of order that delivers a realization of basic truths only made possible by cer-tain arrangements within the practice and in the ring:

> [B]ecause there's so much at stake, and because everyone depends on everyone else, mastery [on the part of performers] here is not a threat, but a necessity and a pleasure, founded on trust and relying on the order of things. . . . The ringmaster represents the necessity, grandeur, and weight of certain hierarchies, which exist for the sake of our well-being and the survival of those whom he intro-duces, who are, people and other animals both, in their own eccen-tric ways, masters as well. He is here to lead us into a kind of understanding that all of us here, in all our diversity—not just of race or background or age or sex, but of species as well—all of us

are in this together. He's the one person in the ring who knows how it all connects, who makes it all come together and make sense. Everything about his presence represents his sense of duty to a higher intention, and we need him.[5]

The ring, the orderliness, the sequencing, the music—all are means for the presentation and rediscovery of the truth of animals with humans, humans as animals, humans as artists, animals as artists. As performance, they are means for the audience's rediscovery and celebration of their own being, their own responsive senses—each person, his or her own body, no matter what its dimensions.

[Consider the animals and human beings in the circus.] Their curious shapes, movements, the texture of their fur and skin, awaken us to all shape and movement and richness. They say, The world is rich, various, odd. Wake up, attend to detail; anything can happen.[6]

And we thought circus was just a relaxing, distracting night out? a refreshment? a trifle? Not for this author; not for this circus!

This particular circus, as Cooper portrays it, delivers not only an experience, an enjoyment. It delivers a range of truth, a manifestation of something basic concerning human beings and other animals. It recalls us to things we are inclined to forget, to let slip. What does it recall and deliver?

First, it recalls us to the truth of the open boundary between human beings and animals, and to the reciprocity of "order," the kind of order to which we give names like "respect." While so many "theories, abstractions, and images of other animals, devised in the witty labyrinths of our minds, form elaborate barriers between us and them," and while "we have altered, sanitized, desexualized, and humanized" the images of animals, this circus gives us real animals with real smells, real grandeur, and a magical presence.[7] "Circus blurs distinctions between people and animals in the manner of myths," and at the same time each creature in it is just what it is: "When the circus horses appear, they embody the distilled, vivid essence of Horse. You can hear them, smell them, almost stroke their glossy necks and haunches. They *are all there*."[8]

Second, on the basis of this perceived melding of human and animal,

[c]ircus demonstrates that there are ways for people and animals living with one another to behave, to prosper, to create something

valuable together. It invents a landscape within which species operate—not by murder or mayhem, nor by isolation, nor by sentimentality—but with this firm resolve: *we will stay here together.* This is courage in the face of the constant possibility of tragedy. It is a world in which animals and people have, together, a stake in something real, and in which something real is always at stake.[9]

Third, circus delivers or provokes or calls forward the individual and shared humanity of the assembled viewers: it is a moment of self-discovery. Even if few people reflect in such a way as to formulate what is happening, "you are carried away, and you are all there."[10] All of the senses are engaged—"a total physical response."[11] Beyond calling attention to what is in the ring, the circus galvanizes an attentiveness beyond its own locality, an attentiveness to what and how we are, and even more to how we "will stay here together" on some enduring level that philosophers call ontological.

It is worth remarking that the circus is not calling for new thoughts, new or revised conceptual constructions (much as they might be needed, especially in revising our habits of assuming exclusions and distinctions as if they were basic). It is a transformation of our being, an "expanded awareness of what it is to be human, and fully alive in your own body. . . . Your hands, heart, lungs, nerves, voice get a good workout, your feet too, if you are a stamper."[12]

This welcoming of truth that circus achieves stands over-against a profound and entrenched cultural habit of a "frightened plan of the world." In this plan, creation is divided into compartments of race, age, nationality, religion, and species such that we "are inaccessible to one another." This plan seeks to "control and dehumanize us by drying us up—deanimalizing us, if you will."[13] Participants in this frightened, control-seeking view of culture, as Cooper sees it, generate various ideologies holding that animals must be sent back to their native habitats (on the assumption that there are such) and should not be involved in training by human beings. The eminent British veterinarian Marthe Kiley-Worthington calls this "animal apartheid" in her extensive study of British circuses. (Dr. Kiley-Worthington's research was commissioned by the Royal Society for the Prevention of Cruelty to Animals which wanted some objective facts to bring to the controversies over circuses. When her results failed to serve the resident ideology, the RSPCA refused to publish it. She had to pay to have it published.)

The fear at the base of this view can get hidden behind the image-oriented and sentimental human constructions of animal being which are so prevalent in our culture. In fact, they are so prevalent as to have almost wiped out any other possibility. Cooper has no kind words for sentimentalism. Worse than a simple issue of taste, sentimentalism is a deception, almost a cultural hallucination. It has everything to do with rendering animals "cute," "pretty," and appreciative of "loving" attention, especially hugs and strokes in the case of domestic animals, and total "freedom" in the case of the rest. She mentions this phenomenon as she has confronted it in dog owners who

> physically recoil—I mean, reel back as if they'd been slapped—at being told that love may not be as important to their dogs as respect. The idea that love is *not* all you need—that an animal might place higher value on a mutually dependent and respectful working relationship—is, to some people, completely offensive.[14]

An aspect of the sentimentalizing and mendacious distortion of animal being is the culture's tendency to turn animals, often nature altogether, over to children—just as history gets turned over to children in distortive theme parks. This phenomenon of handing over once-significant domains of the human experience to children is worthy of study by itself. Cooper's point, and the point to emphasize now, is that it is a major loss and distortion, a sort of illusion that leaves us all diminished.

An objection might be raised to Cooper: isn't circus a minor cultural activity, not available to many people in the world or even in our country? Isn't it an elite form? And isn't it expensive? These are serious and embarrassing questions, perhaps, but the same questions can be raised about the best of the performing arts, visual art, poetry, and all the rest. (In a consumerized society, who cares about any kind of celebration, truth, or enjoyment that is not reducible to "fun"? The least we can hope for, then, are more wake-up calls like Cooper's.)

Cooper's book is not an argument; she does not make a case. She tells a true story, with her own elaborations and condensations and interpretations, so that readers can appreciate secondhand the fact that circus does deliver and does provoke a realization of certain truths about basic dimensions of Being—dimensions as lived by animals and humans, and humans as animals. The re-animalization of human beings, which is a remedy against illusion, could not take place without language; without careful, sustained attention to details; without mutual security and trust between human beings and animals; without the subtle, prolonged disciplines of training (of some animals, and of human beings for their skills of observation and self-criticism). The human task, then, is demanding, urgent, always unfinished—and in the performance of circus, it is a great enjoyment. Circus may be a way to realize that truth is not exclusively something of seriousness, order, gravity, burden, or abstraction. "You are all there." "They are all there." "We will stay here together." Could laughter, senses, colors, movement, sociality, magic, danger, and discipline all be brought back into our concern for truth and ultimacy and Being?

Training

Vicki Hearne, trainer of dogs and horses, toils, so to speak, in the same vineyard as Cooper. She is also a professor trained in philosophy and literary studies, and a published poet. In much of her training, the circle or ring is a key ordering space for the meeting of human and animal; again, those animal libertarians who oppose any and every confinement will register their disapproval. Her book, *Adam's Task: Calling Animals by Name*, is a classic of its kind, but also very idiosyncratic and quirky, and so not amenable to lifting short quotations. Hearne is a sworn opponent of the animal rights movement on the grounds that (1) its ideology promotes fear and contempt not only toward animals but toward human beings who spend a large amount of time in communication with animals, in what she calls "work in the fullest sense"; (2)"[t]he logic of the animal-rights movement places suffering at the iconographic center of a skewed value system" and is a betrayal of the being of human and nonhuman animals; (3) the replacement of working with animals by gratuitous "praise" and "kindness" perverts the basic interrelation of human beings and animals and can corrupt even the smartest animal; and (4) to use my own terms, the movement has no place in its ideology for the sustained attention—and intimacy and acuity of perception—toward other beings which we can witness in training and in such spectacles as the Big Apple Circus. These are strong words: betrayal, perversion, delusion. They can only be justified if there is some truer, more reality-based understanding of bonds between human beings and other beings.

That understanding is properly called communication. A stronger way to say it is that "we are our bonds."[15] It is far more real than just looking at or smiling at an animal. As the great American philosopher Charles Sanders Peirce (1839–1914) said: "Between horse and rider there is a communication which one can explain no better than the other." This sort of communication transpires above—and beyond, or perhaps we should say below—the boundaried, atomistic incidents of command, behavior, response, reward, and so on. In this interspecies communication Hearne plies her craft, and continues it by sharing her reflections with us, her readers. She assumes that we have the ability to catch her meaning, even if we are not trainers and do not keep company with nonhuman animals. She also assumes that she makes sense in using words like "communication" and "listening," and is innocent of undue anthropomorphism. She is aware that accusations of anthropomorphism will be flung at her; and how could they not be? The logic of exclusion applied to the human-animal difference must prescribe that no human names can be validly applied to things animals do or show. Hearne's experience makes sense to her and leads to successful outcomes in animals because there is "understanding" on both sides of the relationship, "respect" on both sides of the relationship, and especially because there is clarity and consistency on both sides, starting with the human.

> With horses as with dogs, the handler must learn to believe, to "read" a language s/he hasn't sufficient neurological apparatus to test or judge, because the handler must become comprehensible to the horse, and to be understood is to be open to understanding, much more than it is to have shared mental phenomena.[16]

As necessary as word-based speech is for the human being, communication across species difference is kinesthetic, probably incapable of being broken into discrete components. Even if we can talk about components, the effective reality of the communication is to have all components at once and integrated—smell, movement, position, touch, voice, timeliness, security, and others. Relating her work with a tracking dog, Hearne moves into philosophical speech:

[S]peaking is always a questioning that wants to be a calling, an invocation, an appeal to obedience which may fail. . . . And we may fail; the creature we ask may indeed respond, hear, obey, but we may then fail to obey. In fact, we usually do, and once that has happened there are no criteria that will take us back to the origin of our own words so that we can find out what has happened.[17]

Two different kinds of excessive power-drive on the human side render communication impossible or at best incoherent. One is the resolve to force an animal to do our will, using violence and pain if necessary, or even starting out with pain, as in the case of "breaking" a horse. The other is to overwhelm the animal, assumed (often wrongly) to be nice and sweet itself, with kind and sweet sentimental praise which says nothing to the animal. Neither extreme allows for listening, for picking up the animal's responses.

But who can really listen who is not aware of his or her own ignorance, his or her own inability to know and anticipate? Here is a major part of Hearne's account: the necessity in the good trainer, the good visitor of animal worlds, to be mindful of imminent and inevitable failure in the normal course of affairs. Whether we should call this "not-knowing" a skill, a learned attitude, an orientation, I do not know. In any event, it is the only way to be responsible—to be capable of response. Its development requires unlearning habits of assuming the constancy of greater knowledge or rationality on the human side. It is the ability to be genuinely surprised, caught off guard, stymied, flummoxed; and then to give the process time so that our failure to be comprehensible to the animal will become clear, and the path out of it will show up. In the training or working situation, correction on both sides might be necessary. Like human beings, each animal has its idiosyncrasies, blind spots, learned oddities. Only sustained attention with intimacy and acuity of perception can get us out of a failed communication. We cannot learn that set of skills from a book or a lecture. But it does help to have an idea about it!

What is it to perceive an animal as an animal, as more than an object? As the phenomenological philosophers have taught us, we can only perceive an object as an object if we assume there is another, unseen side to it. In the case of an animal, to perceive it for real, we assume that we cannot consistently anticipate its next move. Obviously, the unpredictability of animals is one reason for being afraid of them. But even those who are not afraid of them are mindful of the animal's open edge: what next? Between individual animal and individual human, there may come to be a rough anticipation of next moves; but we will never achieve altogether the same "language," or reach final agreement. The same might be said of human communication, but that is another topic.

Correcting an animal, especially if there is some roughness in the process, can, Hearne assures us, stimulate hysterical bleating on the part of human guardians—the kind, or "kind," ones, especially. These are the people who object to bridles on horses because they put the horse in a state of subjection, or say that all training is objectifying, dominating. Michel Foucault takes that line in his attack on the finest of fine equestrian arts, dressage. In fact, Foucault seems to start from the rigid assumption that whoever or whatever is not living *ad lib* is for that reason "dominated."[18] For better or worse, the answers to such complaints have to be worked out in the field, or the ring, or wherever—in other words, in practice. The answers must basically come from the animal. For Hearne, the case is settled. The approach to animals based on "kindness" produces more bad behavior than good, she says. How the animal responds and works, how the dog tracks, how the horse goes—this is where the answer shows up. Citing trainers back to Xenophon (5th century B.C.E., Athens), Hearne reminds us of the extreme difficulty of good training and the rewards in the form of horses whose movements "are at once pleasing and formidable to contemplate" (Xenophon). "For what a horse does under compulsion . . . he does without understanding, and with no more grace than a dancer would display if a person should whip and spur him during his performance."[19] So be it: the proof is in the practice; it cannot be settled by abstractions or myths. If we can learn to see and listen and then communicate kinesthetically, we can argue about limits and syntax and differences.

As a way of recalling us to the realm of the concrete, of practice, Hearne has a chapter entitled "Calling Animals by Name." It begins this way:

> In the course of restoring Drummer Girl [a previously impossible horse] to herself, I obedience-trained her, and in the course of doing this work with me, she learned what her name was.[20]

Anthropomorphism? Our habit, Hearne says, is to use labels rather than names. Labels work for stereotyped, repetitive situations; names work in particular behavioral situations. There are proper names

> that really call, language that is genuinely invocative and unconta-
> minated by writing and thus by the concept of names as labels
> rather than genuine invocations. . . . There has to be a reason for a
> name or else there is no name.[21]

Is calling by name only a human behavior? Possibly not. The founder of "zoo biology," Heini Hediger, gives his own evidence and offers cases from other researchers suggesting that indeed there are proper names *within* the animal kingdom, though they may occur in a nonvocal system (for example, vision, movement).[22] This hypothesis goes well beyond the relatively recent discoveries of territoriality among animals and applies to relations within a species. (In that same paper, Hediger laments that "zoo and circus research have been scientifically taboo."[23])

What I would like to emphasize about Hearne's rich and flinty book is the key place she gives to skepticism, to not-knowing, to humility and, yes, to passivity on the part of a person communicating effectively with an animal. She points to the common "refusal to imagine the limits of our knowledge of Others," and calls "cruelty" the lack of respect which this refusal generates. To validate passivity or openness in this way challenges a long history of assuming activity to be superior to passivity. You can touch an animal actively, as if it were a thing, or over-delicately, as if it were a dangerous monster. Such touching says "I am in charge," or in some situations, "Here I am; listen to me." Or you can touch an animal in a listening way—a way that says "I mean well; please don't bite." Both sorts of messages—both sorts of touching—have their place in communications across species boundaries, but it is crucial to know the difference and to know when to do which one. We can see these differences in human vocalizations and in movements and gestures. Anyone can try the experiment of placing, just placing, their hand on someone, and then later touching as if to listen through the hand; the person touched will more than likely report a decided difference.[24]

This sort of passivity or patience is possibly the most essential skill (other than note-taking) that the great ethologists of our century have shown so well. Some of their findings have taken years of constant observation to develop. You need not be a trainer or rider or circus performer to practice sustained attending and intimate perceiving. Anyone can practice it, anyone who can accept that waiting for sense to arise may take a long time.

Monty Roberts is another lifelong trainer and now an author and teacher. His autobiography, *The Man Who Listens to Horses*, was published shortly before I started this essay.[25] He does not like the term "training," preferring instead "joining up" or "starting up." He says he discovered "the language that horses use to communicate, through position, direction, speed, use of eyes, shoulders, head, in fact the entire body." In short, he discovered that he had to listen and speak with his whole body, and not always put one modality of communication or action in charge. Most especially he discovered, and was certainly not the first to discover, that force, strength, will, and inflicting pain simply do not work. Their use creates the hard boundaries that lead to mutual contempt, distrust, fear, and general craziness. Force and use of pain may be wrong for many reasons; one of them is surely that it assures failure. How do we discover that they produce failure? Only by observing closely and patiently, by experience. This is how Roberts came to develop a method of "starting up" a horse for future riding. One of the more astonishing results of Roberts' methods is their apparent ease; another is the rapidity of achieving the desired result. I should add that Roberts and his wife have a long experience of using the same approach with children— their own and over forty others whom they have welcomed in foster care.

Roberts' story and methods bring to the surface the ancient presupposition that pain—threats of pain, hurting animals or people— really helps, really induces good behavior or corrects bad behavior. We must wonder what are the roots of this presupposition in our belief-systems, our linguistic habits, our politics, our institutions. Answering this question is a task for imaginative scholarship; the work of Roberts and Hearne demonstrates that there is such a presupposition shaping our world and values. Hurtful reactions to hurt and injury are, to use that questionable word, "natural." But to promote hurting in the service of improvement or growth is a cultural habit. It is, to reiterate, the belief and expectation that hurting a being will produce desirable results. It is a deep belief, so deep that the corrective lessons of easily available experience have largely been ignored.

Philosophy

What philosophical issues are engaged by these authors? For one thing, they all show the importance of what I call "positioning" in relation to other beings, perhaps with other human beings as well as nonhuman beings. The successful trainer knows how and when to get into a certain position *vis-à-vis* the animal's perception. Positioning is multisensory or synesthetic; but most especially it is kinesthetic. Roberts' communications with horses are largely a matter of positioning. By saying it is kinesthetic, I mean to avoid implying that perception is only ocular, or communication only verbal or aural. Many authors have presented philosophies and interpretations of experience along the same lines; there is nothing very new about it. But we can underline in the cases of our three authors that they add the crucial importance of structure and syntax in their meetings with beings across species boundaries. In other words, patterns and arrangements can support or compromise or even prevent successful communication. The question is to examine what works. Which structures should we identify as destructive and which as generative? All three authors take issue with the popular image of the "natural" animal as the animal running free, and with the valuation that all animals should be allowed to have that freedom. Such freedom, they agree, is a human fantasy, traceable to fear and loathing. All three authors hold that there are authentic ways to love animals, but they prefer the term "respect" to distinguish themselves from those who presume to speak for animals, whether in the name of loving them or in the name of animal "rights."

Keeping in mind these three works bearing on human-animal co-existence, we must be impressed by the lack of an animal presence in much philosophical thinking about human being. The term "intersubjective" is now in wide currency, after going through a phase of being considered a barbarism by critics. Thanks especially to the phenomenologists of Europe, and more recently the United States, the ideas of corporeality, intersubjectivity, sociality, and transcendence within the fleshly have caught on in many places. The Cartesian ego

or encapsulated subject so important to modern thought and culture
has come under attack from many quarters. The dependence of truth
and truth-seeking on community, and certain structures of community, has been an American staple ever since Peirce. For Maurice
Merleau-Ponty, among others, the "social" is always already there
in the development of the human infant. Merleau-Ponty was a dedi-
cated reader of contemporary biologists and ethologists who con-
ceptualized across-species relationships and within-species forms of
sociality.[26] It is remarkable that he paid so little attention to the presence of animals in the lives and cultures of human beings around the
world. I am tempted to say this neglect was simply a feature of
French humanism and literature generally, but that would be unfair.
There are exceptions. But in the heyday of phenomenology and existentialism, human agonies and revolutions and such held center
stage.

Some biologists, however, were close students of phenomenological philosophy. F. J. J. Buytendijk is a good example, and some of
his works are available in English. One of his more interesting
papers, as far as I know, has not been translated: "*Les Catégories
fondamentales de l'organisation et de la désorganisation de l'existence animale.*"[27] In it Buytendijk discusses the use of "anthropomor-
phic" approaches in studying animal behavior, and reports on an
experiment with rats showing their learning to make sensori-motor
discriminations to re-achieve security within their environments.
His point about security is echoed by all three of the authors we have
been discussing.

Merleau-Ponty coined the term "intercorporeality" to point to
the ways one body overlaps others; and in his later work he elevated
the term "flesh" (*la chair*) to a place of primacy. He saw himself as
working out a new ontology that had already been opened up in the
"teleology" of the modern sciences; in other words, he was taking the
next step in the path already trod by science. Well known for drawing on painting to show how this new ontology already is resident in
human works, what is less well appreciated of Merleau-Ponty's work
is that it all was in a sense about science. He opened his famous late
essay "Eye and Mind" with the regrettable statement that "[s]cience
manipulates things and gives up living in them."[28] It is regrettable
because he already knew that in some areas of science a more
"inhabiting" awareness was taking hold, and because the definite-

ness of the sentence suggests he is anti-science. On the contrary, Merleau-Ponty saw science coming back to ontology and wanted to play a part in this return to the real world. Furthermore, his meditations on painting could be reformatted to apply to human experience with and of animals. What he says referring to the "work" (*l'oeuvre*) in the case of painting could also be said of the "work" described by Cooper, Hearne, and Roberts: I would include all renditions of animality, such as Paleolithic paintings, literature, song, ritual, and actual training and study, in the category of the "work" of human-animal relations.

While the phenomenologists and their epigones make much of the roles of Others in the development of the human individual, they almost always mean human Others, not animal Others. This exclusion is remarkable. It is all the more remarkable today, given the widespread movement of therapeutic and educational involvement of animals with special categories of people. For example, the Thorncroft Equestrian Center outside of Philadelphia teaches handicapped children to ride horses with amazing successes in the overall growth of the young riders. Likewise, the PhillyPAWS project in Philadelphia enables AIDS patients to keep their pets with them through volunteer assistants—obviously the pet has a beneficial effect. Animal-assisted therapy now has its own professional certifying organization, and more and more nursing homes have discovered the morale-boost residents get from the periodic visits of specially trained dogs. The physiological correlates of these therapeutic relationships are well documented and are being studied in several research centers. I have been told that many veterinary schools have added staff trained to address the human-animal relation in view of the well-being of both sides of the relation.

Merleau-Ponty critiques the "aerial perspective" (*pensée de survol*) that has prevailed in science and philosophy, and calls us back to our rootedness in the flesh, the inter-corporeality of existence and our works. He asks us to see things straight on, *en face*, whatever this implies about partiality and multiplicity of perspectives. This way of meeting our questions—and the world and Being—is the corrective to the prestigious habits of pretending to see "from nowhere," or from outside, as if we were not questioned in our questioning. The animal worker has no choice: rising above, conceptualizing too much, or seeking sovereignty by force and pain will, to put it mildly, backfire.

Likewise, the animal worker is a model of sustained attention, a very different kind of perception compared with "just looking" or glimpsing. Only through sustained attention can a perceiver detect the temporal unity of an animal, its style, its way of moving and responding. I doubt that any television editor would allow a display of sustained attention in a production, be it ever so documentary: the attention span for television viewers has been getting shorter, possibly vanishingly shorter, over the years. We might *hear* about sustained attention, as readers of this essay are only hearing about it, but where to learn it, try it out? In short encounters with things or even works of visual art, we easily identify, name, and sometimes assess: the activity is on the viewer's side. In sustained attention to an animal in its movement—or to a work of art, for that matter—we frequently and inevitably find ourselves questioned. That horse Cooper says "is all there" in the performance: how did it come to be all there? We could say the horse is "there!" and we could say the horse is "there?". And how amazing it is! The presence of the question mark means to translate the looks on the faces in the audience at such moments, and the chorus of voices saying "I can't believe it." It is a wake-up experience.

Another way we are questioned, or can be questioned, is in the experience of hanging around attentively and then wondering reflectively: What am I doing in this animal's world? Who am I in that world? (I doubt that this experience is common among pet owners, just because of my experience confronting so many of them for whom ownership settles it all. The exceptions stand out but should strive to become the rule.)

Our three authors maintain the primacy of the real as against the conceptual and the symbolic, not to exclude the conceptual and the symbolic but to uphold and celebrate what we find—ourselves, other beings, the transactions and questions among them all—and what we create together, the work. The work, the mutual transformation and enjoyment, is real and it is limited. The field or ground within which the work happens and proceeds is beyond location, beyond the material array of objects, each one separate from the other. The field of and for communication is not an item in the mix; it underlies the communicants and belongs to all of them. We may call it Being. We can ignore that field, or we can behave so as to open it up and celebrate it, and not just once in a lifetime, as if it were a step in a sequence of projects. Beneath the active respect and conjoint behavior of people and animals in certain situations we might be able to identify something that is very like respect, except that it is not directed toward a being. That something might better be called reverence—a position or orientation. Although they do not use this term as far as I know, our authors all demonstrate an attitude of reverence. It is reverence *within* the fleshly realm, not directed outside it, and especially not expressed as an alternative to fleshly interaction. It is right here. It *is* a firm resolve.

"We will stay here together."

Notes

1. See Jean-Marie Chauvet, E. B. Deschamps, and Christian Hillaire, *La Grotte Chauvet à Vallon Pont-d'Arc* (Paris: Seuil, 1995); also Douglas Mazonowicz, *Voices from the Stone Age: A Search for Cave and Canyon Art* (London: Allen and Unwin, 1975).

2. See Sally Price, *Primitive Art in Civilized Places* (Chicago: University of Chicago Press, 1989), esp. ch. 6.

3. A pioneering text in this kind of observation, what I have called hanging around attentively in order to avoid suggesting primacy of visual, auditory, or manipulative methods, is a collection of research papers under the astonishing title of *The Effect of the Infant on its Caregiver*, eds. Michael Lewis and Leonard Rosenbaum (New York: Wiley, 1974).

4. Diana Starr Cooper, *Night After Night* (Washington, D.C.: Island Press, 1994), p. 10.

5. Ibid., p. 16.

6. Ibid., p. 28.

7. Ibid., pp. 33, 25.

8. Ibid., p. 55.

9. Ibid., p. 153.

10. Ibid., p. 7.

11. Ibid., p. 42.

12. Ibid.

13. Ibid., pp. 86–87.

14. Ibid., p. 151.

15. Carleton Dallery, "Thinking and Being with Beasts," *On the Fifth Day: Animal Rights and Human Ethics*, eds. Richard Knowles Morris and Michael W. Fox (Washington, D.C.: Acropolis Books, 1978), p. 91.

16. Vicki Hearne, *Adam's Task: Calling Animals by Name* (New York: Vintage Books, 1984), p. 107.

17. Ibid., p. 106.

18. David Michael Levin offers a trenchant criticism of this Foucauldian world-picture in "Visions of Narcissism: Intersubjectivity and the Reversals of Reflection," *Merleau-Ponty Vivant*, ed. Martin C. Dillon (Albany: State University of New York Press, 1991), pp. 47–90.

19. Xenophon as quoted by Hearne, pp. 150–151.

20. Ibid., p. 166.

21. Ibid., p. 170.

22. Heini Hediger, "Proper Names in the Animal Kingdom," *Experientia*, 32:11 (November 1976), pp. 1357–1488.

23. Heini Hediger, *Beobachtungen zur Tierpsychologie im Zoo und im Zirkus* (Basel: Reinhardt, 1961). See his path-breaking book *Wild Animals in Captivity: An Outline of the Biology of Zoological Gardens* (New York: Dover Publications, 1964), first published in German in 1942.

24. For extensive and imaginative reflections on this subject, see Gabriel Josipovici, *Touch* (New Haven: Yale University Press, 1996).

25. Monty Roberts, *The Man Who Listens to Horses* (New York: Random House, 1997). His web page is www.MontyRoberts.com.

26. Maurice Merleau-Ponty, *La Nature. Notes, Cours du Collège de France*, ed. Dominique Séglard (Paris: Editions du Seuil, 1995); his courses were given 1956–1961.

27. In *Psychiatrie Animale*, eds. Abel Brion and Henri Ey (Paris: Desclée de Brouwer, 1964), pp. 113–120.

28. Maurice Merleau-Ponty, "Eye and Mind," transl. Carleton Dallery, *The Primacy of Perception*, ed. James M. Edie (Evanston: Northwestern University Press, 1964), p. 159.

ELEVEN

The Animal *as* Animal:
A Plea for Open Conceptuality

 *Steven W. Laycock*

Thomas Nagel's question, "What is it like to be a bat?"—what, that is, is it like *for the bat* (not *for us*) to be a bat?—has, for us, no answer. I want to reject both the realist assumption that there *must* be something it is like to be a bat (the bat's "subjectivity")—even though it is inaccessible to us—and the idealist proposal that what it would be like *for us* to be a bat is what it is like *for the bat* to be a bat—the astonishingly audacious and human-centered presumption that human experience is the measure, not only of all things, all objectivity, but of all forms of subjectivity as well.

Edmund Husserl is luminously insightful in his assertion that "experience is not an opening through which a world, existing prior to all experience, shines into a room of consciousness."[1] And our experience of the purported "world" (or *Umwelt*) of the animate Other could no more be disjoined from consciousness. But human consciousness is not the site of its apodictic givenness. The question, "What is it like . . . ?," while not lapsing into unintelligibility, is nonetheless imponderable, unanswerable, expressing a questioning openness which, in principle, cannot be foreclosed. The attempt to "close" it, to obturate the question through repletion, to bring about the cessation of questioning by filling it, stopping it up with an answer, is an anthropocentric imposition—indeed, the phallocentric insertion of an idealism intent on stopping the leaks in human cognition with the putty of our own substance. No doubt, as Howard Parsons discerns, "[w]e continuously seek closure in our meanings and identities, yet we cannot tolerate the constrictions they lay upon us."[2] Still we credit Maurice Merleau-Ponty's supplemental insight that "the interrogative is not a mode derived by inversion or by reversal of the indicative."[3] The question is not, that is, the simple absence of a responsive presence that, without answer, it would otherwise lack. Thus, "the 'object' of philosophy will never come to fill in the philosophical question, since this obturation would take from it the depth and the distance that are essential to it."[4] Interrogativity is not simply conflatable with answerability, but dilates indefinitely beyond the compactness of the plenary answer. The withdrawal of realism menaces the question with its assumption that unanswerability entails unquestionability. We can, and we do, interrogate a mute reality which offers us only silence in response. Silence is no refutation of the question, but an index to its depth. Questions that inhabit the surface of our concerns can be "answered," abolished as questions, by repletion. But answers that obturate their questions without remainder comprise no more than "information." Such "digital" questions are minimal openings, like the negative internal space of a puzzle piece that awaits a specific extroverted form, or like a specifically designed lock that can offer itself only to a key of particular specifications, thus "giving only dead and circular replies to a dead and circular interrogation."[5] There is a preestablished harmony, a remarkable fit, between digital question and informational response, that would seem no less than astonishing were it not for the purely "rhetorical" character of the question. Info-units fit remainderlessly into the slots prepared for them, absorbing all available interrogative space, exactly because the slots are, indeed, *prepared* for them. There is no information without determinate expectation. The relationship is circular: the question demands the very answer that it receives. Thus, "the impossibility of obtaining for a *directed* question any answer other than *simulated*."[6] "[P]hilosophical interrogation is . . . not," however, "the simple expectation of a signification that would come to fill it."[7] As Patrick Burke affirms, "we do not know a priori what answers are forthcoming."[8] It differs from the informational question in its "formlessness," its ability to absorb multiple responses, and in its self-referentiality. "It is characteristic of the philosophical questioning that it return upon itself, that it ask itself also what to question is and what to respond is."[9] Information, by contrast, is constituted through the binary opposition of presence and absence, "on" and "off," *one* and *zero*. For the question that refuses repletion, the answer does not "fill" or satis/fy, but is rather engulfed, floats. *Zero* remains a possibility, but there is no *one*. Answers deliver themselves to the vastness of interrogative space, and as such are endlessly questionable. As Burke suggests, "if answers come, it will be only as a result of our having recognized the interrogative space, the abyss, within which alone Being can freely and continually manifest itself."[10] Information is a determinate answer. Non-informational response does not so much answer as raise questions, serving thus as the central concretion in a vast field of questions. A philosophical question "obtains not an *answer*, but a confirmation of its astonishment."[11] It has no meaning independent of the questions it raises. Thus, "there is no positive statement that does not have an interrogative halo."[12]

We might demur at the suggestions of Jean-Paul Sartre's claim that "the question is a kind of expectation."[13] For questions do, indeed, go unanswered. And we have no prior guarantee that an answer will, or can be, forthcoming. However, even if the question does not "expect" its own annihilation, it nonetheless exerts the negative pressure of the vacuum. It "invites" rather than "demands" our efforts at repletion. And the philosophical question inscribes the ineluctable failure of these efforts. Our experience is riddled with gaps, lesions, crevasses of unknowing. But a hole that is filled is no longer a hole. Answers an(*nihil*)ate superficial questions, make nothing (*nihil*) of their nothingness, their openness, showing that their openness was merely relative, merely conditional. Informational answers would restore the pocked surface of our experience to an original smoothness and *naïveté*. And if all our questions were appeals for annihilation, we would lapse into the *nihil/ism* of a world of experience that is pure surface, without depth, a world that exemplifies "the violence of a civilisation without secrets."[14] The world of *naïveté* is a world without problem, without solution, without meaning, and without value. It is only with the dawning suspicion that the answer does not "answer," that the apparent "smoothness" of the naïve world is already—*always* already—fragmented, pulverized, reduced to dust in the acidic medium of interrogativity, that the depth of experience is revealed and nihilism evaporates. Again, the digital question is, in a certain sense, "rhetorical." The "key" precedes the "lock." But for the genuinely philosophical question, "no answer ever preceded the question: and what does the question without anguish, without torment mean?"[15] The saturation of interrogative space by information eliminates the anguished possibility of error. Information presents itself as an unquestionable answer. In contradistinction, philosophical inquiry poses unanswerable questions. Philosophy, as Merleau-Ponty attests, "does not raise questions and does not provide answers that would little by little fill in the blanks."[16] And in this sense, "[t]hought is suspended in the daze of the question."[17] If there are imponderables, if there are authentically abyssal and unsurpassable faults in our knowledge, if there are genuine and ineluctable rents in the tapestry of our experience, then a self-satisfied *naïveté* can found itself only upon a deluded apprehension of our cognitive situation. If, as George Bataille proposes, "[k]nowledge is access to the unknown,"[18] it cannot remain knowledge without forfeiting the unknowability of its object. The "known" is always *incognito*, dis/guised: beyond guise, not denuded. Paradoxically, access to the known is not knowledge. Be this as it may, understanding operates *between* the particulate units of knowledge, the digital bits of information, in the spaces, in the gaps, appropriating to itself the structure, the network of relatedness in which these nuggets of positivity are set. Understanding takes unto itself the very interstices in our knowledge, the differences between items of information, the fragmentation, the pattern of lesions and faults that already crackle the crust of knowledge. Jean-Luc Nancy confirms that "[m]any lines of rupture traverse us. . . . [P]hilosophy [is] separated from itself, outside of itself, crossing its own limits—which means, perhaps, . . . that it never did have proper limits, that it never was, in a sense, a 'property.'"[19] And it is assuredly understanding, not positivist knowledge, that philosophy seeks. For Robert Solomon, also, "[p]hilosophy is not a particular body of knowledge." If it is not, as he continues "the vigilance which does not let us forget the source of all knowledge,"[20] it is at least vigilance.

Nagel's question is only a prototype. We find its repetitions and modifications everywhere. "What is it like to be a cat? a slug? an amoeba? a cabbage?" Our world is populated with question marks, indomitable mysteries. Like the Husserlian epoché, "What is it like . . . ?" opens up an authentic dimension of philosophical investigation—in this case, that of the unknowable. Until his abandonment of the "dream" of philosophy as a rigorous—and positivist—science, Husserl sought to ground phenomenological investigation in presence, immediate givenness, thus, ultimately, to put an end to the questions that bedevil this discipline, but thus, also, to reduce philosophy to information. Yet, *der Traum ist ausgeträumt.* While Husserl's declaration expresses a certain despair, we find therein a dawning recognition of philosophy as understanding rather than knowledge. Jean-François Lyotard regards phenomenology as "a combat of language with itself in its effort to attain the originary."[21] And this is because the conceptions of *presence* and *absence* are twin born. And if, in the deeper subtleties of Husserl's thought, absence is itself a modality of presence, if presence, itself embracing the modalities of presence and absence, is elevated to primacy, or accorded originary status, we cannot help but sense the insistence of a higher-order opposition: higher-order presence is ineluctably co-originary with higher-order absence. Phenomenology can have no *arché*, no *principium*, since the archetic "monad" inevitably ruptures into an irresoluble "dyad" of "firsts" neither one of which is genuinely *first*, since both are coeval.

The question, "What is it like . . . ?" funds the possibility of compassionate and sensitive comportment toward the unknown. I cannot know what it is like to be a deer, for example. I cannot know whether the "terror" and "suffering" exhibited by a wounded deer are authentic expressions of an inaccessible subjectivity or my own projection. I can imagine what it might be like—*for me*—to be pursued by hunters intent on taking my life. I can imagine what it would be like—*for me*—to be mortally wounded and to be slipping, in agony, toward the brink of death. And I can also imagine what it would be like—*for me*—to experience mortal terror and to cling desperately to life. The deer, it would seem, mirrors my own projected fears, my own agony. But is the pain that I "see" a reflection or an expression? I do not, and cannot, know. And I must live with the question. It may be, as François Bresson suggests, that "[t]he phenomenological description is at the limit unrealizable and interior experience ineffable,"[22] but animate subjectivity is not merely beyond our capacity to describe or express. John Caputo recognizes that "[i]neffability" is a high-powered discursive resource, the product of a language that has been refined and defined until it is sharp enough and nuanced enough to announce all this ineffability. "Unsayability" is a modification of what is sayable. . . . By the time one has said that something is ineffable, or that one cannot say a thing, one has already been speaking for some time and one has already said too much.[23]

Animate subjectivity is undecidable, not ineffable. There is, in our perception of animals, a qualitative presence, an articulate content. But we cannot, in principle, determine whether it is given "in" or "through" our perception. If we can legitimately "counter Ludwig Wittgenstein by uttering the unutterable,"[24] we must assume that the formless is recognized *as such* in contrast to the formed—in virtue, that is, of its specific form. The inconceivable is conceived *as such*. And as Bataille suggests, "the word silence is still a sound."[25] Wittgenstein counters the counter in his assertion that "if only you do not try to utter what is unutterable, then *nothing* gets lost. But the unutterable will be—unutterably—*contained* in what has been uttered!"[26] We must, in Martin Heidegger's words, maintain "silence about silence."[27] Thus, for Giorgio Agemben, *"[s]ilence comprehends the Abyss as incomprehensible."*[28] But this is silence *beyond* "silence," beyond the contrast of silence and sonority.

It is rather information that is "ineffable." Digital presence and absence is meaningless when dissociated from the interrogative cavity that it fills. It appeals—tragically, mutely, paradoxically—for the very condition of its meaningfulness, like a vacuum that draws into itself that which would fill it and thereby destroy it. But in receiving the response to this appeal, the very possibility of its meaningfulness is abolished. Its meaning is absorbed in its annihilation, and it remains as the site of a mute supplication, a possible meaningfulness, that can in no way be disclosed.

The infamous brutality of Nicolas Malebranche is rooted in his perception of the dog as a machine, an input/output device—*data in*: kick; *data out*: yelp—and assumes an answer to (and thus the answerability of) the question "What is it like . . . ?" It is like nothing at all. The dog has no subjectivity. There is nothing it is like to be a dog any more than there is something it is like to be a clock.

While I would much rather err on the side of a certain human paternalism than that of brutality, it must be recognized that the opposite willingness to see the "terror" of the dog or the deer as a window opening upon an interior state, a transparency to the animal's subjectivity, is likewise, because we truly cannot know, an imposition incompatible with receptivity. *We* penetrate the barrier of unknowing; *we* decide the undecidability of reflection or expression; and *we* insert ourselves at the heart of the purported alterior subjectivity, there to speak for the mute, to give voice to the silent—to give (or rather *impose*), that is, our own voice, not to offer the animate Other a vehicle whereby it may express itself. And to substitute voice for silence is the clearest demonstration that we have not yet attuned ourselves to the silence *beyond* "silence," to the fact that "silence" is still the term of a binary conceptual contrast.

The thirteenth century Zen teacher, Dōgen Zenji, proposed that "[t]o carry yourself forward and experience myriad things is delusion. That myriad things come forth and experience themselves is awakening."[29] Alternatively, "[c]onveying the self to the myriad things to authenticate them is delusion; the myriad things advancing to authenticate the self is enlightenment."[30] To advance toward the Other with our own concepts and theories, to impose our interpretations upon the experience of animate otherness, is a cheap magician's trick: we draw from the hat the very rabbit that we have previously concealed within it. The trick delights the eye to the exact extent that the concealment is forgotten or obscured, to the extent, that is, that an answer appears as a *discovery*. We project our own image upon the manifold objects of our world, and are deceived by this projection much like a parakeet that sees "another" bird in its mirror. We *discover* that the animal is sentient, that it desires to live, feels pain and anguish. Or alternatively, we *discover* that what we call an animate being is merely a complex interaction of organic chemicals, a soulless algorithm devoid of genuine sentience; we discover that there is nothing it is like to be a deer or a dog or a bat. Both "discoveries," the humane and the brutal (or brutalizing), involve ventriloquism. It is we who make it appear that the voice we offer on behalf of the animal is the animal's own, that what we say is what the animal *would* say if it only had a human voice. This, Dōgen perceives, is delusion—taking our own image, our own self-representation, for the presentation of animate subjectivity. My point is not that the opposite is preferable, that the "suffering" we see in the eyes of the wounded deer is merely a projection of our own sensibilities, that, in itself, the deer feels no pain, no anguish, and has no subjectivity at all. My point is rather that the projection/revelation issue is radically undecidable.

An ideally flawless mirror purified of the flaws, the refractions, the distortion, and discoloration that would otherwise call attention to it as an object in its own right, offers an image visually indiscernible from an object presented *in propria persona*. It is *exactly as if* the object were a mirrored representation and, at the same time, *exactly as if* it were given in originary presentation. There is, here, no strictly phenomenological difference between presentation and representation. Or rather, "difference" is a theoretical postulation, a "metaphysic" in the pejorative sense eschewed by rigorous phenomenological method, not a deliverance of positive experience. It is a second-order answer to a question generated by the implosive, assertoric presence of first-order response, and thus a contraction of interrogative space, a movement in the direction of nihilism, the abolition of depth. It is not simply that we cannot know whether the animal does or does not suffer authentic anguish as if there were an answer to this question that, because of the limits of our cognition, we are prevented from knowing, but that the issue is, in principle, undecidable. It is *exactly as if* the deer experienced real terror, real pain, and also *exactly as if* "terror" and "pain" were the echo of our own voice. Suffering is, indeed, a *positive* phenomenon, a compulsive, undeniable insistence. But we cannot locate suffering on either side of the ostensible divide that separates us from the deer. We cannot, that is, discern whether suffering is an asymmetrical "given"or a projective reflux. And this undecidability will continue to disrupt our dualist repose so long as we cling to the primacy of our difference from the deer. If primacy lies, rather, in the gap, if the undecidable manifestation of suffering predates the diremption of human from animal, then a de/cision, a severing of the indissoluble, would capitulate the Adamic fall, the descent into self/Other dualism. It may be, as Bataille proposes, that "[w]ithout night, no one would have to decide."[31] Yet undecidability does not entail the night of agnosticism, but the radiant daybreak in which the dualism of self and Other vanishes with the shadows. Iris Murdoch reminds us that "[o]ur minds are continually active, fabricating an anxious, usually self-preoccupied *veil* which partially conceals the world."[32] If, as Merleau-Ponty affirms, "we ourselves are one sole continued question,"[33] and if "the status of the subject is inseparable from the status of the question,"[34] then human subjectivity is an answer to the unanswerable question of the site of suffering.

The compassion that undecidability engenders is not that of a more "humane" (thus human) imposition, a more "enlightened" paternalism (thus dualism)—though again, if there were an answer that I could know, I would much rather be guilty of human chauvinism than brutality, and I would, like Pascal, wager on the subjectivity of animals on the basis of the associated outcomes. This wager alone would motivate a more compassionate treatment of animals. But paternalism, human chauvinism, is itself a subtle form of violence. Busy imposing our own views, speaking for the animate Other, we are not genuinely open, receptive. And it is no excuse to complain that in attending the Other's voice we hear nothing, that we must speak for the Other because the animate Other cannot speak for itself, that the screen would be blank without our own projection. Let the screen lapse into imageless blankness. Let all lapse into silence. We know that "[t]he absence of language is pregnant with the pure possibility of all language."[35] If silence or incomprehensibility is the expression of the animate Other, we must nonetheless attend. And we must find a voice in this silence, this silence *beyond* "silence," that is not our own. We must attend to "[t]he expression of what is before expression. . . ."[36] And our effort partakes in the "absurdity" that Merleau-Ponty attributes to the philosophical project:

> The philosopher speaks, but this is a weakness in him, and an inexplicable weakness: he should keep silent, coincide in silence, and rejoin in Being a philosophy that is there ready-made. But yet everything comes to pass as though he wished to put into words a certain silence he hearkens to within himself. His entire "work" is this absurd effort. He wrote in order to state his contact with Being; he did not state it, and could not state it, since it is silence. Then he recommences.[37]

Description, representation, formalization, theory-construction all involve a rift, a distantiation, a separation from "silent" being. Thus, "words allow the speaker to remain a word's length away from direct experience."[38] And our task is to "make [being] say . . . what in its silence it means to say."[39] In doing so, "language realizes, by breaking the silence, what the silence wished and did not obtain."[40] The "absurdity" of this project—but also the "enlightenment" of which Dōgen speaks—is the expression of our expressionless immersion in Being.

The legitimation of human paternalism reduces the question of animal subjectivity to trivial decidability. The question is annihilated through repletion. And our openness to the animate Other is thereby foreclosed. In Dōgen's view, when the Other becomes aware of itself in us, when we offer ourselves as the site of its own self-expression, when our gift of voice is genuine, no strings attached, when the expression is not that of ventriloquist projection but a genuine submission of the voice to the Other's disposition—even if what is thus "voiced" is silence (a *silence* before "silence")—*this* is enlightenment. "Enlightened" humanity, human paternalism, the dualism of self and Other, is not Dōgen's enlightenment. It is insensitivity, a diminution, not an enrichment, of our awareness. If we are to imbibe the spirit of the "innocent heart constantly awakening to the shock of wonder, like a child on Christmas morning,"[41] we must not reduce "wonder" to potential answerability. "Wonder," Burke discerns, "is the originary question."[42] Clarice Lispector reminds us that "the explanation of an enigma is the mere repetition of the enigma."[43] To ex/plain, to splay in two-dimensional dis/splay, is to reduce the depths to a glittering surface of information—answer-units that have already annihilated their questions and are now contoured by the form, but lack the lack which is the very being of the question. The Husserlian epoché, as Eugene Fink remarks, is "the awakening of an immeasurable astonishment"[44] over the mysteriousness of the world. And Husserl would have displayed incomparably greater understanding had he been able simply to rest in this astonishment without seeking to resolve it in favor of an unquestioning sunkenness in sullen presence. Yet the interrogativity that transforms *world* into "world,"[45] *world* as that which is naïvely posited into "world" as the object of a neutralized "entertainment" (a possibility poised between the alternatives of affirmation and negation), is foreclosed by the postulation of an idealism that grounds *world* in the positivity of transcendental subjectivity, and to this extent despoils its mystery. "World" cannot be modulated back into *world* without losing its dimension of mystery. And explanation, in anchoring a free-floating "world," a "world" unsupported by the "yes" of compulsive presence, by a grounded positivity, a "world" that is not *bene fundata*, thereby deprives "world" of its liberty, binding it back to affirmation. And if, for Sartre, the epoché "is no longer . . . an intellectual method, an erudite procedure," but "an anxiety,"[46] the metastable resolution of *world* and "world" into one another without cease that bespeaks the ineluctable ambiguity of the for-itself, if, that is, mystery is transformed into instability, then we still find the preservation, as a term in oscillation, of the depthless world.

"What is it like . . . ?," the openness to alterity in its own terms, not in ours, even if this openness can only suspend itself before a voiceless enigma, is at least innocent of the substitution of metaphysics for mystery. It is not Husserlian foundationalism *per se* that transforms the poetry of the world into desiccated prose. For as Jean Baudrillard discerns, "fundamental thought is bottomless. It is, if you wish, an abyss."[47] The world is rendered prosaic, flat, drained of depth and mystery with the assumption of a founding layer of presence, a *fundamentum inconcussum*, beneath which we cannot inquire, a bottom, an origin. Mystery surrounds us. It is an index to the conceptual inviolability of the animate Other, the "coin" with respect to which *self* and *Other* are merely the abstract surfaces.

Notes

1. Edmund Husserl, *Formal and Transcendental Logic*, transl. Dorion Cairns (The Hague: Martinus Nijhoff, 1969), p. 232.

2. Howard L. Parsons, *The Value of Buddhism for the Modern World* (Kandy: Buddhist Publishing Society, 1976), Wheel Publication, No. 232/233, p. 3.

3. Maurice Merleau-Ponty, *The Visible and the Invisible*, transl. Colin Smith (New York: Humanities Press, 1962), p. 129.

4. Ibid., p. 101.

5. Jean Baudrillard, *Simulations*, transl. Paul Foss, Paul Patton, and Philip Beitchman (New York: Semiotext(e), 1983), p. 17.

6. Ibid., pp. 129–30.

7. Merleau-Ponty, *The Visible and the Invisible*, p. 119.

282 Stephen W. Laycock

8. Patrick Burke, "Listening at the Abyss," *Ontology and Alterity in Merleau-Ponty*, eds. Galen A. Johnson and Michael B. Smith (Evanston: Northwestern University Press, 1990), p. 89.

9. Merleau-Ponty, *The Visible and the Invisible*, p. 120.

10. Burke, "Listening at the Abyss," p. 89.

11. Merleau-Ponty, *The Visible and the Invisible*, p. 102.

12. Burke, "Listening at the Abyss," p. 88.

13. Jean-Paul Sartre, *Being and Nothingness: An Essay on Phenomenological Ontology*, transl. Hazel E. Barnes (New York: Washington Square Press, 1971), p. 35.

14. Baudrillard, *Simulations*, p. 21.

15. George Bataille, *Inner Experience*, transl. Leslie Anne Boldt (Albany: State University of New York Press, 1988), p. 36.

16. Merleau-Ponty, *The Visible and the Invisible*, p. 105.

17. Garth Jackson Gillan, "A Question of Method: History and Critical Experience," *Jean-Paul Sartre: Contemporary Approaches to his Philosophy* (Pittsburgh: Duquesne University Press, 1980), p. 142.

18. Bataille, *Inner Experience*, p. 101.

19. Jean-Luc Nancy, "Introduction," *Who Comes After the Subject?*, eds. Eduardo Cadava, Peter Connor, and Jean-Luc Nancy (New York: Routledge, 1991), p. 2.

20. Robert C. Solomon, "General Introduction: What is Phenomenology?," *Phenomenology and Existentialism*, ed. Robert C. Solomon (New York: Harper & Row, 1972), p. 4.

21. Jean-François Lyotard, *La phénoménologie* (Paris: Presses Universitaires de France, 1954), p. 43.

22. François Bresson, "Perception et indices perceptifs," as quoted in Merleau-Ponty, *The Visible and the Invisible*, p. 252.

23. John D. Caputo, *Against Ethics: Contributions to a Poetics of Obligation with Constant Reference to Deconstruction* (Bloomington: Indiana University Press, 1993), p. 75.

24. Theodor W. Adorno, *Negative Dialectics*, transl. E. B. Ashton (New York: Continuum, 1973), p. 9.

25. Bataille, *Inner Experience*, p. 13.

26. Paul Engelmann, *Letters from Ludwig Wittgenstein, with a Memoir* (Oxford: Blackwell, 1967), pp. 82-84.

27. Martin Heidegger, *On the Way to Language* (New York: Harper & Row, 1952), pp. 51–53.

28. Giorgio Agamben, *Language and Death: The Place of Negativity*, transl. Karen E. Pinkus and Michael Hardt (Minneapolis: University of Minnesota Press, 1991), p. 63.

29. Kazuaki Tanahashi, ed., *Moon in a Dewdrop: Writings of Zen Master Dōgen* (San Francisco: North Point Press, 1985), p. 69.

30. Francis H. Cook, *Sounds of Valley Streams: Enlightenment in Dōgen's Zen* (Albany: State University of New York Press, 1989), p. 66.

31. Bataille, *Inner Experience*, p. 26.

32. Iris Murdoch, *The Sovereignty of Good* (London: Routledge & Kegan Paul, 1970), p. 84.

33. Merleau-Ponty, *The Visible and the Invisible*, p. 103.

34. Sylviane Agacinski, "Another Experience of the Question, or Experiencing the Question Other-Wise," *Who Comes After the Subject?*, eds. Eduardo Cadava, Peter Connor, and Jean-Luc Nancy.

35. Harold Coward, *Derrida and Indian Philosophy* (Albany: State University of New York Press, 1990), p. 101.

36. Merleau-Ponty, *The Visible and the Invisible*, p. 167.

37. Ibid., p. 125.

38. Ben-Ami Scharfstein, *Ineffability: The Failure of Words in Philosophy of Religion* (Albany: State University of New York Press, 1993), p. 205.

39. Merleau-Ponty, *The Visible and the Invisible*, p. 39.

40. Ibid., p. 176.

41. Roger J. Corless, *The Vision of Buddhism: The Space Under the Tree* (New York: Paragon House, 1989), p. 281.

42. Burke, "Listening at the Abyss," p. 93.

43. Clarice Lispector, *The Passion According to G. H.*, transl. Ronald W. Sousa (Minneapolis: University of Minnesota Press, 1988), p. 127.

44. Eugen Fink, "The Phenomenological Philosophy of Edmund Husserl and Contemporary Criticism," *The Phenomenology of Husserl: Selected Critical Readings*, ed. and transl. R. O. Elveton (Chicago: Quadrangle Books, 1970), pp. 109–10.

45. See Hans Wagner, "Critical Observations Concerning Husserl's Posthumous Writings," *The Phenomenology of Husserl: Selected Critical Readings*, ed. and transl. R. O. Elveton, p. 221.

46. Jean-Paul Sartre, *The Transcendence of the Ego: An Existentialist Theory of Consciousness*, transl. Forrest Williams and Robert Kirkpatrick (New York: The Noonday Press, 1972), p. 103.

47. Baudrillard, *Simulations*, p. 21.

Contributors

Ralph R. Acampora is Assistant Professor of Philosophy at Hofstra University in Long Island. He has pursued Aboriginal studies on a Fulbright Fellowship in Australia, and has worked as a ranger for the Urban Park Service of New York City. Currently, his attention is focused on forms of animal experience and politics of perception at modern zoos.

Elizabeth A. Behnke is Coordinator and Research Fellow of the Study Project in Phenomenology of the Body and editor of the *SPPB Newsletter*. She has published articles in phenomenology of the body, somatics, and the arts; she also contributed several entries to the *Encyclopedia of Phenomenology* (1997), as well as serving as one of its editors. Her current research interests include phenomenological methodology, embodied ethics, phenomenology of social change, and the theoretical and practical implications of such phenomenological notions as transcendental corporeality and kinaesthetic consciousness.

Lynda Birke is a biologist, whose work has focused on feminist analyses of natural sciences. Her current research explores the interface of biological ideas and social theory, and she is particularly interested in our ideas about, and relationships with, nonhuman animals. Her recent publications include: *Feminism, Animals and Science* (Open University, 1994), and *Reinventing Biology* (with Ruth Hubbard; Indiana University Press, 1995).

Carleton Dallery spent a good portion of his younger years in the company of horses as rider, trainer, and instructor; completed his first career as philosophy professor in 1979, except for guest appearances teaching medical ethics at Haverford College; launched a second career as a clinical and administrative social worker in 1979; and broke—temporarily or not—from that for two years to earn a Master's in Theological Studies (World Religions) at Harvard Divinity School. He is a zealous advocate of animal-human mutual care and respect programs in schools and urban centers, which have been rapidly increasing nationwide.

James G. Hart has taught at Indiana University since 1972. His most important works are a "Precis of a Husserlian Philosophical Theology" in *Essays in Phenomenological Theology*, eds. Laycock and Hart (SUNY Press, 1986) and *The Person and The Common Life* (Kluwer, 1992).

Monika Langer is Associate Professor of Philosophy at the University of Victoria in British Columbia, Canada. She has taught at the University of Toronto, Yale University, the University of Alberta, and Dalhousie University. Principal areas of interest include: continental European philosophy, feminist philosophy, social/political issues, and philosophy of literature. Dr. Langer is the author of *Merleau-Ponty's Phenomenology of Perception: A Guide and Commentary*. Her articles have appeared in such journals as *Philosophy Today, Canadian Journal of Political and Social Theory, Teaching Philosophy, Thesis Eleven, The Trumpeter*, and in the Library of Living Philosophers volume *The Philosophy of Jean-Paul Sartre*. She is a co-editor of *The New Reality: The Politics of Restraint in British Columbia*. At present, she is writing a book on Nietzsche's *The Gay Science*.

Steven W. Laycock has devoted much effort to the elucidation of new dimensions of inquiry at the horizon of traditional phenomenological and existential concerns and has contributed significantly to the elucidation of Buddhist philosophy in light of the concepts and techniques of the Western phenomenological tradition. This endeavor is evidenced by a number of published studies of Ch'an, Hua-yen and Madhyamika Buddhism. His third book, *Mind as Mirror and the Mirroring of Mind*, involves a sustained critical study of Husserl, Sartre, and Merleau-Ponty from a Buddhist perspective. His second book, *Foundations for a Phenomenological Theology*, represents a systematic meditation upon Husserl's philosophical theology. He regularly teaches courses on Husserl, Heidegger, Sartre, and Merleau-Ponty, as well as existentialism, philosophy of religion, and Buddhist philosophy.

Alphonso Lingis is Professor of Philosophy at The Pennsylvania State University. He is the author of *Excesses: Eros and Culture* (1984), *Libido: The French Existential Theories* (1985), *Phenomenological Explanations (1986), Deathbound Subjectivity* (1989), *The Community of Those Who Have Nothing in Common* (1994), *Abuses* (1994), *Foreign Bodies* (1994), *Sensation: Intelligibility in Sensibility* (1995), and *The Imperative*, forthcoming.

William McNeill is Assistant Professor of Philosophy at DePaul University, Chicago. He is co-translator of Heidegger's 1929–30 course *The Fundamental Concepts of Metaphysics: World, Finitude, Solitude*, and author of a forthcoming study on Heidegger and Aristotle.

Luciana Parisi is writing her doctoral dissertation in the Centre for the Study of Women and Gender at the University of Warwick, U.K.

Previously, she did cultural studies and philosophy at the University of Naples in Italy. Her current research focuses on the connections between evolutionary and genetic concepts and philosophy, exploring these in relation to feminist analyses of the reproductive body.

H. Peter Steeves is Assistant Professor of Philosophy at DePaul University, Chicago where he specializes in ethics, social and political philosophy, and phenomenology. He has published the book *Founding Community: A Phenomenological-Ethical Inquiry* (Kluwer, 1998).

After twenty years at Warwick University, England, *David Wood* is now Chairman and Professor of Philosophy at Vanderbilt University. He is the author of *The Deconstruction of Time* (1988), *Philosophy at the Limit*, and the editor of some ten volumes of Continental Philosophy, including *Derrida: A Critical Reader* (1992). He was active in Animal Rights circles in Oxford in the early 1970s, contributing to the collection *Animals, Men and Morals* (1972), and was a founding member of an early, now defunct Oxford group: Ecology Action. He has recently contributed to various discussions on the problem of humanism in Heidegger, Levinas, and Derrida. One of his friends is a black cat.

Index

Abram, David, 119, 122
Adams, Carol, 152–153, 156
Adams, Douglas, 138
Agemben, Giorgio, 276
aliens (extra-terrestrials), 40, 169, 183
analytic philosophy, xi, xii, xiii, 3
angels, 79, 182, 183
Anglicus, Bartholomew, 155
anthropocentrism (anthropomorphism),
    18, 19, 20, 32, 87, 88, 119, 179,
    212–213, 235, 260, 263, 266, 272
apperception, 189, 190, 192, 261
Aquinas, St. Thomas, 182
Aristotle, 28, 51, 52, 56, 65, 79, 138, 156,
    182, 184, 185, 191, 198, 200, 201, 202,
    210, 211, 216, 224, 231, 234, 237, 240
art, 218, 253, 255, 258, 267, 268;
    Paleolithic cave painting, 49–50, 251,
    267
Aspinall, John, 138, 140, 143, 145
Augustine, Saint, 7

babies, 43–44, 45, 52, 106, 173–174, 190,
    191, 254, 266
bacteria, 7, 8, 39, 50, 66, 170, 173–174
Ballard, J. G., 44
Bataille, George, 274, 276, 278
Baudelaire, Charles, 48
Baudrillard, Jean, 281
becoming, 4, 63–71, 79, 86. *See also* Being
Behnke, Elizabeth, 128
Being: of animals, 90, 209, 211, 212, 213,
    215, 220–246, 258, 259; and beings,

difference between, 245; and
carnophallogocentrism, 33; and consciousness, 183; and death, 158, 165;
and fear, 138, 139, 140, 258; Heidegger
and, 28, 197, 209–246 *passim*; human,
213, 214, 218, 219, 235, 236, 243, 244,
257, 258, 259; and language, 239, 268,
280; manifestation of, 273; Man's relation to, 18; Merleau-Ponty and, 95, 97,
98, 100; as objectified, 108; of objects,
143, 213, 239, 240; and organs, 207,
210; responsibility and, 250; and
silence, 279, 280; ways of, 214, 215,
216, 217, 223, 226, 229, 242; in the
world, 219, 242; of world, 237
Bennett, Jane, 123
Bentham, Jeremy, 27
Berger, John, 127
Bergson, Henri, 64, 66
bestiality. *See* sex
Bible, 79–80, 83, 89, 163–164
Binder, Paul, 255
biology, 58, 60, 62, 63, 66, 67, 221, 225,
    230, 263. *See also* science
Bisson, Master Corporal Bob, 160
blood pressure, 106, 107
body: animal, 42, 61, 99, 104, 106, 107,
    109, 110, 125, 144, 167, 208, 226, 238;
    and biology, 58, 62, 63, 106, 107, 108;
    clothed, 46 (*See also* clothing); bodily
    epoché, 102; and fear, 136, 138;
    female, 48, 58, 155–157; flesh, 94, 122,
    123, 124, 165, 265, 266, 269; human,
    43, 45, 47, 137, 170, 173–174, 264; as
    intercorporeal, 7–8, 39, 104, 106, 109,

289